The Millennium Election

Communication, Media, and Politics

Series Editor
Robert E. Denton, Jr., Virginia Tech

This series features a broad range of work dealing with the role and function of communication in the realm of politics, broadly defined. Including general academic books, monographs, and texts for use in graduate and advanced undergraduate courses, the series will encompass humanistic, critical, historical, and empirical studies in political communication in the United States. Primary subject areas include campaigns and elections, media, and political institutions. *Communication, Media, and Politics* books will be of interest to students, teachers, and scholars of political communication from the disciplines of communication, rhetorical studies, political science, journalism, and political sociology.

Titles in the Series

The Millennium Election: Communication in the 2000 Campaign
  Edited by Lynda Lee Kaid, John C. Tedesco, Dianne G. Bystrom, and Mitchell McKinney

Forthcoming

Strategic Political Communication: Rethinking Social Influence, Persuasion, and Propaganda
  By Karen S. Johnson-Cartee and Gary A. Copeland

Campaign 2000: A Functional Analysis of Presidential Campaign Discourse
  By William L. Benoit, John P. McHale, Glenn J. Hansen, P. M. Pier, and John P. McGuire

The Millennium Election

Communication in the 2000 Campaign

Edited by
Lynda Lee Kaid, John C. Tedesco,
Dianne G. Bystrom, and Mitchell S. McKinney

JK
2281
.L55
2003
West

ROWMAN & LITTLEFIELD PUBLISHERS, INC.
Lanham • Boulder • New York • Toronto • Oxford

ROWMAN & LITTLEFIELD PUBLISHERS, INC.

Published in the United States of America
by Rowman & Littlefield Publishers, Inc.
A wholly owned subsidary of the Rowman & Littlefield Publishing Group
4501 Forbes Boulevard, Suite 200, Lanham, Maryland 20706
www.rowmanlittlefield.com

P.O. Box 317, Oxford OX2 9RU, United Kingdom

Copyright © 2003 by Rowman & Littlefield Publishers, Inc.

All rights reserved. No part of this publication may be reproduced, stored in a retrieval system, or transmitted in any form or by any means, electronic, mechanical, photocopying, recording, or otherwise, without the prior permission of the publisher.

British Library Cataloguing in Publication Information Available

Library of Congress Cataloging-in-Publication Data

The millennium election : communication in the 2000 campaign / edited by
  Lynda Lee Kaid . . . [et al.].
     p.   cm.— (Communication, media, and politics)
  Includes bibliographical references and index.
     ISBN 0-7425-2509-0 (cloth : alk. paper)—ISBN 0-7425-2510-4 (pbk. :
  alk. paper)
     1. Political campaigns—United States.   2. Campaign debates—United
  States.   3. Advertising, Political—United States.   4. Communication in
  politics—United States.   5. Journalism—Political aspects—United
  States.   6. Press and politics—United States.   7. Presidents—United
  States—Election—2000.   8. United States. Congress—Elections, 2000.
  9. Elections—United States.   I. Kaid, Lynda Lee.   II. Series.
  JK2281.L55 2003
  324.973'0929—dc21   2003004215

Printed in the United States of America
The paper used in this publication meets the minimum requirements of American
National Standard for Information Sciences—Permanence of Paper for Printed Library
Materials, ANSI/NISO Z39.48-1992.

Contents

Part II: Media Coverage

Part III: New Technologies

Part IV: Socializing the Young Voter in Campaign 2000

Preface

Research collaboration for *The Millennium Election* derived from a research roundtable presented at the 1999 National Communication Association convention. The 2000 National Election Research Team brought together scholars and researchers from across the country, many of whom had worked together on similar projects during the 1996 election. The team was open to all scholars interested in joining the effort. A few of the collaborative research goals included enabling researchers to (1) collect research from geographically diverse research locations, (2) work together to build large-sample, representative data, (3) build common approaches to studying election advertising, debates, Internet use, and campaign news coverage, (4) collect newspapers and videotape local news from across the country, (5) develop and implement a national postelection team survey, and (6) engage researchers in dialogue about valid and reliable instrumentation and operationalization of political campaign research.

Researchers who participated in the 2000 National Election Research Team were asked to (1) participate in advertising experiments during two different times throughout the general election, (2) participate in debate experiments and focus groups for at least one of the presidential or vice presidential debates, (3) tape the highest-rated local newscast in their viewing market from Labor Day to Election Day, (4) subscribe to a local newspaper in order to trap material not otherwise covered by sources such as Lexis/Nexis, and (5) complete a small-sample local postelection telephone survey.

Lynda Lee Kaid directed the 2000 National Election Research Team. Field coordinators John Tedesco (Virginia Tech), Dianne Bystrom (Iowa State), and Mitchell McKinney (Missouri) helped organize and facilitate research. Team researchers came from the following states: Alabama, California, Colorado, Florida, Georgia, Idaho, Illinois, Indiana, Iowa, Kansas, Massachusetts, Missouri, Ohio, Oklahoma, Pennsylvania, South Carolina, Texas, and Virginia. In each location, researchers were encouraged to involve graduate students and under-graduate students in the research effort when possible.

The specific data gathered and used by the team are detailed in the studies that make up this book. The advertising experiments, conducted at two points during the fall campaign, gathered information from nearly 2,000 respondents around the country. The debate experiments were conducted in conjunction with each presidential and vice presidential debate and measured reactions from almost 1,200 respondents. Immediately following real-time viewing of the televised debates, focus groups were conducted at twenty-three sites in nine different states, with a total of 249 citizens joining in these small discussion groups. A telephone survey was planned for the postelection period. This effort was not as successful as a similar effort in 1996, due to the disputed Florida results that kept the final outcome in limbo for many weeks. Nonetheless, the joint efforts of the group did produce a national telephone sample with nearly 300 respondents. Finally, as mentioned above, the team members collected newspapers and taped local television newscasts in their own media markets. The group also collected data on Internet sites of the presidential candidates.

Acknowledgments

The authors would like to express their appreciation to all of the members of the 2000 Election Research Team (Y2E Team). Without so much cooperation from so many people, this project would not have been possible. The book project itself benefited greatly from the editorial assistance of Colleen Connolly-Ahern (University of Florida).

We also wish to express special appreciation for the graphic on the book's cover to Drew Bagley and Phi Anh Nguyen.

Buddy Wiedemann, Jittendra Allu, and Jane Garner also deserve special thanks for their assistance with coordination, computer configuration, programming, and data entry. With their constant support, a lot more went right than went wrong over the course of this complex project.

A 2001 Virginia Tech Humanities Summer Stipend award supported data entry, data analysis, and coding for several research projects reported in this volume. We also thank Tammy Trimble, Kendra Beach, Carey Mosser, and Lindsay Welter at Virginia Tech University for their assistance with data collection, data entry, and content analysis coding.

Mitchell McKinney gratefully acknowledges the receipt of a Research Council grant from the University of Missouri for the preparation of focus group transcripts.

As always, our families and partners made sacrifices and provided support that made this effort possible. We are especially grateful, therefore, to Cliff Jones for thousands of large and small contributions to every phase of the effort; to Keith, Chris, and Beth Bystrom for their understanding and support; and to Bryan Pepper for his encouragement and support.

Introduction: Before Florida, There Was a Campaign . . .

Lynda Lee Kaid, John C. Tedesco,
Dianne G. Bystrom, and Mitchell S. McKinney

Before the 2000 presidential election came to a screeching halt in Florida and left the nation hanging on a result ultimately decided in the courts, the two major party candidates fought a traditional campaign that led to the closest electoral outcome in decades. The first election of the new millennium, even before the Florida stalemate, was the most exciting and most competitive contest in recent U.S. history. Further overshadowed by the presidential outcome was the fact that many other important races took place at the state and local level. The 2000 campaigns were traditional contests in many ways, exhibiting well-known communication patterns among candidates, media, and voters. However, in some very important ways, the 2000 campaign also was the setting for new and innovative communication approaches that may have affected the closeness of the presidential race and the tightening of the competitive margins in the Senate and House of Representatives. This book highlights some of the most important campaign communication of the 2000 election by focusing on the candidates' political messages, the media's coverage of the campaign, the impact of campaign techniques such as the Internet, and the evolving political socialization of young voters.

OVERVIEW OF THE BOOK

A research effort with such diverse goals and techniques did not attempt to dictate a common theoretical or methodological approach for team members.

Members of local research groups were allowed to pursue their own interests from their own theoretical perspectives and to use the team's joint data or any other data they wished to collect on the campaign for their contributions to this book. We believe the book is richer and more useful because of this breadth. We have organized the contributions of team members into four basic sections.

The first part of the book reports research that is rooted in analysis of the candidates' own communication messages. The first three chapters in this section focus on the traditional advertising messages of the candidates (Tedesco and Kaid), on the campaign films produced by the parties for the national conventions (Edwards and Smith), and on the use of issue advertising by special interests groups in 2000 (Walkosz). The televised debates between the candidates are the subject of three chapters in the first section (McKinney, Dudash, and Hodgkinson; Sheckels and Bell; and Roberts and Williams).

The second part of the book contains chapters that report research on the media's coverage of the campaign. This section looks not only at the coverage of the presidential candidates by traditional media such as television and newspapers (D'Angelo and Esser; Larson; and Gaddie and McKinnon) but also at how the candidates are presented to voters through late-night comedy shows on television (Nitz, Cypher, Reichert, and Mueller). Another chapter considers coverage of important elections below the presidential level, comparing coverage of male and female candidates in Senate and gubernatorial campaigns during 2000 (Banwart, Bystrom, Robertson, and Miller).

The use of the Internet for campaigning caught the attention of many campaign observers in 2000 and was the subject of the research projects discussed in the third part of our book. One chapter discusses the pioneering efforts of John McCain in using the Web to raise funds and involve volunteers during the primary stage of the election (Tomlinson). Wicks, Souley, and Verser provide an analysis of the similarities and differences in the content of the presidential candidate websites, and the final chapter in this part addresses the very important question of access, attention, and use of the Web for campaign information (Boyle).

Finally, the fourth part of the book addresses a topic that continues to concern political communication researchers, the lack of civic engagement among young voters. Bernstein analyzes the media use and political discussion characteristics of young voters, and Carlin and Anderson consider differences in reactions to televised debates by young voters and senior citizens. Spiker, Lin, and Wells try to isolate the underlying aspects of political malaise in young voters.

Taken together, the diverse studies and viewpoints in *The Millennium Election* project suggest that there is still much to learn about the traditional forms of candidate-voter interaction—advertising, debates, and newspaper and television coverage. However, the researchers also provide some insight into the evolution of new campaign techniques and new channels of information that may well become the "traditional" media of the new millennium. They also suggest that the traditional channels and new techniques must work together to engage the young generation if they are to become active citizens in the twenty-first century.

I

THE CANDIDATE MESSAGES IN POLITICAL ADVERTISING AND DEBATES

1

Style and Effects of the Bush and Gore Spots

John C. Tedesco and Lynda Lee Kaid

Undoubtedly, the 2000 presidential campaign is one of the most interesting and historic in U.S. history. However, before the postelection voting debacle in Florida and the U.S. Supreme Court election decision there was an interesting and competitive presidential campaign. As the introductory chapter describes, the 2000 campaign offered researchers numerous rich communication circumstances for inquiry. This chapter focuses on the candidates' advertising message strategies and their effects.

As Devlin (2001) describes, the 2000 presidential candidates and their parties spent about $240 million on campaign ads. According to Devlin, the Bush campaign spent $134 million (including $71 million from the Republican Party) compared to $106 million (including $61 million from the Democratic Party) by Gore. Amazingly, the Bush campaign spent 42% more than the $98.2 million spent by Clinton in 1996 (Devlin, 1997).

The content and effects of these tremendous advertising expenditures warrant investigation. Since most polls conducted throughout the traditional hot phase of the campaign (Labor Day to Election Day) indicated that the 2000 battle for the White House would be determined by the large percentage of undecided voters in key battleground states, this chapter will focus on the effects of the ads on both decided and undecided research participants during two separate phases of the campaign. This chapter briefly evaluates the content of the presidential ads and focuses on their differing effects.

ADVERTISING RESEARCH

Candidates spend millions of dollars on campaign advertisements because they expect ads to reinforce their partisans, attract undecided voters, and in some cases convert small percentages of loosely committed voters. Academic research lends some support to these expectations.

Candidate image evaluations are an important predictor of voter decision making (Miller, Wattenberg, & Malanchuck, 1986) and, once formed, often appear resistant to subsequent persuasive appeals (Cundy, 1986, 1990; Mulder, 1979; Pfau & Burgoon, 1989; Surlin & Gordon, 1977). However, the majority of advertising effects research has demonstrated that positive and negative image evaluations of candidates are significantly different following exposure to advertisements (Kaid & Chanslor, 1995; Kaid, Chanslor, & Hovind, 1992; Kaid, Leland, and Whitney 1992; Kaid & Tedesco, 1999; Tedesco, 2002). Merritt (1984) concluded that partisanship produces selective distortion and more favorable emotional response to ads. Whereas partisanship is largely a reinforcing agent, some research has suggested that image evaluations of candidates transcend partisanship (Kaid, 1997; Tedesco, 2002). For example, Tedesco (2002) showed that Virginia Republicans evaluated Democratic Senate candidate Chuck Robb more positively after viewing his advertisements, whereas Kaid (1997) demonstrated that Dole advertisements aired in October 1996 produced negative evaluations from Democrats, independents, and Republicans.

Attempts to explain changes in candidate evaluations have led researchers to suggest negative and emotional advertising content as two significant factors in altered evaluations of candidates. Not surprisingly, negative (e.g., Kaid & Johnston, 1991, 2001; Kaid & Tedesco, 1999) and emotional appeals (Kaid & Johnston, 1991, 2001; Kern, 1989) are dominant features in political spots.

Negative advertisements may evoke a backlash for the sponsoring candidate (e.g., Ansolabehere & Iyengar, 1995; Merritt, 1984). Additionally, powerful evidence exists of a relationship between respondent feelings after viewing ads and candidate image evaluations (e.g., Alwitt, Deighton, & Grimm, 1991; Kaid, Leland, & Whitney, 1992 ; Kaid & Tedesco, 1999; Lang, 1991; Tedesco, 2002). More specifically, positive emotional reactions to ads were positively related to increased image evaluations and negative emotional reactions were correlated with decreased image evaluations (Kaid et al., 1992; Kaid & Tedesco, 1999; Tedesco, 2002).

Despite the strong evidence that ad exposure leads to gains in political candidate issue and image understanding, research shows that advertising exposure increases political cynicism (Kaid, McKinney, & Tedesco, 2000; Tedesco, 2002). Using a cynicism scale adopted from the National Election Survey (Rosenstone et al., 1997), Kaid et al. (2000) and Tedesco (2002) found that advertising exposure significantly increased cynicism levels in experimental research studies.

The research presented here briefly discusses the major content of the Bush and Gore advertisements and presents analysis of viewers' responses to the ads. Specifically, the following hypotheses and research questions are investigated:

RQ_1: Are there differences in ad valence (positive/negative) and appeal strategies (emotion, logic, credibility, fear) used by Bush and Gore?

H_1: Exposure to a series of political advertisements will result in significant image evaluation differences for the candidates involved.

RQ_2: Does exposure to political ads alter candidate image perceptions of both decided and undecided voters?

H_2: Exposure to a series of candidate advertisements will result in increased cynicism.

RQ_3: Are there significant differences in cynicism levels between decided and undecided voters before and after exposure to candidate advertisements?

METHOD

Advertising Content

The general election advertisements for Gore and Bush (including the ads sponsored by the national parties) were content analyzed using the concepts of videostyle articulated by Kaid and Johnston (2001). Ads that began airing following the primary season were included in the sample of 115 Gore and 46 Bush ads. Three trained graduate students coded the sample, which was made available from the University of Oklahoma Political Commercial Archive. Holsti's formula was used to calculate intercoder reliability on a sample of the ads.[1] Intercoder reliability reached +.85 across all categories.

Whereas the advertisements were coded using the entire verbal, nonverbal, and production categories of videostyle described by Kaid and Johnston (2001), only the aspects of advertising valence (positive/negative), appeal strategy (logical, emotional, and ethical), and use of fear appeals are addressed in this chapter.

Advertising Effects

Research participants were recruited on college campuses and in communities at various research sites during two distinct time periods of the campaign. Time 1 (September 30 to October 1) and Time 2 (November 1–3) were chosen as one-month intervals before and after the debates to assess the impact of the ads at various points in the campaign. Research participants included 1,063 participants from twenty-seven research sites in nineteen states during Time 1 and 906 participants at twenty-five research sites in eighteen states during Time 2.[2] Participants during both time periods were shown a series of four spots for both Bush and Gore.[3] The pre-test/post-test design for this study asked participants to (1) complete the pre-test questionnaire, (2) view the series of eight political spots, and (3) complete the post-test. The goal of this study was to explore individual characteristic responses and the causal nature of the relationships between independent and dependent variables. Advertisements receiving the most airplay in various states were selected for use on the stimulus to represent ads aired by each of the candidates during the specific time periods. Information about the ads in use by the candidates was obtained from the website of the *National Journal* (www.nationaljournal.com).

Pre-test/Post-test Questionnaires

In addition to demographic, voter choice, and a host of media exposure questions, the pre- and post-test questionnaires tested repeated measures on a number of highly reliable scales used in previous research. Traditional feeling thermometer scales (0–100) developed by Miller and Levitin (1976) and semantic differential scales developed as measures of candidate image by Sanders and Pace (1977) were used to assess candidate image evaluations.[4] As with previous applications (Kaid, Leland, & Whitney, 1992; Kaid & Tedesco, 1999), these scales produced high reliability in this study: Cronbach's alpha for respective pre-/post-test image scales were .84/.89 for Gore in Time 1, .86/.88 for Bush in Time 1, .86/.89 for Gore in Time 2, and .87/.90 for Bush in Time 2. The semantic differential scales were summed to create a mean score to use in the statistical equations.

Cynicism was assessed on the pre- and post-test through the use of scales that also replicate applications used previously (Kaid, McKinney, & Tedesco, 2000) and adapted from the National Election Studies (Rosenstone, Kinder, & Miller, 1997). Respondents were asked to indicate their level of agreement with eight statements using a five-point Likert scale ranging from strongly agree to strongly disagree.[5] The cynicism questions were summed to create a mean score for each participant's cynicism level in both the pre- and post-test. Cronbach's alpha reliability scores of .67 and .73 for Time 1 and .68 and .74 for Time 2 were recorded for the pre- and post-tests, respectively.

Emotional-response dependent variable measures appearing on the post-test also replicate those used in previous research (Kaid & Tedesco, 1999; Tedesco, 2002). Participants responded to a series of ten adjectives (optimistic, confident, anxious, excited, secure, fearful, bored, patriotic, concerned, and angry) using a three-point scale measuring the extent to which that adjective represented how they felt after viewing the candidate ads. The emotion items were used both independently and grouped by positive (optimistic) and negative (anxious) emotions.

RESULTS

Results of Research Question 1 indicate significant differences between Gore and Bush in the use of negative ads. As table 1.1 shows, the Gore campaign produced and aired significantly more negative ads than the Bush campaign. While the percentages of negative ads are almost twice as high for Gore, the actual advertisement numbers reflect a total of seventy-one negative ads for Gore compared to only seventeen for Bush. Thus, the Gore campaign produced and aired three times more negative ads than Bush. Of additional interest is the appeal strategies used in the ad arguments. Table 1.1 also shows significant differences between Bush and Gore in the use of emotional and fear appeals. While both candidates predominantly used logical appeals in their ad arguments, Gore was almost twice as likely as Bush to use emotional appeals. The difference in the use of fear appeals is very distinct. Gore, mostly through targeting elderly, medical, and health issues, used fear appeals in more than half the ads. Conversely, fear appeals were used sparingly by the Bush campaign.

Table 1.2 shows some interesting support for Hypothesis 1. It is clear from the significant increases in the semantic differential scores for Gore that his September advertising strategy was effective in increasing his image among the groups examined in this study. Exposure to the campaign advertisements significantly increased Gore's image evaluations among women, men, Republicans, Democrats, independents, decided, and undecided voters during Time 1. Interestingly, Bush did not experience any significant increases in image evaluation scores in Time 1. In fact, exposure to the advertising stimulus produced significant decreases in Bush's image score among females, Democrats, and decided voters.

Gore's advertisements during Time 2 continued to work in his favor. During the November exposure condition, Gore's image evaluation increased significantly among females, Democrats, decided, and undecided voters. Bush also experienced significantly increased image evaluations during Time 2 among females, Republicans, and decided voters. In both advertising tests, Gore scored significantly higher among undecided voters in post-test image evaluations, while Bush experienced favorable gains as a result of exposure to his ads aired during Time 2.

Since emotional content was so prevalent in the ads, an assessment of the emotion elicited from the ads and their relationship with image evaluations was completed. Correlations between image evaluations and emotional responses were performed during both Time 1 and Time 2 (see table 1.3). In both Time 1 and Time 2, clear evidence is found to support the correlation between emo-

Table 1.1   Characteristics of the 2000 General Elections Ads

Verbal Content of Ad	Bush (n = 46)	Gore (n = 115)
Ad Focus*		
Positive	63%	38%
Negative	37	62
Use of Appeals		
Logical	89	93
Emotional*	26	47
Ethical	24	37
Fear Appeals*	9	56

*Chi-square test indicates difference is significant at $p < .05$

Table 1.2 Overall Evaluations of Candidate Image with Partisan Breakdown

	Time 1			
	Gore		Bush	
	Pre	Post	Pre	Post
Males (n = 368)	4.44	4.55***	4.57	4.54
Female (n = 677)	4.69	4.90***	4.63	4.52***
Republicans (n = 390)	4.13	4.32***	5.21	5.17
Democrats (n = 400)	5.14	5.35***	4.15	4.00***
Independents (n = 197)	4.54	4.57***	4.46	4.41
Decided (n = 793)	4.65	4.83***	4.69	4.60***
Undecided (n = 194)	4.50	4.67***	4.51	4.45
	Time 2			
	Gore		Bush	
	Pre	Post	Pre	Post
Males (n = 353)	4.45	4.49	4.64	4.66
Female (n = 553)	4.65	4.75***	4.63	4.71***
Republicans (n = 354)	4.03	4.09	5.28	5.43***
Democrats (n = 322)	5.23	5.37***	4.07	4.03
Independents (n = 158)	4.56	4.61	4.46	4.48
Decided (n = 725)	4.61	4.70***	4.70	4.76**
Undecided (n = 92)	4.55	4.66*	4.54	4.62

*** t-test results significant at the $p \leq .001$ level.
** t-test results significant at the $p \leq .01$ level.
* t-test results significant at the $p \leq .05$ level.

tional effect and image evaluation scores as most correlations resulted in statistically significant relationships at the $p < .01$ level. The only emotion not significantly related either positively or negatively to image evaluations was the "anxious" emotion variable.

To assess further the relationship between emotion and image evaluations of the candidates, the emotional indices, party identification, race, post-test cynicism, pre-test cynicism, sex, previous exposure to spots, previous discussion about spots, cumulative media exposure, informed status, and campaign interest variables were entered as predictor variables in a stepwise multiple regression. Post-test image evaluation served as the dependent variable. As table 1.4 shows, emotional indices were the strongest predictors of Bush's post-test image evaluation measures. Optimistic emotions ($R^2 = .41, R = .64, \beta = .54, p \leq .000$) were the strongest predictor, followed by less powerful predictors of anxious emotions ($\beta = -.20, p \leq .000$), party identification ($\beta = .09, p \leq .001$), race ($\beta = -.06, p \leq .017$), and postdebate cynicism ($\beta = -.05, p \leq .037$). During Time 2, only the two emotional indices served to predict the post-test evaluations for Bush:

Table 1.3 Relationship between Emotional Response to Ads and Evaluation of Candidate Image

	Time 1		Time 2	
	Gore	Bush	Gore	Bush
Optimistic	.54*	.56*	.60*	.61*
Confident	.59*	.58*	.63*	.65*
Anxious	−.03	−.02	−.04	−.03
Excited	.42*	.40*	.47*	.47*
Secure	.54*	.57*	.59*	.62*
Fearful	−.45*	−.43*	−.49*	−.52*
Bored	−.38*	−.33*	−.34*	−.42*
Patriotic	.36*	.46*	.40*	.51*
Concerned	−.16*	−.13*	−.24*	−.19*
Angry	−.40*	−.37*	.44*	−.46*

* Pearson correlation is significant at the $p \leq .01$ level.

optimistic emotions ($\beta = .58, p \leq .000$) and anxious emotions ($\beta = −.24, p \leq .000$). While the optimistic emotions were the strongest predictor of post-test image evaluations for Bush in both Time 1 and Time 2, the anxious emotions were the strongest predictors for Gore's post-test image evaluations in both Time 1 ($R^2 = .20, R = .44, \beta = −.28, p \leq .000$) and Time 2 ($R^2 = .24, R = .49, \beta = −.37, p \leq .000$). In both advertising exposures, emotion was a stronger predictor than party identification for both candidates. Interestingly, post-test cynicism ($\beta = −.12, p \leq .000$), sex ($\beta = .10, p \leq .000$), and cumulative media exposure ($\beta = .08, p \leq .003$) helped explain the post-test image evaluations for Gore in Time 1. During Time 2, media exposure ($\beta = .10, p \leq .001$) was the only other predictor of Gore's image evaluation outside of the emotion indices and party identification.

Although the research shows a large amount of anxiety following exposure to the ads, that anxiety did not appear to translate into increased cynicism. Advertisement exposure did not increase cynicism among participants in either Time 1 (pre-test = 3.21, post-test = 3.22) or Time 2 (pre-test = 3.14, post-test = 3.14). Thus, Hypothesis 2 was not supported.

To answer the third research question, differences in cynicism scores were compared for decided and undecided voters. Differences between the decided and undecided participants were significant in both the pre-test (t [1,033] = −4.23, $p < .000$) and the post-test (t [1,012] = −4.53, $p < .000$) for Time 1 and the pre-test (t [872] = −5.02, $p < .000$) and post-test (t [852] = −3.63, $p < .000$) for Time 2. Undecided participants were significantly more cynical than their decided counterparts at both stages of the campaign.

Table 1.4 Post-Ad Regression Analyses of Semantic Differential Image Evaluation Predictors

	R	R²	β	t	signif.
Bush Image Evaluation Time 1					
Step 1: Optimistic Emotions	.64	.41	.54	20.26	.000
Step 2: Anxious Emotions	.67	.45	−.20	−7.46	.000
Step 3: Party ID	.67	.45	.09	3.44	.001
Step 4: Race	.68	.46	−.06	−2.40	.017
Step 5: Post-test Cynicism	.68	.46	−.05	−2.09	.037
				$F = 157.84$	.000
Gore Image Evaluation Time 1					
Step 1: Anxious Emotions	.44	.20	−.28	−9.46	.000
Step 2: Party ID	.51	.26	−.19	−6.93	.000
Step 3: Optimistic Emotions	.56	.31	−.30	−9.74	.000
Step 4: Post-test Cynicism	.58	.33	−.12	−4.40	.000
Step 5: Sex	.58	.34	.10	3.66	.000
Step 6: Media Exposure	.59	.35	.08	2.95	.003
				$F = 81.48$	.000
Bush Image Evaluation Time 2					
Step 1: Optimistic Emotions	.69	.47	.58	20.26	.000
Step 2: Anxious Emotions	.72	.52	−.24	−7.46	.000
				$F = 444.14$	.000
Gore Image Evaluation Time 2					
Step 1: Anxious Emotions	.49	.24	−.37	−11.61	.000
Step 2: Party ID	.55	.30	−.21	−7.39	.000
Step 3: Optimistic Emotions	.59	.35	−.25	−7.81	.000
Step 4: Media Exposure	.60	.35	.10	3.48	.001
				$F = 113.86$	.000

DISCUSSION

It is apparent from this research that Gore's early campaign advertising was more successful in increasing his image evaluations, while Bush's later campaign ads appeared more successful. During Time 1, the image evaluation increases for Gore transcended party identification, gender, and decided/undecided voting status. This finding supports previous research that shows the ability of ads to transcend party identification and work to the benefit of one candidate even among participants in opposing political parties (Kaid, 1997; Tedesco, 2002). During Time 1, Bush's ads appeared to reinforce some of the bad impressions he made among women, Democrats, and decided participants in this study. Interestingly, Bush's early advertisements did not significantly enhance his evaluations even among Republicans. During Time 2, partisanship served a more apparent role in the post-test image evaluations in that Gore's image significantly increased among Democrats and Bush's image significantly increased among

Republicans. While the 2000 campaign marked the second successive election with a gender divide—the majority of women voters for the Democratic candidate and the majority of male voters for the Republican candidate—the research here does not support that trend for advertising effects. Both males and females evaluated Gore more strongly after exposure to his ads at Time 1, and females evaluated Gore's image and Bush's image significantly higher in Time 2.

In an attempt to understand these changes in image evaluations, the stimulus tape was further analyzed. The positive ads aired during the early stages of the campaign appeared to favor Gore more. Even with a balance of positive and negative ads at Time 1, Bush did not perform well among participants. The fact that Bush did better at the later stages of the campaign is also interesting, especially since the advertising stimulus for Time 2 contained more negative ads for both Bush and Gore.

The fact that emotional indices were stronger predictors of the post-test image evaluations for both candidates at both time periods of the study adds convincing power to the argument for the emotional impact of ads on audiences (Kaid & Tedesco, 1999; Lang, 1991; Tedesco, 2002). Emotion was a more powerful predictor of image effects than party identification. Despite the large percentage of fear appeals used by Gore, fear was not inordinately related to the post-test image evaluations.

Despite expectation that exposure to the advertisements would increase participants' cynicism, no significant increases resulted after exposure during either Time 1 or Time 2. Whereas cynicism did not increase among participants, the undecided participants demonstrated significantly higher levels of cynicism than decided participants in the pre-tests and post-tests during both time periods. Although undecided voters are more cynical than decided voters, exposure to advertising messages in both Time 1 and Time 2 assisted large percentages in determining candidate choices. During Time 1, 32% of undecided voters committed to a candidate in the post-test (24% to Gore and 8% to Bush). During Time 2, 35% of undecided voters committed to a candidate (13% to Gore and 22% to Bush). Thus, by the closing days of the campaign, the tide appeared to switch to Bush's favor, with the more sizable shift in undecided voters favoring Bush. Interestingly, in both time periods, a small number of participants switched their candidate preference after exposure; six from Gore to Bush and eleven from Bush to Gore in Time 1, and six from Gore to Bush and six from Bush to Gore in Time 2. Despite the gender divide in the 1996 and 2000 presidential elections, voters did not show increases in image evaluations for Bush at either time during the advertising exposure assessments.

Although advertisements have been demonstrated in previous research to increase cynicism, it appears that campaign context influences whether participants react negatively to ads. Despite the large percentage of negative ads, respondents did not seem to grow more cynical when candidates attacked each other in their spots. The results should encourage researchers to investigate more thoroughly the use and effects of emotion in political spots.

NOTES

1. The formula used to calculate intercoder reliability is that given in North et al. (1963). It is given for two coders and can be modified for any number of coders.

$$R = \frac{2(C_{1,2})}{C_1 + C_2}$$

$C_{1,2}$ = number of category assignments both coders agree on
$C_1 + C_2$ = total category assignments made by both coders

2. States included in the effects assessment during Time 1 and Time 2 include Arkansas, California, Colorado, Florida, Georgia, Idaho, Illinois, Indiana, Iowa, Kansas, Massachusetts, Missouri, Ohio, Oklahoma, Pennsylvania, Texas, Virginia, and South Carolina. Alabama also served as a research site during Time 1.

3. The spots used in the first ad experiment were (1) a positive Gore spot called "Bean-Counters," which features Gore speaking at a rally, attacking the HMO/insurance companies and promoting his patients'-bill-of rights program; (2) a positive Bush spot titled "Hard Things" in which Bush says that America has a chance to focus on tough problems and that there is a budget surplus and a deficit in values; (3) a negative Gore ad called "Judge," which says that the Bush administration did not improve the quality of health care in Texas and states at the end of the spot, "The Bush record. It's becoming an issue"; (4) a Bush ad titled "Compare," which compares Gore and Bush on senior prescription drug plans, school accountability, and tax cuts and states at the end of the spot, "Governor Bush has real plans that work for real people"; (5) a positive Gore ad, "Ian," that features the story of an ill baby boy and his mother talking about how Gore helped reinstate their insurance coverage; (6) a positive Bush ad called "Education Agenda," which itemizes Bush's education agenda, beginning and ending with clips from Bush's convention speech; (7) a negative Gore ad titled "National," which uses split screens to attack Bush's record on the minimum wage and stands on health insurance for children in Texas, ending with the statement that Bush "has real plans that hurt real people"; (8) a Bush ad, "Notebook," that compares Bush and Gore's senior prescription drug plans, using a notebook graphic.

The spots used for the second advertising stimulus, in the order of their appearance, were (1) a positive Bush spot titled "Trust" in which Bush talks about trusting America and renewing America's purpose; (2) a positive Gore ad, "College," in which Gore's college tuition tax deduction for middle-class families is featured; (3) a negative Bush ad, "Gore-Gantuan," that attacks Gore's spending plan and says it will wipe out the surplus and increase governmental spending; (4) a Gore ad titled "Down," which uses a graphic of a dissolving dollar bill to attack Bush's tax-cut plan, ending with the message that Gore will pay down the debt, protect Social Security, and give a tax deduction for college tuition; (5) a Bush ad titled "Education Recession," which suggests that there is a Clinton-Gore education recession and that Bush raised education standards in Texas and tells the viewer how to obtain the "Bush blueprint for education," which features accountability, high standards, and local control; (6) a Gore ad titled "Apron," which attacks Bush on the minimum wage in Texas and promotes the "Al Gore plan" of a higher minimum wage, investment in education, middle-class tax cuts, and a secure retirement; (7) a Bush ad called "Big Relief vs. Big Spending," which compares Bush's tax-cut plan with Gore's spending plan, stating that Gore's spending plan threatens America's prosperity; and (8) a negative Gore ad called "Needle," which opens with a foggy Houston skyline, attacks Bush on his environmental policies in Texas, and ends with a foggy Seattle skyline, asking the viewer to "imagine Bush's Texas-style environmental regulations" in Seattle.

4. The semantic differential scales included twelve bipolar adjective pairs: qualified-unqualified, sophisticated-unsophisticated, honest-dishonest, sincere-insincere, successful-unsuccessful, believable-unbelievable, attractive-unattractive, calm-excitable, aggressive-unaggressive, strong-weak, passive-active, and friendly-unfriendly.

5. The specific items used in the cynicism scale were (1) Whether I vote or not has no influence on what politicians do, (2) One never really knows what politicians think, (3) People like me don't have any say about what the government does, (4) Sometimes politics and government seem so complicated that a person like me can't really understand what's going on, (5) One can be confident that politicians will always do the right thing (reversed in coding), (6) Politicians often quickly forget their election promises after a political campaign is over, (7) Politicians are more interested in power than in what the people think, and (8) One cannot always trust what politicians say.

REFERENCES

Alwitt, L. F., Deighton, J., & Grimm, J. (1991). Reactions to political advertising depend on the nature of the voter-candidate bond. In F. Biocca (Ed.), *Television and political advertising, Volume 1* (pp. 329–350). Hillsdale, NJ: Lawrence Erlbaum Associates.

Ansolabehere, S., & Iyengar, S. (1995). *Going negative: How attack ads shrink and polarize the electorate*. New York: Free Press.

Cundy, D. T. (1986). Political commercials and candidate image: The effects can be substantial. In L. L. Kaid, D. Nimmo, & K. R. Sanders (Eds.), *New perspectives on political advertising*, (pp. 210–234). Carbondale, IL: Southern Illinois University Press.

Cundy, D. T. (1990). Image formation, the low involvement voter, and televised political advertising. *Political Communication and Persuasion, 7*, 41–59.

Devlin, L. P. (1997). Contrasts in presidential campaign commercials of 1996. *American Behavioral Scientist, 37*, 272–290.

Devlin, L. P. (2001). Contrast in presidential campaign commercials of 2000. *American Behavioral Scientist, 44* (12), 2338–2369.

Kaid, L. L. (1997). Effects of the television spots on images of Dole and Clinton. *American Behavioral Scientist, 40* (8), 1085–1094.

Kaid, L. L., & Chanslor, M. (1995). Changing candidate image: The effects of television advertising. In K. Hacker (Ed.), *Candidate images in presidential election campaigns*, (pp. 83–97). New York: Praeger.

Kaid, L. L., Chanslor, M., & Hovind, M. (1992). The influence of program and commercial type on political advertising effectiveness. *Journal of Broadcasting and Electronic Media, 36*(3), 303–320.

Kaid, L. L., & Johnston, A. (1991). Negative versus positive television advertising in U.S. presidential campaigns, 1960–1988. *Journal of Communication, 41*(3), 53–64.

Kaid, L. L., & Johnston, A. (2001). *Videostyle in presidential campaigns.* Westport, CT: Praeger.

Kaid, L. L., Leland, C. M., & Whitney, S. (1992). The impact of televised political ads: Evoking viewer responses in the 1988 presidential campaign. *Southern Communication Journal, 57,* 285–92.

Kaid, L. L., McKinney, M., & Tedesco, J. C. (2000). *Civic dialogue in the 1996 presidential campaign: Candidate, media, and public voices.* Cresskill, NJ: Hampton Press.

Kaid, L. L., & Tedesco, J. C. (1999). Tracking reactions to the television advertising. In L. L. Kaid & D. Bystrom (Eds.), *The electronic election* (pp. 233–245). Mahwah, NJ: Lawrence Erlbaum Associates.

Kern, M. (1989). *30-second politics: Political advertising in the eighties.* New York: Praeger.

Lang, A. (1991). Emotion, formal features, and memory for televised political advertisements. In F. Biocca (Ed.) *Television and political advertising, Volume I* (pp. 221–243). Hillsdale, NJ: Lawrence Erlbaum Associates.

Merritt, S. (1984). Negative political advertising: Some empirical findings. *Journal of Advertising, 13* (3), 27–38.

Miller, A. H., Wattenberg, M. P., & Malanchuk, O. (1986). Schematic assessments of presidential candidates. *American Political Science Review, 80,* 521–540.

Miller, W. E., & Levitin, T. E. (1976). *Leadership and change.* Cambridge, MA: Winthrop Publishers.

Mulder, R. (1979). The effects of televised ads in the 1975 Chicago mayoral election. *Journalism Quarterly, 56,* 336–340.

North, R. C., Holsti, O., Zaninovich, M. G., & Zinnes, D. A. (1963). *Content analysis: A handbook with applications for the study of international crisis.* Evanston, IL: Northwestern University Press.

Pfau, M., & Burgoon, M. (1989). The efficacy of issue and character attack message strategies in political campaign communication. *Communication Reports, 2,* 52–61.

Rosenstone, S. J., Kinder, D., Miller, W. E., & the National Election Studies (1997). *American national election study, 1996: Pre- and post-election survey* [Computer file]. Ann Arbor, MI: University of Michigan, Center for Political Studies [producer], 1997. Ann Arbor, MI: Inter-university Consortium for Political and Social Research [distributor].

Sanders, K., & Pace, T. (1977). The influence of speech communication on the image of a political candidate: "Limited effects" revisited. In B. D. Ruben (Ed.), *Communication yearbook I* (pp. 465–474). New Brunswick, NH: Transaction Books.

Surlin, S. H., & Gordon, T. F. (1977). How values affect attitudes toward direct reference political advertising. *Journalism Quarterly, 54,* 89–98.

Tedesco, J. C. (2002). Televised political advertising effects: Evaluating responses during the 2000 Robb-Allen Senatorial Election. *Journal of Advertising, 31* (1), 37–48.

2

Myth and Anti-Myth in Presidential Campaign Films 2000

Janis L. Edwards and Stacey M. Smith

The presidential campaign film has received close attention in recent years as an important rhetorical genre that "unif[ies] propagandistic image-making traditions of the presidential campaign, the documentary film, and the advertising and public relations fields" (Morreale, 1993, p. 26). Because these films are produced especially for party conventions, they do not receive the extended airplay of traditional candidate ads. However, they serve an important function in providing a more complete image of a candidate than campaign spots can because of their longer format. The fact that they are presented as part of the nominating convention events heightens their significance as a televisual argument in support of the party's nominee and a means by which a candidate's image is reframed as the general election campaign ensues.[1] Kendall and Strachan (2001, p. 2) claim that the campaign film has usurped the role of speech making in providing a formal introduction of the candidate to the delegates.

By combining visual and auditory images with verbal narration, the campaign film builds an image that has immediacy and entertainment value yet retains the reality effect of documentary, as compared with the more overt persuasive techniques of spot advertising. Despite their documentary format, campaign films are produced and crafted as political messages for rhetorical purposes. As Timmerman (1996, p. 365) has noted, the presidential campaign film contributes to a thematic positioning of the candidate for the final phase of the campaign. The films borrow from the techniques of commercials in crafting a multimodal message that "define[s] the character and qualifications of candidates and the broad themes that shape their campaigns" (Morreale, 1994b, p. 141).

The image that emerges from presidential campaign films is highly selective, stemming from an artifact that signifies a campaign's rhetorical strategy in concrete action. Scholars have studied presidential campaign films for insight as to generic or comparative campaign strategies (Kendall & Strachan, 2001; Morreale, 1993, 1994b; Parry-Giles & Parry-Giles, 1996; Timmerman, 1996), determining to what extent a film is "successful" or "unsuccessful" as a strategic narrative. Although strategic issues always inform campaign films, our interest in the Bush and Gore campaign films of 2000 lies primarily in what these messages implicitly reveal about voter attitudes toward presidential politics. Contemporary politics borrows heavily from the techniques of commercial marketing—focus groups, surveys, and the like—to craft campaign messages. Therefore, a singularly important text as the campaign film would be a key framing device for the campaign vision that results from careful analysis and interpretation of the public mind.

Morreale has asserted that campaign films "illustrate the ways that viewers' self images and the wider matrix of a society's image of itself are created through discourse" (1994a, p. 20). Presumably, this dynamic includes the imagining of the country's instrumental and symbolic leader. Moreover, the similarities in rhetorical strategy evidenced by the Bush and Gore films, and their close finish in the election race, suggest that in 2000 these films captured and mirrored a similar construct of voter preference, rendering them particularly useful as sites for evaluation of the American perception of presidential leadership at the turn of the century. We argue that the perception of desirable leadership conveyed by the candidate images constructed in these two films has turned from a traditional "mythic" persona to a contrasting image that we term an "anti-myth." Although the images proffered by George W. Bush and Al Gore in 2000 are prompted, to some extent, by specific contextual events of campaign 2000, we argue that the image construction in their campaign films challenges many characteristics of traditional presidential leadership style that has governed the nation's consciousness of, and accepted candidate strategies for, the office.

THE "MYTHIC" PRESIDENCY

Myths develop as "a socially constructed representation of reality that articulates the central beliefs, values, and preoccupations of a culture" (Morreale, 1991, p. 46). But, as Glassman and Kenney (1994, p. 5) note, the concept of myth "is slippery" and includes the potential for a number of possible interpretations applicable to candidates. Gronbeck (1989), for example, has argued that biographical advertising by presidential candidates may be structured around any one of a number of images that may be described as myths, although he also notes that a message may be more or less mythic. Additionally, Morreale suggests that the mythic construction of candidates is linked to sociohistorical moments

(1994a, p. 21). Our definition of myth, as it pertains to presidential image, focuses on a traditional, idealistic, and prevailing model of political leadership, defined by Misciagno (1996, p. 329) as "a set of expectations and perceptions that are grounded in American political ideology and folklore, by which the president is viewed as larger than life and, above all else, is seen as a strong leader." This "mythic president" ideal has its roots in a hierarchical culture where power has been centralized and is revealed in many of the characteristics of an incumbency campaign, where the candidate emphasizes the symbols of power and mystique that attend the office: remoteness from day-to-day concerns, pageantry, use of legitimized power (through emphasis on accomplishments), and access to power exemplified by world leaders (Trent & Friedenberg, 2000).

Presidential campaign films, as a genre, tend to use a mythic framework. As Morreale has observed, campaign films typically present idealized and archetypal images of the candidates, and of the country (1993, pp. 6–7). The 1984 reelection campaign film for Ronald Reagan illustrates this framework in its presentation of Reagan as a charismatic and omnipotent leader who, in surviving an assassination attempt, forged a connection to the divine.

An antithetical construct would be that of a populist, or Everyman, who is motivated by service more than power. Although there have been populist candidates in our nation's history, prevailing expectations of the presidency incorporate the mythic "great man" construct of the masculine ideal (DeConde, 2000). However, Misciagno (1996) argues that contemporary American society is incompatible with the traditional mythic presidency because the proliferation of the media has eroded the private sphere that creates and protects presidential mystique. Similar arguments are advanced by Parry-Giles and Parry-Giles (2002) in their contention that the media-saturated postmodern age, with the Clinton presidency as the pivotal moment, is redefining traditional expectations of presidential image. Earlier, Jamieson (1988) argued that television is altering expectations concerning the stylistic features of presidential self-presentation. If these arguments are valid, we would expect to find the characteristics of change identified by Misciagno and Parry-Giles and Parry-Giles expressed in market-driven campaign messages such as presidential campaign films. An analysis of the Bush and Gore 2000 campaign films reveals two documents similar in tone and content, where contrast would be expected, that reject the mythic presidency image in favor of the anti-mythic characteristics discussed by Misciagno and suggested by Parry-Giles and Parry-Giles.

MYTH AND ANTI-MYTH

We proceed with our analysis by identifying specific characteristics associated with the traditional, mythic presidential ideal and their contrasting features. Misciagno (1996) proposes the following as characteristics of the mythic presidency:

- The president is a larger-than-life figure.
- Leadership is hierarchical.
- Power is paramount (emphasized in record or deeds).
- Strength is emphasized.
- Masculinity is emphasized (through an emphasis on the figure's connection to male preserves such as the military and sports).
- Man is seen as the embodiment of the "essence and legacy of the American spirit."

An example of the mythic framework in presidential campaign films is the 1984 Reagan reelection film, *A New Beginning*, which emphasized power by associating Reagan with world leaders and the locations of governance, his strong and larger-than-life survival of an assassination attempt, and his position as figurehead of the American people.

In contrast, characteristics of an anti-mythic construction, suggested by Misciagno (1996) and Parry-Giles and Parry-Giles (2002), would include the following:

- The president is a figure who seeks to identify with voters (as opposed to standing apart).
- More personal appeals express greater intimacy.
- An emphasis is placed on everyday human qualities (as opposed to exercise of power).
- Family relationships are emphasized over a record or deeds of governance.
- The message is "feminized" by an intimate, relational tone or content.
- Man is portrayed as Everyman, rather than an embodiment of the collective American spirit.

Campaigns are about contrast. But George W. Bush and Al Gore, despite their deep differences, are positioned in similar fashion in their 2000 campaign films, and in a way that reflects the anti-mythic construct.

The Bush Film

Titled *The Sky's the Limit*, George W. Bush's film is characterized by a down-to-earth personal tone. Identification and a personal quality are established through a combination of narrative content, physical setting, and visual presentation. The film opens with a familiar scene of Americana—Bush and his dog, riding across his ranch in an open jeep. The audience is invited to share vicariously in the personal experience, as the camera sits in the "shotgun" seat. As Bush talks about his personal vision of America's promise, his informality and the camera's position make the viewer feel engaged in a friendly conversation, a conversation about what makes America great, but an ordinary conversation that suggests no remoteness from this candidate.

From Bush's current home, signified by the ranch setting, we travel to the home of memory, the family home in Midland, Texas. Biographical ads and films typically make an account of the candidate's origins. In his recollection, Bush emphasizes the community feeling of people from Midland and how he is a part of the fabric of the place. His mother, Barbara Bush, provides the transition to Bush's unique qualities in an anecdote about the attitude of her "caring little boy" toward his parents after his sister's death. As the parents were consciously giving attention to the boy so he would not feel excluded, George W. felt responsible for distracting his mother from her grief. Whereas this anecdote serves to establish Bush's character in the context of his campaign's promise of "compassionate conservatism," it also maintains the film's initial focus on George W. Bush in a domestic setting, rather than placing him as an actor in the public sphere.

The theme of domestic life is enhanced by archival film footage of the senior Bush family at play in Midland, with familiar home-movie genre scenes. These scenes are followed by pictures of George W. Bush's own family life, as he and his wife recall their courtship, marriage, and the birth of their daughters. Not only are such intimate family stories atypical of past presidential campaign videos, the sense of Bush as an Everyman is accentuated by his own unpolished telling of the story. When he makes a verbal flub, it is not edited out. Rather, his wife pokes good-humored fun at her husband, humanizing the situation. The candidate explains, "I like to laugh. And I like to laugh with people, and sometimes I . . . need to laugh at some of the things I say. I'm a person who likes to smile."

Even when the film shifts description from character to deeds, the transition is framed in terms of family. The first testimonial is from Carlos Ramirez, a Hispanic Democratic mayor of El Paso, Texas, who asserts Bush's dedication to family values, a commitment echoed by Bush's father, the former president. Following comments by George W. Bush on immigration that call attention to the value of inclusiveness, Ernie Ladd, founder of Project P.U.L.L. (Professional United Leadership League) in Houston, describes Bush's involvement in the mentoring program dedicated to helping minority youth. Again, the good deeds accomplished by George Bush are framed in terms of relationships as he tells the story of his feelings about Jimmy Dean, one of the kids in the project who subsequently died, a victim of the "tough circumstances" of his environment. Interestingly, the details of George W. Bush's role and involvement in the program are vague. The example is presented as though it were Bush's initial involvement in civic duty, yet the pictures provided as eyewash are clearly contemporary.

At this point in the film, the mythic "great man" construction is further downplayed as Bush reflects upon his generation in "we" terms rather than "I" terms. Bush embeds his goals in the group goals of a generation of teachers, lawyers, and others. "If we don't help others, if we don't step up and lead, who will?" Bush asks rhetorically. Following this brief reflection, the film returns to the testimonial format as Phyllis Hunter, a teacher in the Texas public schools, speaks about George Bush's support for state school efforts. While Ms. Hunter cites no specific programs and, again, the eyewash clips appear to be contemporary, she attributes improved educational support systems such as teacher training, grant programs, and website availability to Bush's tenure as governor.

Up until this point, the music in the film has been simple and nostalgic, but as the film shifts, so does the music, as a more mythic framework is presented. The tempo picks up and trumpets call as a film montage is presented of images, symbols and icons of America intercut with scenes of a Bush speech. The scenes are varied and include Martin Luther King Jr., John F. Kennedy, the flag raising at Iwo Jima, familiar U.S. cityscapes, the Statue of Liberty, the Lincoln Memorial, the Washington Monument, Ronald Reagan and the collapse of communism, the moon landing, the Jefferson Memorial, baseball, and the American flag. These patriotic scenes seem gratuitous because only the most tenuous link is made between Bush and these symbols of America. Throughout the film, there is no direct and specific mention of his record in public service. The scenes of incumbency style, which could be exploited to substantiate Bush's qualification for office, are bypassed in favor of scenes that establish a more open-ended sense of character. This character is defined as Everyman rather than Great Man, a man whose *heart* is in the right place, even if his actions remain unaddressed.

The Gore Film

Al Gore's film appears to make several specific overtures to women voters but is also "feminized" in other general respects. The film is introduced, narrated, and seemingly created by the candidate's wife, Tipper, who refers to the film as a family album of her snapshots. Gore's film, like Bush's, begins with a focus on family, but here the family is Gore's own nuclear family. Tipper's position as agent of the film is underscored by the beginning point of Al Gore's story, when Tipper and Al first meet as teenagers. The film quickly transitions to Gore's family, or at least its female members. The character of his sister, Nancy, and the accomplishments of his mother, Pauline, are highlighted (an evident ploy to appeal to women voters). When the focus returns to Gore and his decision to enlist in the military during the Vietnam War, the film, much like the Bush film, attempts to make the decision seem somehow common, as Tipper says, "Al realized that if he didn't go, someone else could go in his place." This statement presents Al Gore's view of himself as interchangeable with others.

Gore's motives for public service are presented as motives that are commonly understood and might be shared by anyone. His father, a powerful senator, is his hero, as many boys' fathers are to them. Despite his father's position, Gore began military service at the bottom, as a private. When Gore went to Vietnam, his wife worried as any wife would. Gore's service in Vietnam, his subsequent job decisions, and growing family life are presented as ordinary, even unremarkable. His decision to run for Congress is presented as growing out of an ideal of citizen involvement, painting Gore's motives with the same strokes used in the Bush film. The candidates are just doing what they believe ordinary people should do.

Gore's film does present more information about his record as a politician than does Bush's film, although the details are brief. Tipper cites her husband's twenty-four years in electoral office and "hundreds of open meetings." Two specific accomplishments are attributed to Gore during his congressional tenure: his commitment to the environment, which began with the first hearings regarding protection of *families* from toxic waste, and his role as catalyst for changing a congressional schedule to accommodate *parents* who wanted to participate in Halloween trick-or-treating. The snapshot quality of the still images and their centering on family life underscore the "family first" narrative by Tipper. The focus then shifts more dramatically from the candidate to his family members in recounting his son's accident and his wife's subsequent depression. The candidate's deeds are sublimated to his wife's experience, as he is shown looking on at a White House conference on mental health. As family members are foregrounded in the narrative, the visuals highlight the candidate's involvement with his children and grandson and his feelings over the loss of his father. Character and record are further woven together in a concluding visual montage suggesting past accomplishments and public roles as Gore is depicted in quick succession with others including the Pope, firefighters, military personnel, Nelson Mandela, and the American flag interspersed with numerous family album scenes.

The Bush and Gore films clearly emphasize character over competence, although Gore's film makes somewhat more reference to his record in office. This is not an unusual strategy for challenger campaigns, although both Bush and Gore have enough experience and connection to the presidency to warrant elements of incumbency style in their campaigns. The emphasis on character is likely a response to the perceived weakness of the Clinton presidency, as both candidates seek to differentiate themselves from Clinton and reach out to special constituencies, women, and minorities. However, the stylistic and substantive elements go beyond character references to reflect the anti-myth construction. Rather than being presented as hierarchical or larger than life, both candidates are carefully presented as "of the people," often embedding their decisions and accomplishments in the collective experience of others. Rather than emphasizing power, stories told by and about the candidates emphasize relationships. These candidates are connected to constituents, colleagues, and, most of all, family. They are feminized through appeals that evoke intimacy and emotion above individualism and reason. Family relationships take on far greater significance than deeds. Moreover, women serve as interpreters, especially in Gore's film, which often digresses to his wife's life story. Typical references to the male preserves of sport and war are distinctly downplayed.[2]

The 2000 campaign films of Al Gore and George Bush are not unique in the genre. They express themes and characteristics that are common to many other campaign films as described by Morreale (1993). They include archival photographs and film footage as well as testimonials. However, other commonplaces in campaign films, such as footage of the candidate at work or in the locations of governance that would make them appear presidential, are absent or markedly subordinated to relational themes. Montages associate the candidates with past heroes and American ideals, but these segments are limited and are overshadowed by the emphasis on candidate character. Further, the means by which character is developed is unusually personalized.

CONCLUSION

While the campaign films of the 2000 presidential candidates reflect some of the common features of the genre, they are unusually weighted toward character themes, established through narratives and visuals that emphasize relationships, especially family relationships. Gore's film so thoroughly strikes this theme that it seems sometimes to be more about his wife than about the candidate himself. In a situation where campaigns are built on contrast, the images of Bush and Gore that emerge from their campaign films are strikingly similar. One might argue that the emphasis on character and relationships is a response to the perception problems of the impeached sitting president, Bill Clinton. However, this observation does not adequately explain the tone of the Bush and Gore films. While Clinton's private activities had a considerable negative effect on perceptions of his character, his impeachment had little obvious effect, and he remained highly popular among voters. As documents crafted from a careful analysis of the public mood, the strikingly similar aspects of the 2000 films suggest a confluence of the national mood and a longing for a reinvention of the presidential ideal that departs from the traditional mythic mode of the past.

We must be cautious in assuming the strength of this trend. Although it is implied or argued by Misciagno (1996), Parry-Giles and Parry-Giles (2002), and Jamieson (1988), the events of September 11, 2001, and the subsequent warlike response of the country may reinvigorate a traditional model of presidential leadership that corresponds to war activity in its hypermasculinity and concern with power. Analysis of the 2000 presidential campaign films provides a test case for reevaluation of candidate films in 2004 and subsequent campaigns to determine whether the media-driven changes in presidential image expectations continue to evolve in an "anti-mythic" direction.

NOTES

1. Campaign films are not always televised. The major broadcast channels currently decline to broadcast what they consider to be extended political advertisements, but the films are generally shown on cable channel coverage of the conventions and are sometimes distributed to public interest groups.

2. In Gronbeck's (1989) study of 1988 campaign bio-ads, he describes Gore's ads as presenting "no clear mythic . . . persona" (p. 357).

REFERENCES

DeConde, A. (2000). *Presidential machismo: Executive authority, military intervention, and foreign relations.* Boston: Northeastern University Press.

Glassman, C., & Kenney, K. (1994, Fall). Myths & presidential campaign photographs. *Visual Communication Quarterly, 1* (4), 4–7.

Gronbeck, B. E. (1989). Mythic portraiture in the 1988 Iowa presidential caucus bio-ads. *American Behavioral Scientist, 32,* 351–364.

Jamieson, K. H. (1988). *Eloquence in an electronic age: The transformation of political speechmaking.* New York: Oxford University Press.

Kendall, K., & Strachan, J. C. (2001, November). *Convention films: Finding the prefect image.* Paper presented at the annual meeting of the National Communication Association, Atlanta.

Melder, K. (1989). Creating candidate imagery: The man on horseback. In L. Sabato (Ed.), *Campaigns and elections: A reader in modern American politics* (pp. 5–11). Boston: Scott, Foresman and Company.

Misciagno, P. S. (1996). Rethinking the mythic presidency. *Political Communication, 13,* 329–344.

Morreale, J. (1991). *A new beginning: A textual frame analysis of the political campaign film.* Albany, NY: State University of New York Press.

Morreale, J. (1993). *The presidential campaign film: A critical history.* Westport, CT: Praeger.

Morreale, J. (1994a). American self images and the presidential campaign film, 1964–1992. In A. H. Miller & B. E. Gronbeck (Ed.), *Presidential campaigns and American self images* (pp. 19–39). Boulder, CO: Westview Press.

Morreale, J. (1994b). The Bush and Dukakis convention films. *Journal of Popular Culture, 27*(4), 141–152.

Parry-Giles, S. J., & Parry-Giles, T. (1996). Gendered politics and presidential image construction: A reassessment of the "feminine style." *Communication Monographs, 63,* 337–353.

Parry-Giles, S. J., & Parry-Giles, T. (2002). *Constructing Clinton: Hyperreality & presidential image-making in postmodern politics.* New York: Peter Lang.

Timmerman, D. M. (1996). 1992 presidential candidate films: The contrasting narratives of George Bush and Bill Clinton. *Presidential Studies Quarterly, 26,* 364–373.

Trent, J., & Friedenberg, R. V. (2000). *Political campaign communication: Principles and practices* (4th ed.). Westport, CT: Praeger.

3

Issue Advocacy and Political
Advertising in Election 2000

Barbara J. Walkosz

Television commercials continue to play a prominent role in the American political process. Although political advertisements have been criticized for their negative content and veracity, they remain key to political campaigns, acting as a central source of issue and candidate information for the electorate (Ansolabehere, Behr, & Iyengar, 1993; Devlin, 1995; Jamieson, 1992; Kaid & Johnston, 1991; Kern, 1989). Three significant and related conditions characterize the role of political advertising during the 2000 federal elections. First, the "high-stakes" (Magleby, 2002, p. 4) nature of the 2000 elections—which determined control of both the House and Senate and the presidency—attracted record contributions of soft moneys (Corrado, 2002; Stone, 2000). Second, candidates, political parties, and independent groups expended an unprecedented $629 million on political advertising (Brennan Center, 2001). The increased expenditures resulted in an 82% increase in the number of spots aired in the presidential race from the 1996 to the 2000 election and a 59% growth in congressional campaign advertisements from the 1997–1998 to the 1999–2000 election cycle (Goldstein & Freedman, 2002). Third, the concurrent increase of soft money contributions and issue advocacy advertisements altered the landscape of political advertising from a domain previously controlled by candidates to an arena increasingly colonized by political parties and special interest groups.

The rise in issue advocacy advertisements is the result of the identification of loopholes in Federal Election Commission (FEC) campaign finance regulations that allow unregulated expenditures of large sums of soft moneys for electioneering activities by political parties and groups (Dreyfuss, 1998; Magleby, 2000;

Magleby & Holt, 1999; Starr, 1998; West, 2000). Soft money contributions have raised a number of concerns about the electoral process including the potential breakdown of the campaign financing system, the undue influence of wealthy individuals and private groups on public policy, and the loss of control of campaign themes and strategies by the candidates (Dreyfuss, 1998; Magleby, 2000; West, 2000). Don Simon, general counsel for Common Cause, notes that "this is a problem that threatens to overwhelm all regulation of money in politics, because it provides an avenue for complete evasion of the rules" (quoted in Dreyfuss, 1998, p. 31).

A variety of campaign communications, including television advertisements, debates, interviews, and television appearances, were used by the candidates of Election 2000 to disseminate their policy positions. Issue advocacy advertisements were an integral part of that campaign environment. The intent of this chapter is to determine the role that issue advocacy advertisements played in Election 2000. To achieve this goal, the history of campaign finance regulations, the development of issue advocacy as a normative part of election campaigns, and the characteristics of issue advocacy spots in the 1999–2000 election cycle will be addressed.

CAMPAIGN FINANCE REGULATIONS

The history of campaign finance regulations dates back to 1907 when Congress first sought to restrict the amount of money that corporations could contribute to federal elections. Similar restrictions were applied to labor unions in the 1940s, but it was not until the early 1970s that Congress once again addressed campaign financing (Moramarco, 2000). In 1971, Congress passed the Federal Election Campaign Act (FECA), amended in 1974, 1976, and 1979, to establish the rules that remained in effect for Election 2000. The FECA created the Federal Election Commission (FEC), and, as a response to Watergate and the actions of the Nixon White House, defined a specific set of regulations for campaign disclosure requirements, contribution limits, and spending ceilings for candidates, parties, and groups (Nelson, 2002). Under the spending limits established by the FEC in effect during the 2000 election:

1. Individuals can contribute up to $1,000 each for the primary and general election to candidates running for federal office, for a total of $2,000.
2. The creation of political action committees (PACs) is authorized to allow corporations, labor unions, and political organizations to collect voluntary contributions from interested individuals and pass them on to candidates. PACs are allowed to fund candidates up to $5,000 each for the primary and general election, for a total of $10,000.

3. Annual contributions to parties are capped at $20,000 for individuals and $15,000 for PACs (Moramarco, 2000).

However, soon after the publication of these rules, concerns developed that the FECA regulations would pose a threat to First Amendment rights for individuals who wished to engage in political communication outside of the scope of an election (Moramarco, 2000; West, 2000). In 1976, such a challenge came before the U.S. Supreme Court with the case of *Buckley v. Valeo*, 424 U.S. 1 (1976). In support of the freedom-of-expression argument, the Court ruled that the statutes of the FECA could be applied only to funds related to electioneering activities or to communications that "expressly advocated the election or defeat of a candidate." The Court determined that express advocacy is to be defined by the use of "magic words" such as "elect," "support," "reject," "vote for," "defeat," or "vote against." Thus, if a communication does not expressly advocate for a candidate's election or defeat, it is not subject to the statutes established by the FECA.

While not explicitly defined by the Court, issue advocacy is considered a "communication designed to bring an idea or issue to the public's attention" (Dreyfuss, 1998, p. 32) through "advertising, public relations, voter education, or grass roots mobilization, often with tax-exempt funds" (Faucheux, 1998, p. 20). Prior to the 1990s, issue advocacy was the primary domain for single-issue and ideological groups that were concerned with such subjects as abortion, gun control, and other "hot button" topics (Dreyfuss, 1998). These groups, under FEC regulations, were allowed to spend money on campaign communications to generate support for their cause without reporting their expenditures to the FEC. However, the nature of issue advocacy changed when groups and political parties discovered that they were able to skirt the law and finance electioneering communications by merely avoiding the magic words (Dreyfuss, 1998; West, 2000).

To be clear, the existing definitions and interpretations of issue advocacy differentiate between expenditures for "genuine" issue advocacy, the advocation of a public policy or a piece of legislation, and "electioneering" or "candidate-centered" issue advocacy, communication that intends to elect or defeat a candidate (Annenberg Center, 1998; Brennan Center, 2001). A genuine issue ad is exemplified by the "Harry and Louise" spots, sponsored by the Health Insurance Association of America (HIAA), which criticized the Clinton health care plan (Moramarco, 2000). In a 1999 spot that offers a coverage plan for the uninsured, Harry walks into the kitchen, and he and Louise discuss how to solve the problem of 44 million uninsured Americans:

[Harry]: We can't leave working families and kids without insurance.
[Louise]: Well, someone actually has a workable plan, called InsureUSA. It has tax relief for workers and small businesses, and special help for the working poor.
[On the computer screen the HIAA InsureUSA website comes up.]

[Harry]: But not government-run health care.
[Louise]: I'm e-mailing this to the candidates.
[Harry]: Send 'em a message.
[Announcer]: Coverage is the cure for millions of Americans. Log on to help.

In contrast, an example of an electioneering issue advertisement is this spot run by the Americans for Job Security (AJS) during the 2000 Senate campaign in Michigan between Spence Abraham and Debbie Stabenow:

[Announcer]: The Michigan Chamber of Commerce calls Senator Spence Abraham a champion for Michigan jobs, praising the bipartisan Abraham Plan to train American workers and create new high-tech jobs. So who's smearing Senator Abraham with negative attack ads? An extremist group charged with bigotry and racism. The *Detroit News* says they have "an ugly agenda." Yet Debbie Stabenow is so desperate, she won't denounce this campaign of fear. Call Stabenow, ask her to stop the smear campaign.

Thus, although the AJS ad does not have the magic words of "support" or "reject," it promotes the positive characteristics of Abraham and attacks Stabenow's character. Electioneering issue advertisements often mention or picture the candidates, address candidate personal characteristics and policy positions, and frequently issue a call to action such as asking viewers to call a 1–800 telephone number (Brennan Center, 2002).

Two cases, specifically *FEC v. Christian Action Network Inc.* and *FEC v. State of Colorado Republican Party,* set the precedent for the increased expenditures of independent groups and political parties for electioneering issue advertisements (West, 2000). To explain the former case, in 1992 the Christian Action Network (CAN) decided to run a series of advertisements criticizing Bill Clinton's support of gay rights. The CAN advertisement attacks Clinton's position:

Bill Clinton's vision for America includes job quotas for homosexuals, giving homosexuals special civil rights, allowing homosexuals in the armed forces. Al Gore supports homosexual couples' adopting children and becoming foster parents. Is this your vision for a better America? For more information on traditional family values, contact the Christian Action Network.

CAN spent $2 million on the television commercials and other forms of communication such as direct mail and newspaper advertisements. The group did not register as a political action committee, nor did it report any of its expenditures (West, 2000). The FEC filed suit against CAN for violations of campaign finance regulations and also argued that the magic-word test needed to be amended to address the information carried by the production values in CAN's television commercials. The FEC contended that the nonverbal cues in the voice-over, music, visual images, and visual text carried substantive messages about the defeat or election of a candidate (West, 2000). Thus, even though the CAN advertisement did not contain the magic words, the FEC claimed that the ad conveyed the message that "voters should defeat Clinton and Gore because these candidates favored extremist homosexuals and extremist homosexuals were bad for America" (West, 2000, p. 45). The FEC lost the case and was admonished by the Court for suggesting that the ad, without any magic words, expressly advocated the "defeat" of Bill Clinton (Moramarco, 2000; West, 2000). On the basis of this ruling, soft money began to flow into political communication activities.

A differentiation between hard and soft money can clarify the important and codependent relationship of soft money to issue advocacy. Hard moneys are those funds raised under the contribution limits set by the FECA and are used primarily for express advocacy communications. In contrast, soft moneys are those dollars raised by parties and groups that are unregulated contributions that can legally be used for activities such as issue advocacy or party-building activities (Annenberg Center, 2001). The use of soft money to fund electioneering issue ads has been described as the increased noise in a campaign (Magleby, 2002), "the 800 pound gorilla of campaign finance regulations" (Simon quoted in Dreyfuss, 1998, p. 31), and "checkbook democracy" (West, 2000, p. 7).

THE GROWTH OF ISSUE ADVOCACY
IN ELECTION CAMPAIGNS

The growth of issue advocacy in American politics has been exponential and explosive. The first significant growth spurt occurred during the 1995–1996 election cycle. Dick Morris, a consultant to President Clinton, orchestrated the solicitation and expenditure of massive amounts of soft money to be used by the Democratic National Committee (DNC) to fund an early blitz of advertising to facilitate Clinton's 1996 reelection bid (Morris, 1997). The Republicans responded in kind and employed issue advocacy on behalf of Bob Dole. In a spot run by the Republican National Committee (RNC), Clinton's tax plan is criticized:

> [Announcer]: . . . he gave us the largest tax increase in history. Higher income taxes, income taxes on social security benefits, more payroll taxes. Under Clinton, the typical American family now pays over $1,500 more in federal taxes. A high price to pay for his broken promise. Tell President Clinton: You can't afford higher taxes for more wasteful spending.

In 1996, groups also increased their electioneering activities under the guise of issue advocacy. The AFL-CIO dedicated $34 million to the congressional elections to defeat Republican candidates who were anti-labor. A consortium of business groups countered with a $17 million fund dedicated to the election of

Republican candidates. Corporations, labor unions, political parties, and advocacy groups spent an estimated $135 million to $150 million on unregulated advertisements in the 1996 elections (Moramarco, 2000; West, 2000). This spending trend continued into the 1998 congressional elections, with party and group expenditures estimated at between $250 million and $341 million (Annenberg Center, 1998).

ISSUE ADVOCACY IN THE
1999–2000 ELECTION CYCLE

The role of issue advocacy in the 2000 federal elections can be characterized by three phenomena. First, the expenditure of soft money for issue electioneering spots by groups and political parties was well established, almost normative, creating an environment conducive to the same or increased levels in contributions. Second, the targeting of advertisements to competitive races influenced the content, tone, number, and timing of issue advocacy campaigns (Brennan Center, 2001; Goldstein & Freedman, 2002). Third, network news coverage of the federal elections was so minimal that voters increasingly had to rely on political advertising for campaign information. A Brookings Institution study (Hess, 2000) reported that coverage by the three networks of the 2000 elections was substantially lower than in previous election cycles. In 1996, the three networks provided 25 minutes of nightly coverage of election news or approximately 8 minutes per network per night; however, in 2000, election news coverage decreased to about 12 minutes for all three networks or 4 minutes per network per night (Hess, 2000). Additionally, the majority of the network coverage was devoted to reporting horse-race issues, such as the latest polls and political strategies, rather than issue information. This dearth of coverage underscored the role of political advertisements as an important source of information on campaign issues.

The Brennan Justice Center at the New York University Law School and the Annenberg Public Policy Center each conducted a major study on issue advocacy advertising across all federal elections in the 1999–2000 election cycle. The Brennan Center, working with the Campaign Media Analysis Group (CMAG), analyzed all political commercials televised in the nation's seventy-five largest media markets (Brennan Center, 2001). The Annenberg Public Policy Center tracked over 1,100 distinct spots by 130 groups. The Annenberg Center reported two separate sets of spending totals for the election cycle. The first data set estimates each organization's spending totals and is based on CMAG data combined with journalistic reports and organization self-reports. The second set is based solely on CMAG data and provides an analysis of television issue ad spending for the last eight months of the campaign (Annenberg Center, 2001). The Annenberg Center estimated that issue advocacy spending in the 1999–2000 cycle exceeded

$500 million, with the two major parties and nine groups accounting for 90% of the total spending on issue advertising (Annenberg Center, 2001).

Political Party and Group Expenditures

In 2000, the Republican and Democratic Parties raised $243.1 million and $219.3 million in soft money, respectively (FEC, 2001). A comparison of soft moneys across the last three election cycles provides perspective on the increase in funds. In the 1992 cycle, the Democratic and Republican Parties accrued a total of $84,401,330, compared to the $235,858,899 raised in 1996 and the $463,123,755 amassed in the 1999–2000 election cycle (Common Cause, 2001). In 2000, the parties spent $162 million for issue ads with virtually 100% of the funds dedicated to electioneering spots (Brennan Center, 2001).

Over one hundred groups sponsored issue advocacy advertising in 2000 (Annenberg Center, 2001). The Brennan Center reports that groups spent a total of $91 million on issue advertising with approximately $42 million dedicated to genuine issue ads and $49 million allocated to electioneering advertisements (Brennan Center, 2001). The Annenberg Center estimates a somewhat higher figure and reports that groups expended approximately $348 million for issue ads. (The difference between the spending estimates is the result of reliance upon different databases.) Citizens for Better Medicare, the Coalition to Protect America's Health Care, the U.S. Chamber of Commerce, the AFL-CIO, the National Rifle Association, Pro-Choice Decision, the Sierra Club, the National Abortion Rights Action League, the Pharmaceutical Research and Manufacturers of America, and the National Shooting Sports Federation are the groups that spent the most on issue advocacy advertisements (Annenberg Center, 2001). The major topics or themes addressed in the issue advertisements by both parties and groups included health care, candidates, education, Social Security, and the environment (Annenberg Center, 2001; Brennan Center, 2001).

Presidential Campaign

Election 2000 was the first time in history that political parties outspent the candidates on political advertising in the general election (Brennan Center, 2001). To illustrate, in 1996, Clinton and Dole spent $71 million combined on television advertising while $8 million was spent by the parties. In 2000, the expenditures on media buys for presidential spots were $81.4 million (49%) by the political parties, $70.8 million (43%) by the Bush and Gore campaigns, and $15.2 million (9%) by groups (Brennan Center, 2001).

In 2000, one unique characteristic of the presidential spots was that only 10% of the candidate-sponsored ads, classified as express advocacy and subject to FEC regulations, contained the magic words of express advocacy (Brennan Center, 2001). Thus, the difference between candidate-sponsored and electioneering issue ads became even less distinct. A set of education ads, one sponsored by the Bush-Cheney campaign and the other by the Republican National Committee illustrates the similarities between candidate- and party-sponsored advertisements.

The Bush-Cheney education ad ran as follows:

[Bush]: Seven of 10 fourth graders in our highest poverty schools cannot read a simple children's book. Millions are trapped in schools where violence is common and learning is rare.
[Announcer]: The Bush Education Agenda: Reform Head Start. Focus on reading. Restore local control. Triple funding for character education. Hold schools accountable for results. Now is the time to teach all our children to read and renew the promise of America's public schools.

The RNC ad said:

[Bush]: If we really want to make sure no child gets left behind in America, we need the courage to raise standards in our schools. We need more accountability and more discipline. And we need to stop promoting failing children to the next grade and giving up on them.
[Announcer]: George Bush raised standards. Tests scores soared. Texas leads the country in academic improvement.
[Bush]: It's easy just to spend more. Let's start by expecting more.
[Announcer]: Learn more about the Bush Blueprint for accountability, high standards and local control.

Similarly, a comparison of a set of ads, sponsored by the Gore-Lieberman campaign and the Democratic National Committee, on the Patient Bill of Rights also demonstrates concurrent themes. In the candidate-sponsored advertisement Gore states, "I'm telling you we need a patients' Bill of Rights to take the decisions away from the HMOs and give them back to the doctors and the nurses." In the DNC spot, an announcer proclaims, "The Al Gore plan . . . Taking on the insurance companies to pass a patients' Bill of Rights once and for all." Each set of advertisements exemplifies distinct similarities between the candidates' campaigns and the national parties and demonstrates that literally no difference exists between advertisements that would be classified as express and issue advocacy under the law.

Groups also contributed heavily to the presidential election campaign. The National Rifle Association Political Victory Fund, the National Right to Life PAC, and entrepreneur Stephen Adams ranked as the top three donors to the Bush campaign. The Gore campaign relied primarily on Planned Parenthood, the AFL-CIO, Handgun Control, and the Sierra Club for additional moneys (Nelson, 2002). For example, Planned Parenthood released a number of electioneering issue advertisements to clarify Bush's stance on abortion and to attract Republican and undecided female voters to support Gore (Samuels, 2000). In one spot, a doctor comments on Bush's reluctance to allow women to make their own decisions:

> [Dr. Kate Thompson]: My patients trust me to give them all the facts. And the fact is, George W. Bush does not trust women to make their own choices. Bush supports a gag rule that would let the government limit what doctors can tell their patients. And as governor of Texas Bush tried to restrict family planning and sex education. Bush could appoint Supreme Court justices who agree with him on taking away our right to choose. Get Planned Parenthood's voter guide. See for yourself.

Sponsorship of the ads, stage of the campaign, and competitiveness of the race determined the tone of the advertisements (Brennan Center, 2001). For example, group- and party-sponsored ads, 70% and 44% respectively, were decidedly more negative than candidate-sponsored ads, 60% of which were rated as positive (Brennan Center, 2001). As the campaign margin narrowed and the election came to a close, the electioneering issue ads became more negative. The DNC released this ad attacking Bush's position on health care on September 6:

> [Announcer]: George W. Bush says he has a plan for children's health care. But why hasn't he done it in Texas? Texas ranks 49th out of 50 in providing health care coverage to kids. It's so bad, a federal judge just ruled Texas must take immediate corrective action. The judge's findings: Bush's administration broke a promise to improve health care for kids. The needs of abused kids are neglected. Texas failed to inform families of health coverage available to a million children. The Bush record. It's becoming an issue.

The DNC noted that it did not release the ad earlier in the campaign because it was too negative but made the decision to air it as the race became more competitive (Samuels, 2000).

In the presidential campaign, the race was narrowed to ten states (Florida, Illinois, Iowa, Michigan, Missouri, Ohio, Oregon, Pennsylvania, Washington, and Wisconsin) and the targeted expenditures for political advertising reflected the competitiveness of those races (Brennan Center, 2001). To demonstrate, the Sierra Club launched its Voter Project in late September with a series of ads designed to inform voters of the presidential and congressional candidates' positions on the environment (Braverman, 2000). In the spot scheduled to air in Michigan, entitled "Great Lakes," Al Gore's "Clean Water Action plan to clean up polluted runoff" is contrasted with Bush's "weakened clean water standard for rivers and lakes in Texas." In a parallel message in Wisconsin, voters were reminded that clean water is important to Wisconsin and that "under George Bush, Texas is 46th in the nation in spending to protect drinking water." The NACCP joined with the Sierra Club to produce a spot aired during the Senate race in Michigan to criticize Senator Abraham's relationship with polluting businesses at the expense of the health of Michigan citizens. The spot intended to mobilize African Americans to vote for Debbie Stabenow, Abraham's Democratic opponent (Braverman, 2000).

Although California was not a competitive state and is a traditional Democratic stronghold, the Republicans decided to spend over $12 million there, while Gore and the Democratic Party limited their expenditures to $107,000. The Gore campaign's decision to limit expenses in California allowed for the reallocation of funds to other close contests, including Florida. *Buying Time* (Brennan Center, 2001) observes that if Bush had lost Florida, the decision to spend the moneys in California would have been chronicled as a phenomenal campaign blunder. In Florida, considered a favored state for Bush, the race was closer than anticipated in the last month of the campaign. Although Gore was outspent by Bush and the Republicans by a margin of $4 million, the Gore campaign received over $2 million from independent groups to bolster its efforts.

Congressional Elections

In contrast to expenditures on the presidential campaigns, candidate campaign buys for political advertising exceeded those of both parties and groups. In the Senate races, candidate campaigns accounted for 74% of the spending, and parties and groups for 17% and 9%, respectively. In the House elections, candidates sponsored 60.7% of the spots, with parties contributing 22.4% and groups spending 16.9% (Brennan Center, 2001). As expected, the majority of the spending in the congressional elections also occurred in competitive races.

A central concern about issue advertising is that as advocacy money is injected into Senate and House races, the nature of those races may be altered owing to the agenda of either the party or the group sponsoring the communication. Citizens for Better Medical Care (CBMC), a PAC sponsored by the pharmaceutical companies, expended the most dollars, $65 million, of all groups on issue advocacy (Annenberg Center, 2001). In a set of campaign spots aired during the Montana Senate race between Republican Conrad Burns and Democrat Brian Schweitzer, CBMC and the Democratic Congressional Senatorial Committee (DCSC) engaged in a "conversation" about Schweitzer's position on prescription drug costs. CBMC initiated the dialogue in response to Schweitzer's publicized bus trips that took senior citizens to Canada to buy lower-priced prescription drugs. The CBMC claimed that Schweitzer was advocating for "Canadian-style government controls on prescription medicines" and that this was a bad recommendation because the Canadian health system is "in crisis" (Dems help Schweitzer, 2000; Pharmaceutical, 2000). The DCSC-sponsored ad responded:

[Announcer]: Brian Schweitzer is on a crusade for fairer, cheaper drug prices. And his "bus runs for the border" have saved seniors thousands. Now a front group for the big drug companies is trying to run Brian Schweitzer off the road—spending hundreds of thousands of Washington dollars on ads the *Missoulian* calls "distorted" and "not true." . . . Call the big drug companies and tell them to get out of the way of Brian Schweitzer's fair prices drug plan. *[On screen: Call the big drug companies 202–835–3400; Tell them to get out of Brian Schweitzer's way; Paid for by Democratic Senatorial Committee]*

Although Schweitzer raised the issue about prescription drug costs, the campaign discourse on the issue might not have continued without the infusion of the soft money spots sponsored by CBMC and the DSCS. Even though the discussion about prescription drugs might have been considered a positive development because it brought attention to the issue, the focus of Schweitzer's campaign was determined by the soft money dialogue, possibly to the exclusion of other important issues, and the frame of the issue provided by the advertisements may have differed from the one he intended.

EFFECTS OF ISSUE ADVOCACY ADVERTISING

A consensus has been reached that political advertising can affect voters' attitudes, thoughts, and behaviors (Kaid, 1981). Television commercials can also stimulate voter turnout (Jamieson, 2000) and provide voters with issue and candidate information (Jamieson, 1992; Kaid & Johnston, 1991). Further, the research on negative advertising concludes that to their merit, negative ads can help voters distinguish candidate policy positions and performance more easily than other types of political information and increase voter involvement by generating strong feelings toward the candidate (Garramone, 1984; Jamieson, 1992). The downside of negative advertising is that it can evoke negative affect toward both the ad and the ad sponsor (Garramone, 1984; Pfau & Kenski, 1991) and adversely affect the political process by disgusting voters and driving them away from the polls (Ansolabehere & Iyengar, 1995). Because of similarities that have been identified between candidate-, group-, and party-sponsored ads, the potential for similar effects for issue advocacy advertising exists. However, there is scant research on the specific effects of issue advocacy advertisements.

Jamieson (2000) notes that "when the issue is complex, reporting on it deficient, adwatching minimal, and one side substantially outspends the other, [issue] ads can influence public attitudes" (p. 140). In one of few studies conducted specifically on issue advocacy spots, Pfau et al. (2001) determined that issue ad influence is related to party affiliation in that for Republicans, candidate- and party-sponsored ads are the most influential while for unaffiliated voters, positive candidate-sponsored ads carried the most influence and party-sponsored ads the least. An inoculation message provided a possible "antidote" to exposure to issue advocacy messages in that subjects who received a warning about exposure to soft money advertising, upon viewing party-sponsored spots, were more knowledgeable about the candidates and their positions, displayed more interest in the campaigns, and were more likely to vote.

DISCUSSION

The codependent relationship of issue advocacy and soft money intensified in the 1999–2000 election cycle. Although a precise determination of the impact of issue advocacy on the 2000 election outcomes cannot be determined, its prominent role can be addressed. To start, the increase in soft money strengthened the relationship between campaign finance sources and campaign strategy decisions, resulting in a decrease in candidates' control over their campaigns and an increase in the influence of special interests and issue advocacy advertisements. Magleby (2002) writes that "in competitive races campaigning has become a team sport with the candidate no longer in control" (p. 15).

The themes, number of exposures, tone, and timing of campaign communications were determined as much by the amount of soft money contributions as they were by candidate-centered strategies (Brennan Center, 2001). For example, in Election 2000, health care was the number-one topic addressed in the political advertising of candidates, parties, and groups, ranking second only to education in George W. Bush's campaign. To the credit of the campaign strategists, health care was also frequently identified by voters as one of the most important problems facing the nation. Citizens for Better Medicare, the Coalition to Protect America's Health Care, and the Pharmaceutical Research and Manufacturers of America were among the top sponsors of issue advocacy (Annenberg Center, 2002). In this case, the concern about soft money is not that it moved the topic of health care to the top of the campaign agenda but rather that the issue advocacy advertisements produced by these special interest groups influenced the framing of the health care debate during the election.

The influx of large amounts of soft money also has the potential to saturate, immobilize, and confuse voters. Soft money provides election campaigns with the ability to inundate voters with political advertisements, direct mailings, and telephone messages. Consequently, simply because of the sheer number of exposures, the electorate, particularly in a targeted area, may choose to tune out the messages rather than engage in the political process (Magleby, 2002). Further, issue spots are more likely to disguise their backing—compounding the problems that voters already have in distinguishing the sponsorship of campaign communications (Annenberg Center, 2001; Magleby, 2000). Thus, in the midst of the "noise," voters cannot determine, and are deprived of information about, the message source, which is a central part of assessing source credibility (Jamieson, 2001).

The increase in the total money now required to finance a campaign also affects candidates as they are forced to spend time and energy on fundraising in order to remain competitive (Magleby, 2002; Nelson, 2002). Fundraising demands can exclude, discourage, and restrict qualified candidates from entering the political arena while privileging wealthy candidates like Steve Forbes and Mark Dayton, who are able to spend unrestricted amounts of their personal wealth (Magleby, 2002). The viability of candidates is now more often determined by their ability to bring in funds than by their policy positions.

The role of issue advocacy in campaigns is receiving increased attention, and the findings from Election 2000 provide an agenda for future research. Magleby (2000) recommends that expenditures related to the "ground wars," including direct mailers, voter slates, telephone banks, and get-out-the-vote drives, be included in future research efforts in order to broaden our understanding of issue advocacy. Additionally, the role of targeted advertising in national elections raises the issue of how restricting expenditures to certain geographic locations alters the national discourse on public policy given that a substantial number of voters do not receive the information on the candidates' policy positions. Finally, efforts to investigate the potential of education as an antidote to the undue influence of issue advocacy advertisements (Pfau et al., 2001) bears further study, particularly in the context of decreasing media coverage of campaigns.

The growth of issue advocacy appears to have taken us back to where we started from. The original intent of the FEC was to ensure full disclosure of campaign finance expenditures. The regulations were intended to keep big money out of politics; however, the loopholes in the FEC regulations have acted as barriers to those goals (Magleby, 2000; West & Loomis, 1999).

The fundamental question that needs to be asked is: Does issue advocacy threaten our electoral democratic processes? (Magleby, 2000). The response is yes if issue advocacy hinders the ability of citizens to engage in informed deliberations about public policy, privileges the agendas of contributors of large donations to election campaigns and special interest groups, and does not hold candidates, parties, or groups accountable for their activities.

Campaign finance reform has been put forward as the solution to problems raised by issue advocacy expenditures. On March 27, 2002, President George W. Bush signed into law H.R. 2356, the Bipartisan Campaign Reform Act of 2002. The law bans soft money contributions, improves disclosure requirements, and makes electioneering issue advertisements subject to campaign finance laws.

However, opponents of the reforms have turned to the courts to prevent enforcement of the law. Further, the FEC's rulemaking on the soft money provisions of the new law have essentially reestablished the loophole that was closed by the Finance Reform Act (Oppel, 2002). At the end of the rulemaking session, Commissioner Scott Thomas said to the FEC, "You have so tortured this law, it's beyond silly." The role of soft money and its relationship to issue advocacy in elections may once again be left to the determination of the Court.

REFERENCES

Annenberg Public Policy Center (1998). *Issue advocacy during the 1997–1998 election cycle.* Retrieved April 29, 2000, from www.accp.org.

Annenberg Public Policy Center (2001). *Issue advocacy during the 1999–2000 election cycle.* Retrieved July 25, 2002, from www.accp.org.

Ansolabehere, S., Behr, R., & Iyengar, S. (1993). *The media game.* New York: Macmillan.

Ansolabehere, S., & Iyengar, S. (1995). *Going negative: How political advertisements shrink & polarize the electorate.* New York: Free Press.

Braverman, A. (2000, Sept. 20). Sierra Club, NAACP hit three hopefuls. Retrieved July 31, 2002, from www.nationaljournal.com.

Brennan Center for Justice (2001). *Buying time 2000: Television advertising in the 2000 federal elections.* Retrieved July 24, 2002, from www.buyingtime.org.

Common Cause (2001). National parties raise record $463 million in soft money during 1999–2000 election cycle. Retrieved July 26, 2002, from http://commoncause.org/publications.

Corrado, A. (2002). Financing the 2000 presidential general election. In D. B. Magleby (Ed.), *Financing the 2000 election,* (pp. 79–105). Washington, DC: Brookings Institution Press.

Dems help Schweitzer get back on road (2000, May 3). Retrieved July 31, 2002, from www.nationaljournal.com.

Devlin, L. P. (1995). Political commercials in American presidential elections. In L. L. Kaid & C. Holt-Bacha (Eds.), *Political advertising in western democracies,* (pp. 186–205). Thousand Oaks, CA: Sage.

Dreyfuss, R. (1998, January/February). Harder than soft money. *American Prospect, 36,* pp. 30–37.

Faucheux, R. (1998). The indirect approach. *Campaigns & Elections, 19,* 18–24.

FEC (2001, May 15). FEC reports increase in party fundraising for 2000. Press release. Retrieved May 26, 2002, from http://fecweb1.fec.gov/press/051501partyfund.

Garramone, G. (1984). Voter responses to negative political ads. *Journalism Quarterly, 61,* 250–259.

Goldstein, K., & Freedman, K. (2002). Lessons learned: Campaign advertising in the 2000 elections. *Political Communication, 19,* 5–28.

Hess, S. J. (2000). The Hess report on campaign coverage in nightly news. Retrieved July 6, 2002, from www.brook.edu/hessreport.

Jamieson, K. H. (1992). *Dirty politics: Deception, distraction, and democracy.* New York: Oxford University Press.

Jamieson, K. H. (2000). *Everything you think you know about politics . . . and why you're wrong.* New York: Basic Books.

Kaid, L. L. (1981). Political advertising. In D. Nimmo & K. R. Sanders (Eds.), *Handbook of political communication* (pp. 249–271). Beverly Hills, CA: Sage.

Kaid, L. L., & Johnston, A. (1991). Negative versus positive television advertising in U.S. presidential campaigns. *Journal of Communication, 41* (3), 53–64.

Kern, M. (1989). *30-second politics: Political advertising in the eighties.* New York: Praeger.

Magleby, D. B. (2000). The expanded role of interest groups and political parties in competitive U.S. congressional elections. In D. B. Magleby (Ed.), *Outside money: Soft money and issue advocacy in the 1998 congressional elections* (pp.1–16). New York: Rowman & Littlefield.

Magleby, D. B. (2002). A high stakes election. In D. B. Magleby (Ed.), *Financing the 2000 election*, (pp.1–22).Washington, DC: Brooking Institution Press.

Magleby, D. B., & Holt, M. (1999, May). The long shadow of soft money and issue advocacy ads. *Campaign & Elections, 20* (4), 22–28.

Moramarco, G. L. (2000). *Regulating electioneering: Distinguishing between "express advocacy" & issue advocacy.* New York: New York University Law School, Brennan Center for Justice.

Morris, D. (1997). *Behind the Oval Office: Winning the presidency in the nineties.* New York: Random House.

Nelson, C. J. (2002). Spending in the 2000 elections. In D. B. Magleby (Ed.), *Financing the 2000 election*, (pp. 22–48). Washington, DC: Brookings Institution Press.

Oppel, R. A. (2002, June 23). Soft money ban goes into effect, but the effect is uncertain. *New York Times*, B-25.

Pharmaceutical industry injected into Montana's Senate campaign (2000, April 25). Retrieved July 31, 2002, from www.nationaljournal.com.

Pfau, M., & Kenski, H. (1991). *Attack politics: Strategy and defense.* New York: Praeger.

Pfau, M., Park, D., Holbert, R. L., & Cho, J. (2001). The effects of party- and PAC-sponsored advertising and the potential of inoculation to combat its impact on the democratic process. *American Behavioral Scientist, 44* (12), 2379–2397.

Popkin, S. (1991). *The reasoning voter.* Chicago: University of Chicago Press.

Samuels, J. (2000, Sept. 3). Planned parenthood releases ad blitz. Retrieved July 31, 2002 from www.nationaljournal.com.

Starr, P. (1998, Jan./Feb.). The loophole we can't close. *American Prospect*, pp. 6–9.

Stone, P. (2000, October 10). Campaign finance: Going for the gold. *National Journal, 32*, p. 3228. Retrieved July 31, 2002, from www.nationaljournal.com.

West, D. M. (2000). *Checkbook democracy.* Boston: Northeastern University Press.

West, D. M., & Loomis, B. A. (1999). *The sound of money.* New York: W. W. Norton.

4

Viewer Reactions to the 2000 Presidential Debates

Learning Issue and Image Information

Mitchell S. McKinney, Elizabeth A. Dudash,
and Georgine Hodgkinson

While the historic 2000 presidential campaign between Governor George W. Bush of Texas and Vice President Al Gore will likely be remembered for its tumultuous conclusion, the impact of the campaign's presidential debates should not go unnoticed. First, the election's virtual tie in presidential balloting was presciently forecast by public reactions to the campaign's three debates occurring in early to mid-October. The major media's "snap polls" following each of the debates, asking the public who won show that most viewers gave the first debate to Gore, the second to Bush, and rated the third a toss-up between the two candidates.[1]

That public evaluation of Bush's and Gore's debate performance was somewhat evenly matched might actually be construed as a win for George W. Bush. In the game of predebate expectations, it was Gore, the more experienced national leader and frequently touted superior debater, who many believed would benefit most from debates. Ironically, while Bush was seen as reluctant to debate, one could argue that his debate performance actually served as the catalyst to his eventual election victory. Support for such an assertion can be found in the national daily tracking polls during the two-week period in which the three debates occurred. Both CNN's and Gallup's daily polls showed Gore registering a slight to moderate lead on October 3, the day of the first debate (Gallup shows Gore leading Bush by eight points, while CNN has Gore leading Bush by two points). Two weeks later, following the final debate on October 17, both of the tracking polls reveal something of a reversal in public support (both CNN and Gallup registered Bush with a ten-point lead over Gore). Thus, during the period in which the dominant campaign story was the candidates' performance in their three debates, Bush was able to take a lead in public support that he would hold until Election Day. For Gore, the fact that the debate series ended with nearly three weeks remaining until the election was actually a blessing. Once the two campaigns and media turned their attention away from the debates, and perhaps with a fading public memory of Gore's verbal aggressiveness and excessive sighing during his debate performances, the vice president was able to erase his post-debate public opinion deficit and pull nearly even with Governor Bush by the time voters cast their ballots.

Of course, the questions of who "won" a given debate and how debates may or may not affect the outcome of an election are usually followed most closely by campaign operatives and media pundits. Such matters, however, have not been the primary concern of presidential-debate scholars. Rather, debate researchers have typically viewed the debate as a campaign message designed to create a more informed electorate, and thus scholars have been more interested in examining if, what, and how citizens learn from their debate viewing. Debate-learning studies have focused specifically on the issue and image dimensions of televised debate messages, with a large body of research examining debate viewers' acquisition of issue knowledge, as well as how debate exposure affects perceptions of candidate image. In short, a robust body of empirical findings has demonstrated rather convincingly that debate viewing does increase knowledge of candidate issue positions and also affects voters' perceptions of candidates' image or personality traits (see Benoit, McKinney, & Holbert, 2001, for a review of this literature).

Whereas issue knowledge and image perception effects have been well established in the extant debate literature, a persistent and unresolved question centers on the relative or proportional nature of such debate-viewing effects. In short, the question remains as to which influence is greatest—does debate exposure have a larger impact on perceptions of candidate image or on the acquisition of issue knowledge? Certainly, one answer to this question might be that issue and image learning are two message variables that work in tandem. Hellweg (1993), for example, has argued that candidates' debate messages incorporate a dual strategy of highlighting issue differences while also emphasizing a positive self-image and a negative opponent image. However, other scholars have claimed that televised debates actually privilege one of the message components—issues or image—over the other. Zhu, Milavsky, and Biswas (1994) provide a review of thirty-two empirical studies that test issue learning and image formation from debate exposure. Of these studies, only five offer a direct comparison of issue learning versus image formation. Zhu et al. concluded that these few studies "suggest that issue knowledge learning is greater than image perception formation" (p. 311). Also, Zhu et al. (1994) conducted their own direct comparison of issue learning/image formation effects on viewers of the first 1992 presidential debate. Their findings revealed a "sizable effect on audiences' issue knowledge but no impact at all on the perception of candidates' personalities" (p. 325).

Yet, these researchers point out that such a conclusion should be regarded as highly tentative owing to the small number of studies that actually provide a direct comparison of issue versus image learning and also owing to various methodological weaknesses in several of the existing studies. Furthermore, they note that other scholars, having reviewed many of the same studies, have reached a very different conclusion. Lanoue and Schrott (1991), for example, argue that "viewers are far more likely to use debates to gain insight into each candidate's personality and character. . . . A superior 'personal' presentation appears to be more important to voters than accumulation of issue-oriented debating 'points'" (p. 96).

PURPOSE

Clearly, the issue versus image influence of televised debates merits additional scholarly attention. On the basis of the limited analysis presently available, and with such contradictory claims attributed to these findings, the current research seeks to provide greater insight into what viewers learn from watching televised debates. Our study will analyze viewer reactions to the three George W. Bush–Al Gore campaign 2000 debates. Our analysis will explore what viewers report learning after they have watched one of these debates—examining specifically whether such learning takes the form of issue knowledge acquisition or the formation of candidate image perceptions. We also examine viewers' specific reactions to George W. Bush and Al Gore. Finally, as our study includes viewer reactions to all three of the 2000 debates, and as each debate used a different format, we examine possible debate format effects on voter learning. The following research questions guide our analysis:

RQ$_1$: When asked to describe what they learned about the candidates or their issue positions immediately following their viewing of a presidential debate, do viewers cite more claims of issue learning or more claims relating to candidate image?

As discussed previously, a number of empirical debate studies have measured candidate image perception and issue knowledge acquisition as dependent variables, using exposure to debate as the independent variable (again, see Zhu et al., 1994, for a review of this work). The most common measures of issue learning have included "scoring" a viewer's ability to accurately identify candidates' issue positions on the basis of actual debate content or the ability to correctly discriminate the issue positions of competing candidates. Common image measures have included various scales that rate candidates on selected personality traits.

Our study, however, takes a very different approach in answering the question of how debate exposure may affect viewer learning. Very simply, we asked debate watchers assembled in multiple, small focus groups immediately following the nationally televised debate broadcast, "Did you learn anything about the candidates or the issues that you didn't know before watching tonight's debate?" This open-ended question, as well as related follow-up probes, was designed to elicit responses relating to either candidate image perceptions or issues discussed during the debate (or both). In the content analytic method we applied (described in greater detail in our methodology section), our unit of analysis was each individual's response to this question, coded as a claim either of issue acquisition or of candidate image evaluation (or both). Not only does our empirical qualitative data allow us to analyze the *amount* of learning, comparing the number of issues to image learning claims, but also the rich nature of our focus group data— explanations of learning offered by viewers in their own words—allows us to better understand the content or substance of their learning.

RQ$_2$: How do issue and image learning claims differ for George W. Bush and Al Gore?

Beyond the broad question of which type of learning is greater—issue or image—we are also interested in specific reactions to the two candidates involved in these debates. We analyze both the quantity and the substance of issue and image learning attributed to both candidates.

RQ$_3$: Are there differences in issue and image learning based on debate format?

The series of three 2000 debates presented researchers with a rather unique design for a debate-learning study as each debate adopted a different structure or format. The first debate, which we have labeled the podium debate, had the two candidates standing behind lecterns and responding to questions from the debate moderator. The second debate, identified as the chat debate, featured the two candidates and the debate moderator seated at a table engaged in what moderator Jim Lehrer referred to as a "conversation." The third debate was a town hall forum in which the candidates walked freely about the stage responding to questions asked by selected "undecided" citizens. A very limited amount of previous research has suggested that the structure of a debate may well influence the actual debate dialogue and candidate interaction patterns and thus could potentially have an effect on such variables as issue and image learning (see McKinney, in press, for a review of the available research on this topic). In responding to this research question, our analysis will treat debate format as an independent variable and examine possible format effects on issue and image learning.

METHOD

Procedures

This study utilized debate viewer responses provided in twelve focus group discussions conducted immediately after viewing the three 2000 presidential debates. Following each of the three debates, four discussions were conducted at viewing sites throughout the United States.[2] A total of 127 debate viewers participated in these group discussions, with 38 (or 30% of all participants) participating in discussions following the first debate, 33 (26%) participating in focus groups after the second debate, and 56 (44%) of the discussants participating in the third debate viewing and discussion. Groups ranged from 5 to 15 discussants, with an average group size of 10.6.

Group facilitators at the viewing and discussion sites adopted two approaches for recruiting participants. The broader study for which these data were collected was designed to compare younger voters' attitudes toward the political process to those of older or adult populations. Thus, half of the focus groups consisted of traditional-age college students. The method of selecting these participants followed the usual approach of recruiting from undergraduate courses and offering extra credit for participation. The adult participants were recruited from the communities in which the discussions took place, and facilitators applied a quota sampling technique to assemble a group of participants reflecting their communities. Average participant age was thirty-two, with ages ranging from eighteen to eighty. Sixty percent of the participants were female. Forty-two percent of the participants indicated Democratic Party affiliation, 38% Republican, 16% identified as independent voters, and 4% chose "other" as their political party option. Finally, 86% of the participants were Caucasian, 5% were African American, 4% identified as multiracial/mixed, and Asian, Spanish/Hispanic, and Native American each represented 2% of the participants.

Participants were asked to arrive at the viewing site thirty minutes before the 9 P.M. EST debate began to complete required research forms. Immediately following their viewing of the ninety-minute debate—and not allowing exposure to any postdebate media commentary—a short break was taken. Participants then took part in the focus group discussion, which lasted approximately one hour. In addition to the initial questions relating specifically to voter learning, other topics of discussion included voter alienation, the role of media in the political process, and national community. The entire session lasted approximately 3 1/2 hours. Audio and video recordings were produced, and trained student aides created verbatim transcripts of the discussions.

Data Analysis

To guide our analysis of the discussion transcripts, the first step was to define the primary coding categories of issue learning and candidate image evaluation. Issue learning included any reference to a candidate's policy-related ideas or positions, including past policy-related actions (such as votes cast or programs supported), or assertions of future or desired policy deeds. Image learning responses were defined as any observation or evaluation relating to candidate image traits, personality features, or references to candidate character. The following excerpt illustrates issue versus image learning claims. When discussants in California were asked, "Did you learn anything about the candidates or the issues that you didn't know prior to viewing tonight's debate?" a male respondent replied, "Yes. I learned a bit more about the personalities of the candidates, which . . . one I feel was more personable, one less personable." The facilitator then followed with, "Anyone else learn anything new?" and a female participant responded, "Yes, but it had nothing to do with personality. It was what Texas had done in their education system with the top 10 percent of high school students being automatically enrolled into higher education. I'd never heard of that before, and I think that's good." In these two responses, we find the male participant offering a claim of image learning, while the female responds with a claim of issue learning. In some cases, a single response might include both issue and image learning claims, and thus the response would be categorized as both issue and image learning. Responses also might include multiple issue and/or image evaluations and would therefore be coded for each separate issue or image observation made.

Next, for the two dominant categories of issue and image learning, subcategories were developed. Here, a grounded-theory approach to category construction was taken, as two researchers first reviewed each of the twelve transcripts and noted how participants described their claims of issue and image learning. Issue learning was divided into seven subcategories and image learning into nine categories (see table 4.1 for a listing of these categories). When discussing issues learned, participants would most often attribute their issue learning to a specific candidate, Bush or Gore. Furthermore, when attributing learning of an issue to a particular candidate, discussants would frequently note that they agreed with the candidate's issue position (coded Bush/Gore issue learning +) or that they disagreed with the candidate's issue position (coded Bush/Gore issue learning −). Often, however, discussants would cite an issue learned without indicating whether they agreed or disagreed with the position (coded Bush/Gore issue learning general). The previous example of the female California discussant who learned during the debate that the top 10% of high school seniors were automatically admitted to a Texas institution of higher education would be coded as Bush issue learning + . An example of "negative" learning or an instance where a participant experienced issue learning but disagreed with the candidate's position was illustrated when a male participant in Ohio noted, "I did not know Gore was for the death penalty. I was under the impression that he was against capital punishment and that's one of my main criteria for voting, so that really pissed me off, angered me!" This comment would be coded Gore issue learning − . A final issue learning category, issue learning general, was created for those comments in which an issue learning claim was made but the learning was not attributed to a specific candidate. An example of this type of learning claim was illustrated by a female participant in Ohio who claimed to have learned about two specific issues: "I thought the stuff they said about education and also the environment was important, 'cause that's stuff that directly affects me."

Image learning was divided into nine categories. Comments regarding both candidates' image were categorized as positive, negative, or neutral. The following comment from an Oklahoma male was coded as Gore −, a negative image assessment for Al Gore: "Gore looked very plastic to me tonight." A female participant in California offered the following image observation coded as both Bush + and Gore −: "I thought that Bush was really calm . . . relaxed. I liked it. I think it was because with each question, he actually thought about it. Gore was so . . . was like 'blah, blah, blah' attacking Bush on every plan." In addition to the six candidate-specific (Bush/Gore) positive, negative, and neutral categories, three image subcategories (positive, negative, and neutral) were developed for image evaluations directed at both candidates. For example, a female in Idaho offered the following Both Candidates − observation, "Well, I thought they both were just so childish, acting petty tonight."

Our approach to data collection and analysis in this study relies upon a "combination" or "interplay" of qualitative and quantitative methods as described by

Table 4.1 Debate Viewers' Issue and Image Learning Claims by Category

	1st Debate	2nd Debate	3rd Debate	Totals
ISSUE Learning	n =	n =	n =	n =
General	6	13	4	23
Bush Gen	4	3	0	7
Bush +	3	3	8	14
Bush −	4	3	14	21
Gore Gen	2	4	4	10
Gore +	7	1	3	11
Gore −	1	4	5	10
Totals	27	31	38	96
IMAGE Learning				
Bush +	7	4	19	30
Bush −	22	12	16	50
Bush Neutral	5	1	5	11
Gore +	13	4	10	27
Gore −	18	11	27	56
Gore Neutral	4	0	3	7
Both Candidates +	1	0	2	3
Both Candidates −	1	3	6	10
Both Neutral	2	0	1	3
Totals	73	35	89	197

Strauss and Corbin (1998). First, the nature of our data—focus group discussions—provides us with rich qualitative evidence of what citizens learn from watching a televised debate. Our study design does not attempt to measure evaluation of candidate image with preset image scales or lists of personality traits, nor do we attempt to measure issue learning with forced-choice candidate issue positions (in which a certain degree of supposed "learning" could occur simply by luck in selecting correct responses). Rather, our method of data collection allows viewers to describe for us exactly what they learned, with participants often interpreting how such issue learning affected their view of the candidates and offering in their own words their assessments of candidate image. Yet, once these qualitative data were collected, we were interested in applying a more systematic approach to data analysis in order to determine the dominant responses to our principal research questions.

Applying the coding categories described previously, the first two authors independently coded one-third of the twelve transcripts. Of the total number of coding decisions made, agreement approached 95%. Most coding decisions were rather straightforward, as comments were easily identified as either an issue or image observation. Also, whether an observation was positive or negative was usually fairly obvious. The few instances of disagreement, which were resolved following discussion by the two coders, usually centered on coding decisions involving the neutral subcategories under image evaluation. The remaining eight transcripts were divided evenly between the two researchers and coded separately.

In reporting our results, we continue our interplay of qualitative and quantitative data analysis.[3] First, results from the quantitative content analysis of the discussion transcripts are provided in our discussion of findings. In our discussion section, we draw upon our qualitative data, using discussants' own explanations, to illustrate key conclusions.

RESULTS

Issue Learning versus Image Evaluations

The first research question related to the effect of debate exposure on issue and image learning. As table 4.1 indicates, for the three debates combined there were 293 specific claims of learning by discussants following their debate viewing, including 96 (33%) claims of issue learning and 197 (67%) candidate image assessments. Thus, two-thirds of all debate-learning reactions were candidate image evaluations, while one-third of the focus group participants' claims of learning from the debate dealt with campaign issues.

The second research question compared issue and image learning from the two candidates. First, in assessing viewers' reported issue learning from the two candidates across the three debates, the total number of learning claims favored George W. Bush. When combining each candidate's general, positive, and negative claims of issue learning, Bush was credited with 42 claims and Gore with 31. Perhaps more telling than the overall number of learning claims, however, is an examination of the number of positive and negative evaluations regarding specific issues learned. This analysis revealed a more negative assessment of issue learning claims for Bush, as 21 (60%) of his issue learning evaluations were negative reactions and 14 (40%) were positive issue evaluations. Issue learning for Gore positions, on the other hand, was almost equal (with 11 positive assessments and 10 negative evaluations of Gore issue learning).

When comparing the two candidates' overall image evaluations across the three debates, the total number of image assessments was almost exactly the same (91 positive, negative, and neutral image evaluations were offered of Bush, and 90 such image evaluations were made of Gore). In analyzing the two candidates' positive and negative image assessment totals, two rather interesting results emerged. First, Gore netted a higher overall "negative image" evaluation across the three debates than did Bush. When combining each candidate's positive, negative, and neutral image evaluations, 50 (55%) of Bush's total 91 image evaluations were negative assessments. Gore's overall negative image evaluation, however, was even higher: 56 (62%) of his 90 image evaluations were negative.

Also, across the three debates, a trend assessment of positive and negative image evaluations shows that as the debates progressed from the first to the third encounter, Bush's image assessments became increasingly positive; for Gore, however, image assessments became increasingly negative. These trends can be found by calculating a net image score (subtracting negative image evaluations from positive assessments). This calculation shows that in Debate 1, Bush achieved a − 15 image score; in Debate 2 his score improved to a − 8; and by the time of the third and final debate, Bush's net image score was a 3 (as his third debate performance netted 19 positive image evaluations to 16 negative assessments). Gore's net image score became increasingly negative as the debate series progressed. In Debate 1, Gore registered a − 5 image score; his image evaluation in Debate 2 deteriorated, netting a − 7 assessment. Finally, he achieved his greatest negative assessment in the third and final debate, a − 17, as his debate performance netted only 10 positive image evaluations to 27 negative assessments. Thus, not only did assessments of Gore's image become increasingly negative as the debate series wore on, but also, unlike Bush, Gore *never* achieved a positive image assessment score during any of the three debates.

Effect of Debate Format on Issue and Image Learning

The third research question concerned the effect of debate type on learning. Across the three debates, viewers of the first debate (the podium debate) generated a total of 100 learning claims, of which 27 (27%) were issue-based claims of learning and 73 (73%) were candidate image evaluations. Reactions to the second debate (the chat debate) resulted in 66 total learning claims, with 31 (47%) of these claims based on issue learning and 35 (53%) candidate image observations. Finally, the viewing of the third debate (the town hall debate) netted a total of 127 learning claims, of which 38 (30%) were issue-based claims of learning and 89 (70%) were candidate-image-based evaluations. The results of issue versus image learning according to debate type reveal a noticeable difference in the ratio of issue to image learning. As table 4.1 shows, while the issue to image learning comparison in Debates 1 and 3 is very similar to the overall finding of two-thirds image evaluations to one-third issue learning reported above, the chat debate resulted in a nearly equal amount of issue learning and image assessments (47% issue learning and 53% image evaluations).

In assessing the total number of learning claims (issue and image) across the three types of debates, it is clear that an uneven number of claims were reported for each. As table 4.1 indicates, the podium debate resulted in 100 issue and image observations; the chat debate featured 66 such claims of learning; and the town hall debate featured 127 overall learning claims. These discrepancies across debate type are less evidence of any debate-format effect on the *amount* of viewer learning than, perhaps, a reflection of the overall number of participants in the four group discussions held following each of the three debates. As table 4.2 reveals, the percentage of learning claims per debate mirrored almost exactly the percentage of discussants involved in the set of focus groups conducted following each debate.

DISCUSSION

Perhaps the most apparent finding from our analysis is the extent to which debate viewing seems to affect perceptions of candidate images, much more so than the acquisition of issue knowledge. By a margin of approximately two to one, focus group participants cited image observations over their reporting of issue learning. Indeed, when discussing their image evaluations of the candidates, discussants often acknowledged finding televised debates most useful for understanding candidate image or personality. For example, a Florida female stated, "I feel very strongly about the character of the person . . . and a debate gives me an

Table 4.2   Comparison of Learning Claims Made to Number of Discussants by Debate

	Total Issue & Image Learning Claims	*# of Focus Group Participants*
Podium Debate	100 (34%)	38 (30%)
Chat Debate	66 (23%)	33 (26%)
Town Hall Debate	127 (43%)	56 (44%)

opportunity to study their personality." Other respondents described something of the performance nature of a televised debate. A debate, unlike other sources of campaign information, places candidates on a stage—literally—and thus personality or image features become paramount. An Ohio female seemed somewhat reluctant to acknowledge this fact when she claimed, "I hate to admit this, but when I watch a debate like this, it seems like their personality just keeps popping out at me." A female in Idaho claimed, "This is the first debate that I've seen, and it's the first time I've actually seen Bush, especially, talk; what I've heard, it might be from . . . newspapers . . . so, umm . . . the debate was very interesting to get to actually see the candidates live and see their reactions to one another."

Viewers' assessments of George W. Bush and Al Gore revealed something of an issue-image split between the two candidates. Bush's most negative assessments were related to issue learning, while Gore's most negative assessments were associated with image evaluations. As reported in the previous section, more issue learning claims were attributed to Bush than Gore (42 claims versus 31). The greater amount of issue learning from Bush may be due to the fact that the Texas governor was the lesser-known political figure and thus some viewers were seeing and hearing him for the first time. Although discussants reported learning more about Bush's issue positions, he also received the highest percentage of negative issue-learning reactions (receiving 21 negative to 14 positive issue assessments), while Gore's positive and negative learning assessments were almost equal (with 11 positive assessments and 10 negative evaluations). Across all discussion sessions, the issue positions that discussants most often claimed to have learned from Bush included his plans for testing in elementary education, privatization of Social Security, and his position on the so-called abortion pill. Most often, when discussants noted learning of these issues, their reaction to Bush's position was negative. For example, an Idaho male reacted this way to Bush's education-testing ideas:

> This is the first time I heard him say he wants to test every year from one through eight. And I think that would be foolish, I just don't think . . . we would be doing so much testing, that that's all we'd do is testing. . . . I didn't realize until tonight that he was actually proposing that we would test every year and I don't think that would make much sense at all.

A female in Ohio reacted this way to Bush's ideas regarding Social Security:

> I just think it's interesting that Bush keeps referring to young people managing their own money. I think that sounds kind of scary because there are so many young people today . . . [*group laughter*]. No, seriously, I see it all the time in the car business, all the time; these young kids are going bankrupt, they have no concerns, they know . . . don't know about management of money; and he wants to turn everything

over to the young people to manage on their own? I don't think that's going to work.

Finally, a Missouri female discussant seemed to find Bush's position on the abortion pill not forceful enough:

> I think Republicans have always been really specifically pro-life, and I don't think Bush tonight was really taking a good pro-life stand. He was, you know, when they asked him about, you know . . . the FDA-approved abortion pill, he really didn't say "I'm going to fight this, this is wrong, this is not pro-life." He was like, "You know, I'm just going to see what happens, and if the FDA approves it and it is safe, then okay." He didn't really stand up and say "Oh my gosh get the picketers out on the line today!"

While Bush received more criticism for his issue positions, Gore's greatest negative evaluations were directed toward his image assessments. Again, the previous section pointed out that Gore's total negativity score was 62% (whereas Bush's was 55%). Also, Gore's image assessments became increasingly negative over the course of the three debates; he never achieved a net positive image evaluation following any of the three debates. The dominant criticisms of Gore's debate performance included viewers' dislike of his verbally aggressive and attack-oriented style and his tendency to rely too heavily on facts and figures to support his positions.

A female participant in Texas, following the first debate, offered this comparative evaluation of Gore's and Bush's debate performance:

> I was just going to say that I've been out of the country for a long time, so I haven't followed Gore or anything, but it was interesting to see how . . . their demeanor . . . I found Bush to be very calm, and he didn't . . . like . . . interrupt the speaker, as opposed to Gore who was always interrupting the speaker and trying to get extra time in and was just generally rude in the debate. I was very surprised. That's not the image of Gore that I got before.

The following exchange between two female discussants in California after the third debate exemplifies the negative reactions to Gore's aggressive debate style. The first participant noted, "I think Gore was just way too cocky tonight. He was like 'I know it all.'" This comment was then supported by the observation, "Yes. He seemed so defensive to me, with every single point." Finally, the first participant concluded, "I think we should ask, which is the real Al Gore? Is it the polite Al Gore from the last debate, or this Al Gore tonight? Because obviously . . . he was so rehearsed."

In analyzing the negative reactions to Gore's debate performance, and particularly the comments relating to his aggressive debate style, it was noteworthy that female viewers proffered the vast majority of such comments. Indeed, the idea of a possible gender difference in reactions to Gore's aggressiveness was prompted by this explanation from a Missouri female discussant following the first debate:

> I think . . . I guess . . . as a young female voter who . . . Gore supposedly has so much more of the female vote . . . I was really turned off by Gore's aggressiveness; and I don't know if it's because my female instincts of being the listener, and . . . you know, you hear each other out rather than interrupt and cut someone off, including the moderator of the whole debate. It was really a turn-off in my opinion about, you know . . . his aggressiveness; and it's like do we really want a president who's so aggressive, and like . . . it's "this way" and "this is what I think" and "look at this statistic."

The previous comment also touches upon a common objection expressed regarding Gore's approach to debate, that of his overreliance on facts and figures to support his positions. A female participant in Ohio after the third debate voiced this view:

> I think in terms of style, Gore seems to always detail his attacks, he's always 1-2-3-4 and then 5; and Bush always simplifies; and because he simplifies I think people understand him more than Gore. His message and his issues, although I don't agree with them, are clearer than Gore's. But I think people are more receptive, in my opinion . . . because Gore is like 1-2-3-4-5-6, and people get confused and don't know; and Bush is just like, "I trust you." It sounds pathetic, but he's simplifying the argument in two sentences instead of saying like Gore, "Can I get two more minutes, can I respond more?"

Finally, the evidence provided by this study suggests that debate format does affect viewer learning. Specifically, the chat debate appears to create the type of communicative dynamic that allows viewers to focus less on candidate performance and image considerations and more on issue appeals. Again, as reported in the previous section, reactions to the chat debate resulted in an almost equal amount of reported issue and image learning, while the podium and town hall debates spurred almost three times as many candidate-image observations as issue evaluations.

A group of three female discussants in Florida, meeting after the chat debate, provided this comparison between the first and second debate formats. The first discussant claimed, "I thought they could talk a little bit more freely about controversial issues than they did in the first one . . . because they would have been standing up at the podium. Some of the issues today were better with them sitting closer together for discussion of more controversial issues." A second discussant agreed: "It was more conversational for explaining their position . . . explaining examples. . . . I think they did a better job of that this time." The third participant seemed to suggest the chat debate was a model that contributed to greater issue focus by observing that "they could state their positions without being interrupted, without having to, like, counterattack or defend themselves or anything like that. And the informal manner . . . because you're right . . . the issues did not come out last time. . . . [W]e learned things today that we did not hear last week . . . and it's kind of like, 'Oh, he didn't say that last week.'"

While the podium debate may have featured a more combative candidate dialogue than the chat encounter, thus possibly limiting issue learning, the town hall debate may function to highlight the more performance-style communicative elements of debate and thus serve to emphasize candidate image. A California female viewer assessed the candidates' town hall performance this way:

> I think, I have to say that I was . . . it was fun. I thought it was a neat way to handle it; but I thought that it gave the candidates too much opportunity to show their emotion. We want the candidates to be able to show their emotions, and show that they are strong about a point and their feelings . . . really . . . but I feel like, I have to say, I mean I like him . . . but Gore was too jumping up, walking around and getting excited.

Two Missouri female discussants, while disagreeing on their overall assessment of the town hall format, both noted the debate's performance dimensions. The first participant claimed, "I think if I had listened to it on the radio it would have been a much better debate; but if you watch it on TV, and watch them both walk into each other's frames . . . [it] annoyed the hell out of me." The second discussant disagreed: "I think that's what made it good. And it made it much more natural and you got to see them a little bit better than just in a stiff position. I thought it made it a lot better, you could see a lot more of them."

CONCLUSION

The current study advances our knowledge of what viewers learn from watching televised debates, provides insight into viewer reactions to George W. Bush's and Al Gore's campaign 2000 debate performances, and suggests that the structure of a debate dialogue does affect candidate communicative behaviors and learning outcomes. First, our results clearly support the "image" camp of dominant debate-viewing effects. Whereas some may believe such a finding diminishes the significance of televised debates, we disagree. First, comprehending the sort of president we are electing, including a better understanding of personality and/or character traits, is a very important factor in candidate selection. The ability of televised debates to provide such information should not be devalued. Our analysis also reveals that, while image effects may be predominant, valuable issue-knowledge acquisition does result from debate exposure.

In assessing debate viewers' reactions to Bush and Gore in the fall of 2000, our findings tend to support the popular notion that whereas voters may have found Bush's policy explanations sometimes a bit too simplistic, Gore was just not very likable as a debater. Furthermore, the increased public approval of Bush following the debates may be explained by our findings that suggest that televised debates function more on the level of image analysis than issue knowledge. Viewer reactions to Gore also may provide a valuable lesson for future campaign debaters. Apparently, a televised debate is not the best medium for a meticulous recitation of facts and figures to support one's positions.

Finally, our conclusions regarding debate format have implications for debate scholars as well as debate planners. First, future research should compare differing debate designs, examining how such dependent measures as issue learning and candidate-image evaluations, as well as other debate-content and viewer-reaction variables, may be influenced by format. For debate planners, our analysis suggests that viewers seem to prefer, and perhaps learn differently from, different types of debates. Like the debates of 2000, future debate series should attempt to incorporate a range of debate structures that facilitate varied candidate interactions.

NOTES

1. The USA Today/CNN/Gallup Poll asked "Who did better?" while both ABC News and CBS News asked "Who won?"

	USA Today/CNN/Gallup	*ABC News*	*CBS News*
Debate 1			
Bush:	41%	39%	42%
Gore:	48%	42%	56%
Debate 2			
Bush:	49%	46%	51%
Gore:	36%	30%	48%
Debate 3			
Bush:	46%	41%	40%
Gore:	44%	41%	45%

2. For the first presidential debate, citizen reaction was gathered from groups in Athens and Akron, Ohio; Denton, Texas; and Columbia, Missouri. For the second debate, participants were located in the following locations: Norman, Oklahoma; Akron, Ohio; Denton, Texas; and Gainesville, Florida. Finally, groups for the third debate were located in Columbia, Missouri; Moscow, Idaho; Akron, Ohio; and Sacramento, California.

3. The results of our content analysis are not subjected to statistical calculations in order to claim significant differences. Such an approach to data analysis would violate the assumptions of our qualitative data collection techniques. For example, participants in the focus group discussions were not required to respond to questions asked by the facilitator, nor did each discussant provide an equal number of candidate and/or issue observa-

tions. Our content analysis of the discussion transcripts provides a description of the type and frequency of viewer responses.

REFERENCES

Benoit, W. L., McKinney, M. S., & Holbert, R. L. (2001). Beyond learning and persona: Extending the scope of presidential debate effects. *Communication Monographs, 68,* 259–273.

Hellweg, S. A. (1993). Introduction. *Argumentation and Advocacy, 30,* 59–61.

Lanoue, D. J., & Schrott, P. R. (1991). *The joint press conference: The history, impact, and prospects of American presidential debates.* New York: Greenwood.

McKinney, M. S. (in press). The evolution of presidential debate formats: Responding to citizen needs. In M. S. McKinney, D. G. Bystrom, L. L. Kaid, & D. B. Carlin (Eds.) *Communicating politics: Engaging the public in democratic life.* New York: Peter Lang.

Strauss, A., & Corbin, J. (1998). *Basics of qualitative research: Techniques and procedures for developing grounded theory* (2nd ed.). Thousand Oaks, CA: Sage.

Zhu, J., Milavsky, J. R., & Biswas, R. (1994). Do televised debates affect image perception more than issue knowledge? A study of the first 1992 presidential debate. *Human Communication Research, 20,* 302–333.

5

Character versus Competence

Evidence from the 2000 Presidential Debates and Election

Theodore F. Sheckels and Lauren Cohen Bell

We join others in and out of the communication discipline in believing that the quadrennial presidential debates do matter. We are interested, however, in determining *how* they matter. This chapter examines voters' responses to the 2000 debates between Republican George W. Bush and Democrat Al Gore that suggest an answer to this question.

Research on presidential debates has tended to focus on actual debate content and on the specific moments in the debates that effected change (Friedenberg, 1994). Both the initial commentary and the limited research on the 2000 debates conform to this pattern by arguing that they did effect change and that Gore's aggressiveness and exaggerations in the first debate were the decisive moments (Ceaser & Busch, 2001). Our research suggests that the debates' effects were along these lines but not as simple as this analysis suggests. The debates did provide crucial information to voters about two specific dimensions, candidate character and candidate competence. Specifically, the debates provided voters who cared about character with confirming relevant information, and they pushed voters who cared about competence to focus more on character.

After briefly discussing the background for this study and the methodology we employ, we focus on four questions: (1) Did viewers recall the Gore-Bush debates in terms of issue information or ethos information? (2) Was the ethos-related information recalled for each candidate character-related or competence-related, and how did this information vary between Gore voters and Bush voters? (3) Did voters' overall impressions of the candidates' character and competence vary with the number of debates viewed? (4) Did voters' impressions correspond to what they claimed was important in the election and with how they voted?

The answers to these questions suggest that issues seem to matter very little to voters, at least in terms of information gathering during the debates. Moreover, by examining what kind of ethos-oriented information voters recalled about Bush and Gore, we can conclude that, at least in 2000, character information was more important than information about the candidates' competence. These results do not vary significantly with the number of debates viewed and only partially conform to the factors that voters claimed were important to them in determining their vote for president. An analysis of this partial agreement suggests that the debates did provide voters with information relevant to their decision. Since studies have suggested that, in recent elections, 31% of voters made their voting decision in the campaign's last month (Ceaser & Busch, 2001), one would assume that the debates can play an important role in determining voting behavior. Several studies (Payne et al., 1989; Tannenbaum et al., 1962; Wall et al., 1988) have suggested that this role may be to reinforce people's preexisting impressions of each of the candidates. Our study suggests that while debates may reinforce, they may also effect a shift in how the different aspects of candidate ethos are weighted and, as a result, perhaps change voting decisions.

BACKGROUND

Previous studies have suggested that viewers learn about issues and the candidates' positions on issues from the debates (Carlin & Bicak, 1993; Chaffee, 1978; Davis, 1992; Drew & Weaver, 1991; Friedenberg, 1994; Hellweg, Pfau, & Brydon, 1992; Holbrook, 1996; Lanoue & Schrott, 1991; McKinnon, Tedesco, and Kaid, 1993; Mitchell, 1979; Ornstein, 1988; Pfau, 1988; Wall, Golden, & James, 1988; Zhu, Milavsky, & Biswas, 1994). This learning is possible, claim these authors, because as other studies have shown, the debates exhibit both content (Bitzer & Reuter, 1980; Hart & Jarvis, 1997; Leon, 1993; Meadow, 1983; Prentice et al., 1981; Riley & Hollihan, 1981; Riley, Hollihan, & Cooley, 1980; Tiemens et al., 1985) and candidate clash (Benoit & Wells, 1996; Bilmes, 1999; Carlin et al., 1991).

However, this issue-oriented information may be less telling than other information provided by debates. As another set of studies has suggested, for the overwhelming majority of voters, the debates provide what one might call "image" information. Sears and Chaffee's 1979 review of research on the 1976 Ford-Carter debates notes that, despite voters' expressed desire for issue-oriented information, they came away from the debates with global impressions of the candidates that had as much to do with matters of competence and personality as with issues. Glass (1985) found that the candidates' personal attributes mattered as much as, or more than, issues in all elections dominated by two candidates between 1952 and 1984, and that competence and character were the crucial attributes for 83% of voters. Other studies have reached similar conclusions. For example, Pfau and Kang (1991) argue that, to the extent the 1988 debates influenced voters, they did so through relational messages that primarily expressed similarity/involvement (defined to include "cooperative attitude, equality, the absence of a superior attitude, warmth, interest, similarity, friendliness, sincerity, and honesty" [p. 119]) and, secondarily, composure (defined to include "lack of tension, comfort, poise, and relaxation" [p. 119]). The dominance of the visual in televised debates is crucial in conveying these relational messages, according to Pfau and Kang. Similarly, according to Conrad (1993), the dominance of narrative in television programming accounts for the dominance of character information over issue information in viewers' processing of debates. Finally, Hinck (1993) argues that "an audience apprehends a debate in its entirety . . . not as a discursive argument over policies" (p. 215). What proves important, then, is that the candidates present "desirable images of presidential character" (p. 3) and that they "enact qualities of leadership" (p. 5).

We believe that the polarized conclusions reached in the literature on presidential debates may in part be the result of semantics. The terms "image" and "issue" in these studies may be of limited utility, as evolving definitions of the terms (Hellweg, 1979; Hellweg et al., 1985; Hellweg, 1995; Wakshlag & Edison, 1979) have blurred the distinction between them, causing several scholars to suggest their inherent interrelatedness (Hacker, 1995; Nimmo, 1995; Patterson & McClure, 1976). We believe that more useful than the term "image" is the rhetorical term "ethos," which is traditionally thought of as having a character dimension and a competence dimension (McCroskey, 1993). In fact, character, competence, and assessments that blend the two seem to be the crucial information categories that voters acquire from the debates, as the analysis below will demonstrate.

METHOD

To determine the effects of the debates on viewers, and the extent to which viewers' perceptions of Bush and Gore were ethos-related or issue-related, we examined 353 exit surveys completed by Hanover County, Virginia, voters in the 2000 presidential election. The 353 surveys represent approximately 25% of the total number of respondents (1,421) to an exit poll administered by Randolph-Macon College and the *Hanover (Va.) Herald-Progress* newspaper. That poll had a margin of error of less than 2.5%. The surveys we used in this analysis include all forms on which meaningful responses were recorded on a set of open-ended questions that asked "What moment during the debates best characterized George W. Bush?" and "What moment during the debates best characterized Al

Gore?" The questions were designed to identify what impressions of the candidates voters brought from viewing the debates to the polling place.

Once the 353 surveys were identified, data from each were coded and recorded using an SPSS (Statistical Package for the Social Sciences) spreadsheet. We coded each respondent's vote for president (1 = Bush, 2 = Gore, 3 = other), which candidate qualities mattered most in deciding how to vote for president (1 = character, 2 = competency, 3 = hybrid, 4 = other), party affiliation (1 = Democrat, 2 = Republican, 3 = independent, 4 = something else), the number of debates watched (zero through three), view of Gore's personal character (Likert scaled, where 1 = strongly positive and 5 = strongly negative), and view of Bush's personal character (Likert scaled, where 1 = strongly positive and 5 = strongly negative). We then coded each respondent's general responses to Bush and Gore, respectively, based upon the individual's answers to the open-ended questions that probed the moments remembered from each candidate's performance during the debates. These responses were coded as follows: 1 = issue response; 2 = positive character assessment; 3 = negative character assessment; 4 = positive competency assessment; 5 = negative competency assessment; 6 = positive hybrid assessment; 7 = negative hybrid assessment. Each of the 353 surveys was coded by each author, and overall intercoder reliability rates ranged between 92% and 99%, suggesting very high levels of agreement.

Before we present the results of our study, one caveat is necessary: of the 353 respondents to the survey, 251 identified themselves as Bush voters. This may account for the overwhelmingly negative responses to Gore based upon these survey data. For that reason, all data are presented as percentages of the totals, and not as raw numbers. While these data accurately reflect the partisan demographics of Hanover County, Virginia, they are unlikely to reflect accurately the partisan demographics of other areas. Nonetheless, the information presented below sheds some light on the ways in which voters learn from the presidential debates and the ways in which those debates matter to voters' assessments of the candidates.

RESULTS

Before turning to a discussion of how the debates seemed to matter to voters in 2000, it is important to discuss what voters said was "most important" to them with regard to "deciding how to vote for president." Respondents to the survey suggested that "competence" was most important to them (48%), followed by "hybrid" (a category that included both competence and character responses [40%]), followed by "character" (10%). Issue positions were mentioned in just 2% of the cases. There were, however, differences between those who voted for Bush and those who voted for Gore. Bush voters were slightly more interested in character than were Gore voters, while Gore voters were dramatically more interested than Bush voters in choosing a candidate who was competent. Table 5.1 summarizes these results.

Table 5.1 Most Important Factor in Deciding for Whom to Vote for President (%)

	All Voters	Gore Voters	Bush Voters
Character	10	7	12
Competence	48	71	38
Hybrid	40	19	48
Issues	2	3	2
N	353	88	251

Not only were Bush voters slightly more interested in character than were Gore voters, Bush voters were also more critical of Gore's character than Gore voters were of Bush's. As table 5.2 demonstrates, Gore received "strongly negative" character assessments from nearly twice as many Bush voters (42%) as Bush received from Gore voters (22%).

Thus, we see that Bush voters were looking for a president whose character, in their view, was strongly positive. It is clear that Bush voters did not believe that Gore's character fit that requirement. This, perhaps, might help to explain their votes for Bush, especially since these results held true across party lines (82% of Democrats gave Gore positive marks, compared to 94% of Republicans who gave Bush positive marks). This emphasis on character in the 2000 election has also been noted by Trent et al. (2001). Their analysis showed a marked shift away from competence, which had proved dominant in 1988, 1992, and 1996.

In addition to understanding what voters in 2000 claimed to be looking for in their next president, our data allow us to judge the ways in which the debates provided voters with particular kinds of cues about each of the candidates. Not surprisingly, given the low percentage who suggested that issues were most important in deciding how to vote for president, very few voters indicated that they recalled the candidates in issue-specific terms. As table 5.3 shows, just 16%

Table 5.2 Character Evaluations of Presidential Candidates (%)

	All Voters		Gore Voters		Bush Voters	
	Bush	Gore	Bush	Gore	Bush	Gore
Strongly Positive	45	16	5	56	59	3
Moderately Positive	30	16	15	32	35	13
Neutral	10	12	25	8	5	11
Moderately Negative	9	23	32	2	1	30
Strongly Negative	6	32	23	1	0.4	4
Don't Know/Unable To Judge	0.6	2	2	1	—	2
N	336		88		248	
Chi-square results	202.6***	189.6***				

*** = p < .001

of Bush voters recalled him in issue terms, while 84% recalled him on the ethos dimension, with 56% of respondents recalling Bush in character terms, 21% recalling him in competence terms, and just one individual out of 353 (0.4%) describing him by blending character and competence. With regard to Gore, 12% of voters recalled him in issue-specific terms, while 88% of voters used the ethos character or competence terminology to describe him: 74% recalled him using character terminology, while 14% recalled him in terms of his competence. Again, just one respondent of 353 (0.4%) discussed Gore in a description that blended character and competence.

There were, of course, clear differences in the direction of the responses (positive or negative) for each candidate, and the responses varied as well according to which candidate ultimately won the respondent's vote. Table 5.3 breaks down the general responses more fully to describe the respondents' reactions to each of the candidates. What is clear from table 5.3 is that voters recall their own candidate far more positively than they recall his opponent. With regard to substantive differences, the data in table 5.3 suggest that voters tended to focus somewhat more heavily on issues and competence for Gore and on character for Bush, although, again, the direction of the mentions varied depending upon for whom the respondent ultimately voted.

These results demonstrate that ethos-related assessments of candidates dominate respondents' recollections of the 2000 presidential debates. This seems to be the case regardless of the number of debates the respondents viewed. Table 5.4 reports respondents' evaluation of each of the candidates by the number of debates watched. Although there are some clear differences between the candidates and across the number of debates watched, none of these differences were statistically significant using standard chi-square analysis of association. However, it is possible to draw some inferences from the data. Bush received his most favorable assessments from those respondents who watched all three of the presi-

Table 5.3   Generalized Responses to Both Candidates (%)

	All Voters		Gore Voters		Bush Voters	
	Bush	Gore	Bush	Gore	Bush	Gore
Issue Mention	16	12	9	27	19	6
Positive Character Mention	44	7	7	22	6	2
Negative Character Mention	12	67	34	13	3	86
Positive Competence Mention	9	10	—	34	13	2
Negative Competence Mention	19	4	51	2	5	5
Positive Hybrid Mention	0.4	0.4	—	2	0.5	—
Negative Hybrid Mention	—	—	—	—	—	—
N	353		88		251	
Chi-square results	47.8***	137.4***				

*** = p < .001

dential debates. Among those respondents who watched all three debates, 25% of respondents evaluated him negatively. Likewise, Bush did well among voters who watched only one debate, with just 25% of those respondents giving him a negative evaluation. On the basis of the data presented here, Bush did poorest among those viewers who watched two debates, with 37% of respondents giving him negative marks.

Gore's numbers were significantly different from Bush's. Eighty-one percent of those viewers who watched only one debate evaluated Gore in negative terms. (In this case, the respondents who evaluated him negatively were unanimous in giving him a negative character rating.) Among those voters who watched two debates, Gore did somewhat better, with the percentage of people giving him negative marks falling to 60%. (It should be noted, however, that slightly more Democrats than Republicans indicated that they had watched only two debates, which may explain these findings as well as those regarding two debates and Bush, above.) Among those viewers who watched all three of the presidential debates, 73% gave him a negative rating on either the character or the competence dimension. Since it is likely that the single debate viewed was the first—the one now infamous for Gore's exaggerations and aggressive nonverbal behavior— one might conjecture that this one debate played a crucial role in defining Gore and, to a lesser extent, Bush and that these impressions were only slightly altered by further debate viewing.

Finally, we turn to the question of whether respondents' recollections of the debates conform to their preferred candidate qualities and their ultimate choice for president in 2000. As table 5.1 notes, 10% of respondents indicated that the candidate's character was most important to them in determining for whom to vote, 48% of respondents indicated that the candidate's competence was most important to them, and 40% of respondents gave a response that was a hybrid, suggesting that both character and competence mattered to them. However, when we compared these stated preferences with their recollections of the

Table 5.4   Responses to Candidates by Number of Debates Watched (All Voters) (%)

	One Debate		Two Debates		Three Debates	
	Bush	Gore	Bush	Gore	Bush	Gore
Issue Mention	18	15	18	16	15	9
Positive Character Mention	46	4	40	6	49	8
Negative Character Mention	11	81	17	53	7	70
Positive Competence Mention	11	—	5	16	11	10
Negative Competence Mention	14	—	21	7	17	3
Positive Hybrid Mention	—	—	—	1	1	0.4
Negative Hybrid Mention	—	—	—	—	—	—
n	28	26	78	73	150	142

debates, some interesting results emerged. These results are presented in table 5.5.

In table 5.5, we have aggregated the character and hybrid categories and separated them from the competence category, since the data in table 5.3 suggest that most respondents gave a character-related response to the debates. Our hypothesis is that Bush voters are more likely to care more about character (alone or in combination) than Gore voters and that they are more likely than Gore voters to respond to the debates in character terms. Indeed, the data presented in table 5.5 bear out this assessment.

Among those individuals who voted for Bush, 59% expressed the view that character was among the most important qualities that determined their vote. By comparison, only 26% of Gore voters expressed the view that character was most important. The overwhelming majority of Bush voters did indeed recall Bush's debate performance in positive character terms and Gore's in low character terms, regardless of whether they had initially indicated that character mattered most to them. Gore voters, on the other hand, were more likely to recall both candidates in terms of competence, positively for Gore and negatively for Bush. Just as the Bush voters recalled the candidate in character terms regardless of which ethos dimension they felt was more important, Gore voters seemed to recall both candidates' performance in the debates in competence terms regardless of which ethos dimension they felt was more important.

CONCLUSION

Those who value and enjoy the quadrennial presidential debates have been intent on defending them against charges that they are "counterfeit." Thus, they have focused on the debates per se, examining content and clash, or on the immediate effects, finding that learning does occur. We would suggest that the better focus is on how the debates are remembered on Election Day. We suggest that debates are recalled in ethos-related terms and that the dynamics of character and competence can explain *how* debates may matter when citizens vote.

We posed four questions that we felt needed to be answered if we were to understand how the debates matter on Election Day. We wanted to know what kind of information the debates provided. We found that the information was overwhelmingly about the candidates' ethos. Our conclusion at first glance would seem to confirm some research and disconfirm other studies; but, in actuality, our conclusion provides different information because most studies focus on the immediate impact of debates, and our analysis focused on the impact weeks later. Based on our findings, one might hypothesize that most specific issue-oriented information fades with time, causing ethos-oriented information, which is more holistic and may be quite visual, to become more dominant than immediately after the debates. The voters' failure to store the information in

Table 5.5 Comparison of Preferred Candidate Qualities and Debate Recollections and Vote for President (%)

Vote for President	Preferred Candidate Quality	Response to Debates (Bush)				Response to Debates (Gore)			
		Character or Hybrid, positive	Character or Hybrid, negative	Comp. positive	Comp. negative	Character or Hybrid, positive	Character or Hybrid, negative	Comp. positive	Comp. negative
Bush	Character or Hybrid (59%)	73	5	19	3	3	86	5	6
	Competence (38%)	76	2	15	8	1	96	—	3
Gore	Character or Hybrid (26%)	9	41	—	50	36	18	42	3
	Competence (70.5%)	8	15	—	77	25	25	50	—

long-term memory may explain some of the fading. However, we also conjecture that the debates may not be especially good at providing issue-oriented information to voters. Some formats may be better than others (Carlin, Morris, & Smith, 2001), but all may be limited because of the constraints of time for detailed answers, at-home viewing behavior that is both casual and characterized by distractions, and short-term memory limitations. On the basis of our study, one might also hypothesize that, regardless of the kind of information viewers immediately (or, allowing for some mediation, almost immediately) receive, voters recall ethos-related information. Recognizing this hypothesis, candidates would become less concerned with specific responses and more concerned with how they come across or with, in Hinck's terms, how they enact the presidency.

A second purpose of our study was to probe the ethos-oriented information voters recalled. We found that in 2000 it was more related to the character dimension than the competence dimension. We found this to be especially true among Bush voters, who recalled positive character information about Bush and negative character information about Gore. We found that the number of debates viewed did not significantly alter this picture; however, we did notice that those who watched only one debate were especially negative in recalling Gore's character. We conjecture that the one debate they watched was probably the first.

When we put these findings about the dimensions of ethos associated with the debates in the context of what voters said was important to them in assessing a presidential candidate, the dynamics of the 2000 election and the role the debates played in them become clearer. On the one hand, voters who cared primarily about character tended to recall the debates in character terms. Thus, the debates gave them confirming relevant information, although not information for which they were necessarily dependent on the debates. The majority of Bush voters consistently fell into this category, and they valued character and remembered the debates in character terms.

Voters who cared primarily about competence, on the other hand, also recalled the debates in character terms. Thus, the debates gave them information that would seem less relevant. The majority of Gore voters fell into this category; and, inconsistently, they valued competence but recalled the debates in character terms. The primary impact of the 2000 presidential debates may well have been to push character ahead of competence in voters' minds. This change in focus may well have played a role in shifting support from Gore to Bush (or from undecided to Bush) by inviting voters to examine character (Bush's strength) and overlook competence, which was demonstrably Gore's strength. Note that in our survey voters who valued competence and recalled the debates in competence terms were 1.5 times more likely to give Gore a positive competence assessment than Bush and 5.1 times more likely to give Bush a negative competence assessment than Gore. One can hypothesize, then, that the debates are potentially volatile when they alter the character-versus-competence dynamics of the electorate. In this case, the character information received about Gore was so powerful as to cause the majority of those who cared primarily about competence (Gore's strength) to set aside that dimension of ethos and focus on the character dimension. We conjecture that, in the aftermath of the Clinton impeachment, voters were especially sensitive to issues of character and therefore easily drawn from competence to character. We suggest that character-competence dynamics may well be an effective lens through which to see not just the Bush-Gore debates but also other presidential debates, past and future.

REFERENCES

Benoit, W. L., & Wells, W. T. (1996). *Candidates in conflict: Persuasive attack and defense in the 1992 presidential debates.* Tuscaloosa: University of Alabama Press.

Bilmes, J. (1999). Questions, answers, and the organization of talk in the 1992 vice presidential debate: Fundamental considerations. *Research on Language and Social Interaction, 32* (3), 213–242.

Bitzer, L., & Reuter, T. (1980). *Carter v. Ford: The counterfeit debates of 1976.* Madison: University of Wisconsin Press.

Carlin, D. P., & Bicak, P. J. (1993). Toward a theory of vice presidential debate purposes: An analysis of the 1992 vice presidential debate. *Argumentation and Advocacy, 30,* 119–130.

Carlin, D. P., Howard, C., Stanfield, S., & Reynolds, L. (1991). The effects of presidential debate formats on clash: A comparative analysis. *Argumentation and Advocacy, 27,* 126–136.

Carlin, D. P., Morris, E., & Smith, S. (2001). The influence of format and questions on candidates' strategic argument choices in the 2000 presidential debates. *American Behavioral Scientist, 44,* 2196–2218.

Ceaser, J. W., & Busch, A. E. (2001). *The perfect tie: The true story of the 2000 presidential election.* Lanham, MD: Rowman & Littlefield.

Chaffee, S. H. (1978). Presidential debates—are they helpful to voters? *Communication Monographs, 45,* 330–346.

Conrad, C. (1993). Political debates as televisual form. *Argumentation and Advocacy, 30,* 106–118.

Davis, R. (1992). *The press and American politics: The new mediator.* New York: Longman.

Drew, D., & Weaver, D. (1991). Voter learning in the 1988 presidential election: Did the debates and the media matter? *Journalism Quarterly, 69,* 27–37.

Friedenberg, R. V., ed. (1994). *Rhetorical studies of national political debates, 1960–1992.* 2nd ed. Westport, CT: Praeger.

Glass, D. P. (1985). Evaluating presidential candidates: Who focuses on their personal attributes? *Public Opinion Quarterly, 49,* 517–534.

Hacker, K. L. (1995). Introduction: The importance of candidate image in presidential elections. In K. L. Hacker (Ed.), *Candidate images in presidential elections* (pp. xi–xix). Westport, CT: Praeger.

Hart, R. P., & Jarvis, S. E. (1997). Political debate: Forms, styles, and media. *American Behavioral Scientist, 40,* 1095–1122.

Hellweg, S. A. (1979). An examination of voter conceptualizations of the ideal political candidate. *Southern Speech Communication Journal, 44,* 373–385.

Hellweg, S. A. (1995). Campaigns and candidate images in American presidential elections. In K. L. Hacker (Ed.), *Candidate images in presidential elections* (pp. 1–17). Westport, CT: Praeger.

Hellweg, S. A., Dionosopoulos, G. N., & Kugler, D. B. (1985). Political candidate image: A state-of-the-art review. *Progress in Communication Sciences, 9,* 44–78.

Hellweg, S. A., Pfau, M., & Brydon, S. R. (1992). *Televised presidential debates: Advocacy in contemporary America.* New York: Praeger.

Hinck, E. A. (1993). *Enacting the presidency: Political argument, presidential debates, and presidential character.* Westport, CT: Praeger.

Holbrook, T. M. (1996). *Do campaigns matter?* Thousand Oaks, CA: Sage.

Kranish, M. (2000, October 11). Bush plans new defense of tax cut; Gore likely to attack in debate tonight. *Boston Globe,* p. A1.

Leon, M. (1993). Revealing character and addressing voters' needs in the 1992 presidential debates: A content analysis. *Argumentation and Advocacy, 30,* 88–106.

McCroskey, J. C. (1993). *An introduction to rhetorical communication* (6th ed.). Englewood Cliffs, NJ: Prentice Hall.

McKinnon, L. M., Tedesco, J. C., & Kaid, L. L. (1993). The third 1992 presidential debate: Channel and commentary effects. *Argumentation and Advocacy, 30,* 106–118.

Meadow, R. (1983). *Televised campaign debates as whistle-stop speeches.* In W. Adams (Ed.), *Television coverage of the 1980 presidential campaign* (pp. 89–102). Norwood, NJ: Ablex.

Mitchell, L. M. (1979). Background paper. In *With the nation watching: Report of the Twentieth Century Fund Task Force on televised presidential debates* (pp. 17–105). Lexington, MA: Heath.

Nimmo, S. (1995). The formation of candidate images during presidential campaigns. In K. L. Hacker (Ed.), *Candidate images in presidential elections* (pp. 51–63). Westport, CT: Praeger.

Ornstein, N. (1988). Non-presidential debate. In J. Swerdlow (Ed.), *Presidential debates and beyond.* Washington, DC: Congressional Quarterly Press.

Patterson, T. E., & McClure, R. D. (1976). *The unseeing eye: The myth of television power in national politics.* New York: G. P. Putnam's Sons.

Payne, J. G., Golden, J. L., Marlier, J., & Ratzan, S. C. (1989). Perceptions of the 1988 presidential and vice presidential debates. *American Behavioral Scientist, 32,* 425–435.

Pfau, M. (1988). Intra-party political debates and issue learning. *Journal of Applied Communication, 16,* 99–112.

Pfau, M., & Kang, J. G. (1991). The impact of relational messages on candidate influence in televised political debates. *Communication Studies, 42,* 114–128.

Prentice, D. B., Larsen, J. K., & Sobnosky, M. J. (1981, November). *The Carter-Reagan debate: A comparison of clash in the dual format.* Paper presented at the meeting of the Speech Communication Association, Anaheim, CA.

Riley, P., & Hollihan, T. (1981). The 1980 presidential debate: A content analysis of the issues and arguments. *Speaker and Gavel, 18,* 47–59.

Riley, P., Hollihan, T., & Cooley, D. (1980, April). *The 1976 presidential debate: An analysis of the issues and arguments.* Paper presented at the meeting of the Central States Speech Association, Chicago.

Sears, D. O., & Chaffee, S. H. (1979). Uses and effects of the 1976 debates: An overview of empirical studies. In S. Kraus (Ed.), *The great debates: Carter vs. Ford, 1976* (pp. 223–261). Bloomington: Indiana University Press.

Tannenbaum, P., Greenberg, B., & Silverman, F. (1962). Candidate Images. In S. Kraus (Ed.), *The great debates: Background, perspective, effects* (pp. 271–288). Bloomington: Indiana University Press.

Tiemens, R. K., Hellweg, S. A., Kipper, P., & Phillips, S. L. (1985). An integrative verbal and visual analysis of the Carter-Reagan debate. *Communication Quarterly, 33,* 34–43.

Trent, J. S., Short-Thompson, C., Mongeau, P. A., Nusz, A. K., & Trent, J. D. (2001). Image, media bias, and voter characteristics: The ideal candidate from 1988–2000. *American Behavioral Scientist 44,* 2101–2124.

Wakshlag, J. J., & Edison, N. G. (1979). Attraction, credibility, perceived similarity, and the image of public figures. *Communication Quarterly, 27,* 27–34.

Wall, B., Golden, J., & James, H. (1988). Perceptions of the 1984 presidential debates and a select 1988 presidential primary debate. *Presidential Studies Quarterly, 18,* 541–563.

Zhu, J. H., Milavsky, J. R., & Biswas, R. (1994). Do televised debates affect image perception more than issue knowledge? A study of the first 1992 presidential debate. *Human Communication Research, 20,* 302–333.

6

Lockbox and Fuzzy Math

Associations of Viewers' Debate Recall and Partisan Strength in the 2000 Presidential Campaign

Marilyn S. Roberts and Andrew Paul Williams

Much has been written about the 2000 presidential campaign, the election-night debacle, and the aftermath—popularly referred to as the Florida recount. But for some, the defining moments of this tumultuous political season came from the three debates between Vice President Al Gore and Texas governor George W. Bush. Upon a review of the CNN/USA Today/Gallup polling conducted across all election phases, four major turning points led to the election's historic outcome (Moore, 2000). The first turning point came when the yearlong double-digit lead enjoyed by Bush, who had been reelected governor of Texas in a landslide, was shaken by the emergence of Senator John McCain of Arizona as a serious challenger for the Republican nomination. Bush's loss of the New Hampshire primary to McCain significantly reduced the governor's lead over Gore.

According to Moore, the second major turning point came during the two parties' nominating conventions. Bush's support was buoyed by the selection of Richard Cheney as his running mate. According to CNN/USA Today/Gallup polling, Bush headed to the Republican National Convention with an eleven-point lead, and his post-convention "bounce" was six points, resulting in a seventeen-point lead over Gore. After the Democratic National Convention concluded, Gore's "bounce" placed him within one point of Bush. This dead heat generated a new post-convention presidential campaign dynamic.

The 2000 presidential debates were the third major turning point for Bush and Gore. Just as the 1960 Kennedy-Nixon debate left contradictory impressions of who "won" the debates, depending upon whether they were watched on television or heard on the radio (Rubin, 1967), Gore was perceived as the winner in the first and third debates by those who had watched the debates live (Moore, 2000). Bush was perceived as the overall beneficiary across all debates as "Bush moved into the lead for the first time since the GOP convention" (Moore, 2000). Media opinion of who won was inconsistent.

The fourth major turning point appeared in the final days of the campaign, including Election Day itself. The last-minute surges in the polls, given the margin of error of the final Gallup and other polls, gave the candidates, citizens, and the media an election that was too close to call.

This chapter's aim is to examine the third major turning point, the presidential debates, more closely. By examining the telephone survey results of nearly three hundred respondents, the researchers seek to better understand the impact of viewership and non-viewership on recall and the impact of the 2000 presidential debates. This study focuses on three research questions. First, what debate recall is significantly associated with Bush and Gore? Second, how does debate recall relate to partisan strength toward Bush and Gore? Third, what is the relationship between news coverage about the debates and partisan strength toward Bush and Gore?

LITERATURE REVIEW

Debate Impact

Political communication scholars largely agree that televised debates have become an institutionalized part of the American political process and serve a ritual function in our democratic system (Friedenberg, 1994; Benoit & Harthcock, 1999; Benoit, McKinney, & Holbert, 2001). "Since their inception in 1960, and then from 1976 forward, political debates emerged as central events in presidential campaigns" (Kaid, McKinney, & Tedesco, 2000, p. 67). "The potential for influence from presidential debates is significant. These events attract more viewers than other campaign events . . . [and] research has suggested that debates may have become the single most important influence on voters" (Benoit & Currie, 2001, p. 28).

Kaid, McKinney, and Tedesco (2000) acknowledge that candidates approach debates with varying objectives, including to reinforce their major campaign issues, "to confront or attack personally their opponent" (p. 72), to perpetuate their image as a leader, and, at times, even to attempt to educate viewers. Benoit and Harthcock (1999) note "that presidential campaign discourse can occur on both policy (issue) and character (image) grounds" (p. 343). "Research on political messages often analyzes this discourse using two key dimensions: functions (positive and negative attack messages) and topic (issues or policy along with image or character)" (Benoit & Currie, 2001, p. 29). Best and Hubbard (1999) argue that debates perform three "normative" functions: engaging viewers in the campaign process; informing viewers about the campaign issues; and informing viewers about the individuals who are running. Trent and Friedenberg (1995) argue that debates serve eight functions: increasing audiences; reinforcing audiences; shifting voters' intent; setting voters' agendas; increasing voters' issue knowledge levels; modifying candidate images; "freezing" campaigns; and building confidence in American democracy (pp. 229–236). Benoit, McKinney, and Holbert (2001) note that "watching presidential debates can foster voter knowledge of candidates and their issue positions" (p. 260) and influence viewers' overall perceptions of candidates.

Viewer Recall

Scholars have aptly noted that candidates' on-screen appearance is one of the most significant aspects of how viewers evaluate debate performance. Such research has focused on the impact of television to influence the public perception of candidates and one scholar has concluded "that what a candidate looked like was more persuasive than what he or she said" (Kraus, 1996, p. 78). Consider the role of candidate image in the famous Kennedy-Nixon debate: "[T]he pale Nixon—underweight, still recovering from a knee operation, and unwilling to submit to a professional makeup job—was outshone by the tanned and telegenic Kennedy, whose victory in that debate prepared the way for his triumph in November" (Cornog, 2000).

In addition to recalling broad image characteristics, viewers also recall specific moments, stinging comments, or humorous incidents from a debate as the defining aspects of the political event. For example, "In 1980, a single debate was held between President Carter and Ronald Reagan, where Reagan ended up winning the debate with his now famous question, 'Are you better off today than you were four years ago?'" (Roberts & Owen, 1997, p. 3).

Media Impact

A key concern among political communication scholars is the effects media coverage of political events has on shaping public perception. Kendall (1997) notes that "there is much evidence of the influence of the media's interpretation of debates. Studies comparing the perceptions of viewers exposed to post-debate commentary with those not exposed have established that the groups differ significantly in their impressions of which candidate did the better job" (p. 8). Trent and Friedenberg (1995) discuss the significance of the post-debate analysis:

> Political debates are not over when the last word is uttered. Who won? Who made a grievous error? Who seemed best in control? Questions like these immediately fol-

low the debate, and their answers are often as important as the debate itself. After all, it is what the audience perceives to have happened in the debate that is of consequence. (p. 226)

Concern over media instant analysis is that it may misrepresent or sensationalize. For example, in a study focusing on the Mondale and Reagan debates of 1984, Morello (1988) posits that the media's depiction of them "misrepresented the amount of verbal clash [that actually occurred] in the debates" (p. 277). Such journalistic commentary is often overly simplistic, and "in some cases a single compelling remark or interactional exchange becomes the primary focus of attention as it is extensively replayed, quoted, paraphrased, referred to, and discussed. This process creates a defining moment, one that is taken to symbolize the event in its entirety" (Clayman, 1995, p. 118).

It is suggested that the potential for media impact is most salient for audience members immediately after the debates. "It is during these hours, when interpersonal influence and media influence are often operating, that the campaign engages in the post-debate strategy of favorably influencing perceptions of the debate" (Trent and Friedenberg, 1995, p. 227).

Often, commentators not only disagree but also note that the public views things very differently. For example, after the first 2000 presidential debate, "pundits were nearly unanimous: George W. Bush didn't mangle his words or screw up his facts, so under the diminished expectations set by the prognosticators themselves, he 'won' the debate" (Kurtz, 2000, p. C1); but numerous other pundits declared Gore the winner, even though "Bush gained in [the] polls" (James, 2000, p. A29).

Despite such mixed results, in terms of affecting pubic opinion, some researchers take a reactive, even dramatic stance against such journalistic practices. For instance, "Kathleen Hall Jamieson, news media expert, advised viewers to avoid post-debate commentary as meaningless and dangerous" (Marks, 2000, p. A24).

THE 2000 PRESIDENTIAL DEBATES

The first presidential debate, which was held October 3 at the University of Massachusetts in Boston, reached a viewership of 44.6 million and was conducted in the traditional, formal format in which each candidate stood on stage behind a podium (Commission on Presidential Debates, 2000). This event was hyped by the media as "a big night of both politics and show biz" (Thompson, 2000, p. B2), and it became the most-watched debate of the 2000 campaign.

The second debate, held October 11 at Wake Forest University in Winston-Salem, North Carolina, reached a smaller viewership of 37.5 million. It was conducted in a more informal format, in which each candidate sat at a table with the moderator seated between them (Commission on Presidential Debates, 2000). In this rematch both Bush and Gore attempted to fine-tune their images and stances on issues. "In contrast to their contentious first debate in Boston last week, Bush and Gore were on such good behavior that it was sometimes difficult to see how sharply they disagree on many issues" (Balz, 2000, p. A1).

The third debate, held October 17 at Washington University in St. Louis, Missouri, reached a viewership of 37.7 million and was in the town hall format (Commission on Presidential Debates, 2000). This final debate featured two tense candidates who were in a dead heat in the polls and were still attempting to reach key undecided voters.

A "New York Times/CBS News Poll [found] that even after absorbing three debates and months of campaigning, American voters [were] thoroughly ambivalent about their choice for president"—with Bush at 44% and Gore at 42% (Berke & Elder, 2000, p. A1). In contrast, a CNN/USA Today/Gallup poll showed that Bush led with 50% and Gore with 41% following the final debate (Holland, 2000).

METHOD

The current study utilized telephone survey research to measure respondents' recall of the 2000 presidential debates. The survey was conducted between October 2000 and December 2000 and was part of a larger, multi-method national study conducted by Y2E (Political Communication Election Project). Respondents were asked the opened-ended question, "What moment during the debates most sticks in your mind as characterizing Bush/Gore?" Each respondent was asked whether he or she personally watched each of the three presidential debates, as well as the vice presidential debate. Open-ended responses were examined and a coding scheme developed to identify positive versus negative recall and broad versus specific recall. Using Holsti's formula (North et al., 1963), intercoder reliability was calculated using a sample of 10% and yielded an intercoder reliability of .93; differences were reconciled.

Other questions included five-point Likert-type questions about respondents' interest in politics generally; interest in the 2000 presidential election; media use for election information; frequency of reading or hearing media coverage about the debates; and usefulness of the media's post-debate coverage. Standard demographic information collected included gender, age, educational level, household income, racial/ethnic heritage, partisanship, partisan strength of belief, 1996 presidential vote, and 2000 presidential vote intention.

To answer the research questions, data analysis was conducted using the Statistical Package for Social Science (SPSS). The purpose of the study is to examine more closely the debate moment recall that most characterized the Bush and

Gore debates and the associations that debate recall may have with partisan strength.

The sample contained a total of 291 respondents residing in eleven states. The states with the highest percentages of respondents were Oklahoma, Texas, Idaho, Missouri, and Virginia. States represented at lesser levels were South Carolina, Utah, California, Alabama, and Georgia.

The sample was comprised of 47% males and 53% females. The average age of the respondents was thirty-nine. Participants were predominantly non-Hispanic whites (84%) with all other groups totaling 16%. The sample's average annual household income was between $40,000 and $49,000. The average number of years of education was 14.8 years, indicating some college or technical training.

Significant associations were found across all cross tabulations between viewership of each debate and interest in politics in general, as well as interest in the 2000 election. No difference was found between gender and interest in the 2000 election. Male respondents had a greater percentage of above average and high interest in politics in general than females did, chi-square $(3, N = 274) = 15.41$, $p < .01$.

Regarding party affiliation, 35% reported being a Democrat ($n = 98$), 129 respondents (45%) described themselves as Republicans, and 20% reported themselves as independents or other party affiliations ($n = 57$). Asked to identify the strength of their partisan affiliation on a five-point scale with 5 being strong and 1 being weak, 30% ($n = 71$) were considered Democratic Favorables. More than 40% were classified as Republican Favorables. Respondents who reported themselves as independent or other or as neutral or weak partisans were considered to be Campaign Impressionables, or potential swing voters.

Nearly two-thirds of the sample reported voting in the 1996 presidential election. Votes for President Bill Clinton and Senator Robert Dole were evenly split (31%, 32%), while 4% reported voting for Ross Perot, and one-third said that they did not vote in 1996.

Of those who reported their 2000 presidential voting intention or actual vote, half (50%) reported voting for Bush ($n = 144$), one-third (32%, $n = 94$) for Gore, and 42 participants (14%) reported not voting. Ten respondents reported voting for other candidates, and only one refused to answer.

RESULTS

The first debate was seen by 61% of the sample, the second debate was viewed by 52%, and the third debate was watched by 57% of the sample. Thus, a majority of the sample watched all three presidential debates, while about a third viewed the vice presidential debate. Cross tabulations were calculated across all four debates, and there were no significant differences between the number of men and women who viewed each debate. When examining age and debate viewership, a relationship was found between age and who watched the vice presidential debate. More persons thirty-five years and older watched this debate than persons under thirty years of age, chi-square (3, N = 274) = 8.75, $p < .05$.

When examining educational differences, the first debate was watched by more persons with advanced degrees than lesser or no degrees, chi-square (3, N = 274) = 17.67, $p < .01$. Similarly, more persons with advanced degrees also watched the vice presidential debate, chi-square (3, N = 274) = 11.19, $p < .01$.

A significant relationship was found between viewing the second presidential debate and party affiliation. More Democrats and Republicans watched than independents or those with other affiliations, chi-square (2, N = 274) = 7.43, $p < .05$. However, no differences were found between viewership and strength of partisan affiliation.

One significant association was found between annual household income and debate viewership. More persons with incomes of over $60,000 tended to view the first presidential debate, chi-square (2, N = 274) = 13.73, $p < .01$.

Debate Moment Characterizing Bush and Gore

The first research question asked, "What debate recall is significantly associated with Bush and Gore?" Open-ended survey responses were coded as broad positive/negative, specific positive/negative, and neutral recall (table 6.1).

The results suggest that Bush received more broad and specific positive recall from males, as well as the largest percentage of neutral debate comments. Examples of broad positive recall include characterizations of Bush as "calm, relaxed, concerned, self-confident, honest, sincere, a gentleman, friendly, having a warm personality, stately, and charismatic." The most frequent example of specific positive recall from males was when Bush "called Gore's numbers 'fuzzy math.'" Other males noted Bush's composure and politeness "when Gore physically charged him from across the stage and constantly interrupted him."

In contrast, female respondents provided the largest percentage of no recall for Bush, as well as the greater number of broad and specific negative debate recall. Examples of broad negative recall include characterizations of Bush as "sarcastic, a smart-aleck, having a limited vocabulary, smirking, and snippy." Examples of specific negative recall include when Bush "smiled while discussing executions; couldn't answer a question about Social Security; and avoided answering a question about affirmative action."

The cross-tabulation result for Gore suggests that females had less debate recall, while males had the largest percentage of neutral recall. However, males produced the greater broad and specific negative recall for Gore. Examples of respondents' broad negative recall include characterizations of Gore as "pushy, a bully, constantly interrupting, harsh, inconsistent, evasive, dishonest, rude, attacking, smug, and overbearing." The most frequent comment coded as specific negative recall characterizing Gore was his "overuse of the term 'Lockbox.'"

Table 6.1   Debate Moments That Characterize Candidates

Debate Moment That Characterizes Bush (by gender)

Moment	No recall		Broad positive recall		Specific positive recall		Broad negative recall		Specific negative recall		Neutral recall		Total	
	n	%	n	%	n	%	n	%	n	%	n	%	n	%
Gender														
Male	47	40	23	52	8	73	14	35	12	48	24	65	128	47
Female	70	60	21	48	3	23	26	65	13	52	13	35	146	53
Total	117	100	44	100	11	100	40	100	25	100	37	100	274	100

Debate Moment That Characterizes Gore (by gender)

Moment	No recall		Broad positive recall		Specific positive recall		Broad negative recall		Specific negative recall		Neutral recall		Total	
	n	%	n	%	n	%	n	%	n	%	n	%	n	%
Gender														
Male	39	39	4	19	3	38	44	54	19	59	19	58	128	47
Female	60	61	17	81	5	62	37	46	13	41	14	42	146	53
Total	99	100	21	100	8	100	81	100	32	100	33	100	274	100

Chi-square = 14.37, d.f. 5, $p < .01$

Other female recall included his "trying to intimidate Bush with his body; being insincere when telling stories about 'real people'; wearing too much makeup; and sighing heavily."

Female respondents also provided the highest percentage of broad positive recall, which included characterizations of Gore as "knowing issues, confident, and professional." Examples of the small percentage of specific positive responses included when Gore "told stories about real audience members; told the 'old-lady' story; talked about education; and said Bush's tax plan was only for the wealthy."

Debate Recall Impact on Partisan Strength

The second research question asked, "What was the relationship between debate recall and partisan strength toward Bush and Gore?" To examine this question, a cross tabulation was run between debate recall (positive, negative, neutral, or no recall) and partisan strength (Democratic Favorables, Republican Favorables, or Campaign Impressionables). The results produced significant associations for both candidates when controlling for gender.

Bush debate recall by partisan strength. Results of the cross tabulation of Bush debate recall by partisan strength for male respondents fell along partisan lines, with Republicans providing the majority of positive recall and Democrats reporting the most negative debate recall (see table 6.2). However, Campaign Impressionables most often reported no debate recall or were evenly split between positive and negative recall. Campaign Impressionables had more neutral Bush recall than Democrats but less than Republicans.

When examining recall by females, the majority of Republican Favorables reported no debate moment for Bush (see table 6.2). Democratic Favorables reported the highest negative recall, while Republican Favorables gave positive comments. Less than half of the Campaign Impressionables reported no debate recall. While positive and negative recall were relatively even, the data suggest a slight edge among Campaign Impressionables.

Gore debate recall by partisan strength. The debate recall for Gore by male Democratic Favorables was either reported as negative or no recall (see table 6.3). Two-thirds of Republican Favorable males reported negative Gore debate recall. Of male Campaign Impressionables, Gore had either no recall or negative or neutral recall; only one comment was reported as positive.

Female respondents reporting no debate recall for Gore appear to be spread evenly across partisan strength (see table 6.3). Democratic Favorable females reported positive recall. While Republican females provided the highest level of negative recall, nearly 30% of Campaign Impressionables also reported negative recall.

Table 6.2　Bush Debate Recall by Partisan Strength and Gender

Male Respondents

	Democrat Favorables		Republican Favorables		Campaign Impressionables		Total	
Debate Recall	n	%	n	%	n	%	n	%
No Recall	6	25	14	30	13	43	33	33
Positive Recall	4	17	16	35	5	17	25	25
Negative Recall	10	42	4	9	5	17	19	19
Neutral Recall	4	17	12	26	7	23	23	23
Total	24	100	46	100	30	100	100	100

Chi-square = 14.55, d.f. 6, $p < .05$

Female Respondents

	Democrat Favorables		Republican Favorables		Campaign Impressionables		Total	
Debate Recall	n	%	n	%	n	%	n	%
No Recall	12	27	26	58	16	47	54	44
Positive Recall	1	2	13	29	8	24	22	18
Negative Recall	25	57	3	7	7	21	35	29
Neutral Recall	6	14	3	7	3	9	12	10
Total	44	100	45	100	34	100	123	100

Chi-square = 14.55, d.f. 6, $p < .05$

Debate News Coverage and Partisan Strength

The third research question asked, "What is the relationship between news coverage about the debates and partisan strength toward Bush and Gore?" The cross tabulation between how often news coverage about the debates was read or heard and partisan strength did not produce any significant differences among female respondents. However, there was a statistical difference among male respondents (see table 6.4). Republican Favorables and Campaign Impressionables reported lesser amounts of debate coverage exposure. Republican Favorables reported higher levels of average and moderate frequency. High frequency was reported evenly among Democratic and Republican Favorables, while fewer Campaign Impressionables reported high frequency for reading or hearing debate coverage.

When asked how useful respondents thought the post-debate media coverage was, there was no difference among males regarding partisan strength. However, a significant difference resulted for female respondents (see table 6.5). Democratic and Republican Favorables and Campaign Impressionables were spread fairly evenly across those who saw post-debate news coverage as being of little

Table 6.3 Gore Debate Recall by Partisan Strength and Gender

Male Respondents

Debate Recall	Democrat Favorables		Republican Favorables		Campaign Impressionables		Total	
	n	%	n	%	n	%	n	%
No Recall	5	21	9	20	12	40	26	26
Positive Recall	4	17	0	0	1	3	5	5
Negative Recall	11	46	31	67	9	30	51	51
Neutral Recall	4	17	6	13	8	27	18	18
Total	24	100	46	100	30	100	100	100

Chi-square = 19.29, d.f. 6, $p < .01$

Female Respondents

Debate Recall	Democrat Favorables		Republican Favorables		Campaign Impressionables		Total	
	n	%	n	%	n	%	n	%
No Recall	16	36	17	38	15	44	48	39
Positive Recall	17	39	0	0	2	6	19	15
Negative Recall	9	21	24	53	10	29	43	35
Neutral Recall	2	5	4	9	7	21	13	11
Total	44	100	45	100	34	100	123	100

Chi-square = 36.7, d.f. 6, $p < .01$

Table 6.4 Debate News Coverage, by Partisan Strength and Male Respondents

	Democrat Favorables		Republican Favorables		Campaign Impressionables		Total	
	n	%	n	%	n	%	n	%
Frequency of hearing								
Heard less	2	8	11	48	10	44	23	100
About average	2	14	8	57	4	29	14	100
Moderate frequency	4	17	16	67	4	17	24	100
High frequency	16	36	16	36	14	24	58	100

Chi-square = 12.43, d.f. 6, $p < .05$

usefulness or as somewhat useful. Female Campaign Impressionables reported lower percentages of moderate and high usefulness.

No statistical differences were found between partisan strength and the usefulness of post-debate news coverage and age, educational level, or annual household income.

CONCLUSIONS

The purpose of this chapter was to examine more closely the third turning point in the 2000 presidential campaign, the presidential debates, by focusing on viewer recall. Though media coverage appeared mixed about who won, the current study suggests that viewers' recall heavily favored Bush over Gore. The findings further indicate that 60% of female respondents had no debate recall that characterized either candidate. Bush received the highest percentage of broad and specific positive recall from male respondents, as well as the highest neutral recall. He also received the highest percentage of broad and specific negative recall from females. While Gore received the highest positive recall from females, negative recall was more evenly split between males and females.

When examining the association between debate recall and partisan strength, results indicate that Bush's debate recall fell along partisan lines for male respondents. However, female Republican Favorables largely recalled no debate moment for Bush. Campaign Impressionables either did not recall, or had mixed reactions to, Bush's debate performance. For Gore, most male Democratic Favorables reported either negative or no debate recall. Conversely, Democratic Favorable females recalled Gore positively from the debates. Campaign Impressionables overwhelmingly reported neutral or negative recall.

Because many respondents did not actually view the debates but relied instead on the media's debate coverage, the study examined the exposure and usefulness

Table 6.5   Usefulness of Post-Debate Media Coverage by Partisan Strength by Female Respondents

	Democrat Favorables		Republican Favorables		Campaign Impressionables		Total	
	n	%	n	%	n	%	n 125	%
Usefulness of post-debate coverage								
Little usefulness	11	33	11	33	11	33	33	100
Somewhat useful	20	33	19	31	22	36	61	100
Moderate to high usefulness	15	48	14	45	2	7	31	100

Chi-square = 9.59, d.f. 4, $p < .05$

of this coverage by gender. A significant difference was found among male respondents. Republican Favorable males and Campaign Impressionable males reported reading or hearing less debate news coverage than did Democratic Favorable males. Both Republican and Democratic Favorable males reported higher percentages of average and moderate frequency of media exposure than did Campaign Impressionable males.

There was no difference among males regarding the perceived usefulness of post-debate coverage. However, female Democratic and Republican Favorables found post-debate coverage more moderate or highly useful than did female Campaign Impressionables.

As in any study, there are limitations. Certainly the standard limitations of all survey research applies here. Additional limitations include that only eleven of fifty states are represented in the sample; therefore, the results cannot be generalized to the nation. Furthermore, the sample was overwhelmingly composed of non-Hispanic whites. Also, the time span necessary to complete the interview process may have eroded recall among some respondents. Building upon the implications of the current study, the researchers will continue to examine differences between debate recall and issue concerns, and attitudes toward the candidates, the media, and government in general, among a more diverse population.

REFERENCES

Balz, D. (2000, Oct. 12). Tests passed, but questions remain. *Washington Post*, p. A1.

Benoit, W. L., & Currie, H. (2001). Inaccuracies in media coverage of the 1996 and 2000 presidential debates. *Argumentation and Advocacy, 38* (1), 28–39.

Benoit, W. L., & Harthcock, A. (1999). Functions of the great debates: Acclaims, attacks, and defenses in the 1960 presidential debates. *Communication Monographs, 66*, 341–357.

Benoit, W. L., McKinney, M. S., & Holbert, R. L. (2001). Beyond learning and persona: Extending the scope of presidential debate effects. *Communication Monographs, 68*, 259–273.

Berke, R., & Elder, J. (2000, Oct. 2). In final days, voters still wrestle with doubts on Bush and Gore. *New York Times*, p. A1.

Best, S. J., & Hubbard, C. (1999). Maximizing "minimal effects": The impact of early primary season debates on voter preferences. *American Politics Quarterly, 27*, 450–467.

Clayman, S. E. (1995). Defining moments, presidential debates, and the dynamics of quotability. *Journal of Communication, 45*, 118–134.

Commission on Presidential Debates (2000). Debates History: 2000 Debates. Retrieved December 10, 2002, from www.debates.org/pages/debhis2000.html.

Cornog, E. (2000, November–December). High noon in prime time [Electronic version]. *Columbia Journalism Review.*

Friedenberg, R. V. (1994). *Rhetorical studies of national political debates, 1962–1992.* Westport, CT: Praeger.

Holland, K. (2000). CNN poll: Bush maintains post-debate lead. Retrieved October 22,

2000 from *allpolitics.com*, www.cnn.com/2000ALLPOLITICS/stories/10/22/tracking.-poll/index.html.

James, C. (2000, October 19). Debates leave instant analysts hedging their bets. *New York Times,* p. A29.

Kaid, L. L., McKinney, M. S., & Tedesco, J. C. (2000). *Civic dialogue in the 1996 presidential campaign.* Cresskill, NJ: Hampton Press.

Kendall, K. E. (1997). Presidential debates through media eyes. *American Behavioral Scientist, 40,* 1193–2002.

Kraus, S. (1996). Winners of the first 1960 televised presidential debate between Kennedy and Nixon. *Journal of Communication, 46,* 78–96.

Kurtz, H. (2000, Oct. 5). Instant, ephemeral analysis: Debating the debates. *Washington Post,* p. C1.

Marks, P. (2000, Oct. 13). Instant media analysis often proves at odds with public opinion. *New York Times,* p. A24.

Moore, D. W. (2000). Major turning points in 2000 election: Primary season, party conventions and debates. *The Gallup Organization,* November 7, 2000. Retrieved November 10, 2000, from www.gallup.com/poll/releases/pr00107c.asp.

Morello, J. T. (1988). Argument and visual structuring in the 1984 Mondale-Reagan debates: The medium's influence on the perception of clash. *Western Journal of Speech Communication, 52,* 277–290.

North, R. C., Holsti, O., Zaninovich, M. G., & Zinnes, D. A. (1963). *Content analysis: A handbook with applications for the study of international crisis.* Evanston, IL: Northwestern University Press.

Roberts, M. S., & Owen, E. J. (1997, May). *Interpreting the debates online: Opinions and perspective of America Online members.* Paper presented at the International Communication Association Annual Conference, Montreal.

Rubin, B. (1967). *Political television.* Belmont, CA: Wadsworth.

Thompson, R. (2000, October 8). There was no debate about it. *Washington Post,* p. B02.

Trent, J. S., & Friedenberg, R. V. (1995). *Political campaign communication: Principles and practices* (3rd ed.). Westport, CT: Praeger Publishers.

II

MEDIA COVERAGE

7

Metacoverage of the Press and Publicity in Campaign 2000 Network News

Paul D'Angelo and Frank Esser

When the Democratic Party implemented suggestions from the McGovern-Fraser Commission in the early 1970s, the role of political parties as traditional intermediaries between voters and presidential candidates was irrevocably weakened and gradually replaced, albeit unintentionally, with the news media (Arterton, 1984; Joslyn, 1984; Patterson, 1980, 1993; Polsby, 1983; Wattenberg, 1994). "One of the major unintended by-products" of party reform, states Davis (1992), "has been an increased dependency on the mass media as an electoral intermediary and the emergence of the press as an independent force in the electoral process" (p. 205). Scholars have long discussed the implications of this structural shift toward the so-called modern campaign as leading to personalized—or candidate-centered (Agranoff, 1976)—and professionalized presidential elections. In candidate-centered elections, candidates are less oriented toward the collective goals of the party and more focused on raising money and articulating their "own" policy positions (Patterson, 1993; Wattenberg, 1994). In turn, candidates need the news media to transmit policy and image messages to the electorate. As Graber (1997) states, candidates and the news media are "inextricably intertwined . . . those who aspire to elective office must play the new politics, which is *media politics*" (p. 264, emphasis added). To effectively play media politics, candidates require the assistance of professional advisers and consultants whose main tasks are to garner, react to, and control messages conveyed to the electorate through increasingly fragmented media outlets (Blumler & Kavanagh, 1999; Esser, Reinemann, & Fan, 2001; Sabato, 1981). Ansolabehere, Behr, and Iyengar (1991) state, "Electoral politics in the United States is, for better or worse, increasingly contingent upon the candidates' media strategies and media treatment of political events" (p. 109).

The institutional context of the modern campaign and the relational dynamics of media politics provide the setting for coverage of (a) the behaviors and roles of the news media as political agents who participate in, and shape, campaign events and outcomes, and (b) the presence and roles of communications media in candidates' publicity efforts, including their advertising and public relations strategies, use of allotted media (e.g., debates) and soft media (e.g., appearances on entertainment programs), and activities of their media advisers and consultants. News stories that to some extent cover the press or publicity reflect the view among journalists that a campaign is a composite reality that cannot be covered fully and accurately unless news stories at times consider how the behaviors of news media and political publicity intersect with each other. A growing body of literature examines the organizational antecedents, narrative structures, cognitive outcomes, and political ramifications of news about press and publicity dimensions of media politics (D'Angelo, 1999, 2002; Esser et al., 2001; Johnson, Boudreau, & Glowaki, 1996; Kerbel, 1997, 1998; Kerbel, Apee, & Ross, 2000; Tankard & Sumpter, 1993; Stempel & Windhauser, 1991). This chapter follows Esser and D'Angelo (2003), who argue that both of these forms of news—press and publicity—constitute metacoverage. They claim, with some empirical support, that metacoverage is a logical outcome of media politics, that metacoverage occurs in conjunction with other campaign topics, that press and publicity dimensions of metacoverage occur in relatively distinct fashion from each other, and that campaign journalists frame press behaviors and publicity processes in the course of creating metacoverage. This article adds to the findings of Esser and D'Angelo (2003) by shedding empirical light on (a) the extent to which press behaviors and publicity processes co-occur as topics in Campaign 2000 network news, and (b) the topics of Campaign 2000 network news that are most prone to contain press and publicity frames.

DISTINGUISHING PRESS AND PUBLICITY AS TOPICS OF METACOVERAGE

The two dimensions of metacoverage would seem to co-occur regularly in campaign news stories. In fact, the two benchmark content analyses of Kerbel (1998) and Johnson et al. (1996) pursue the operational strategy that both merges and differentiates press and publicity dimensions of metacoverage. Kerbel (1998) examined stories about the 1992 presidential election on ABC's *World News Tonight* and the first thirty minutes of CNN's *Prime News* (excluding special programming) from January 1 to November 3. He identified five categories of self-referential/process news: (1) general references, (2) campaign behavior, (3) candidate motivation, (4) candidate-press relations, and (5) technical matters. Using sentence-length utterances as the unit of analysis, he found that about 20% of all utterances ($n = 10,329$) were self-referential. Statements in the campaign behavior category included those about "staging events, running campaign ads, timing activities conveniently for television broadcast, carefully selecting attractive or emotional backdrops for a presentation" (p. 38)—all of which are about publicity. Conversely, statements in the candidate-press relations category were about "direct interaction with the press corps . . . [rather than] indirect activities such as staging rallies or running campaign ads" (p. 42). Yet the campaign behavior category also includes statements about "attempts to *influence coverage* [that] concentrated on behind-the-scenes activities such as creating and marketing campaign ads, staging rallies for television, and getting a candidate's supporters on the air" (p. 39, emphasis added)—all of which involve *direct* interactions with the news media, as in the candidate-press relations category.

Johnson et al. (1996) analyzed hard news stories (excluding editorials, op-ed pieces, and commentary) in print news (*New York Times* and *Chicago Tribune*) and broadcast news (ABC, NBC, and CBS) from January 1991 to November 1992. Using the story theme as the unit of analysis, they found four categories: (1) media performance/impact, (2) media coverage of policy issues and campaign issues, (3) candidate media strategy/candidate media performance, and (4) general media stories. They found that "the press, the communication technology, or the campaign advertisement was central to the story" (p. 660) in 441 cases, or about 8% of the universe of over 4,700 stories. Stories coded as candidate media strategy discussed "how candidates tried to attract media attention or how they used the media to get across their message to the voters" (p. 658). Yet stories coded as candidate media performance—part of the same category cluster as candidate media strategy—"judged whether a candidate had an effective media presence . . . on television talk shows or television in general" (p. 658). Similarly, media performance stories "have an evaluation element, critiquing such issues as whether coverage of a candidate has been fair or whether the media have paid enough attention to issues in the campaign" (p. 658). But media impact stories, which are in the same category cluster as media performance, examined "ways in which candidates conduct their campaign" (p. 658), with some evaluating the effectiveness of ad campaigns.

Although the strategy of merging and differentiating press and publicity dimensions of metacoverage enables the construction of rich content-analysis categories, it remains unclear the extent to which these dimensions actually co-occur in campaign stories. Accordingly, the following research question is posed:

RQ$_1$: To what extent are press and publicity topics present in the same story in Campaign 2000 network news?

PRESS AND PUBLICITY FRAMES IN THE TOPICAL
STRUCTURE OF CAMPAIGN NEWS

When press behaviors or publicity processes are a salient part of a campaign news story, the opportunity exists for journalists to frame the press or the publicity process (D'Angelo, 2002; Esser and D'Angelo, 2003; Kerbel et al., 2000). Contrary to the position of Kerbel (1997; see also Kerbel et al., 2000) that self-referential news presents a singular, strategy-oriented frame around press behaviors and roles (and by extension, around candidates who interact with the press), D'Angelo (1999, 2002) conducted a qualitative examination in which he showed that there are enough different propositions and scriptlike structures in campaign news to sustain the conceptual rationale for identifying three different press and publicity frames. In both dimensions of metacoverage, these frames are called conduit, strategy, and accountability. Esser and D'Angelo (2003) quantitatively measured press and publicity propositions in Campaign 2000 network news that constitute press and publicity scripts, which, in turn, constitute press and publicity frames. Again, contrary to the received view, Esser and D'Angelo (2003) found that stories contained more propositions about the connectivity functions of the press and publicity process (sample script: "Mass media are conveyors of publicity acts") than about strategy functions of the press and publicity process (sample script: "Publicity requires technical expertise.") However, Esser and D'Angelo (2003) found that while conduit scripts used more propositions overall than strategy scripts, strategy frames were more prevalent than conduit frames in actual campaign news stories.

In light of the relational nature of media politics, in which the instrumental goals of journalists and candidates are enmeshed (Blumler & Gurevitch, 1981), it appears to be a conceptual error to think that the press or publicity process can be the sole topic of a news story without there also being a pretext for journalists to cover the press or publicity vis-à-vis another aspect of the campaign (D'Angelo, 2002). In other words, journalists frame the press and the publicity process within a broader topical architecture. Drawing from Kerbel (1998), Esser and D'Angelo (2003) identified eight campaign topics that are classified into three categories: politics and process, policy issues, and personality. Table 7.1 lists and defines these topics.

The literature on framing and campaign news suggests that the media politics environment has fostered within the press corps a schema dominated by the viewpoint that electoral politics is a strategic game (Cappella & Jamieson, 1997). Policy issues are either covered in terms of competition for advantage or are tokens in stories that are mainly about the competitive process (Patterson, 1993). Kerbel (1997) adapts this normative positive, claiming that metacoverage implicates the news media in a "mediated saturated process of winning the political game" (p. 100). It seems likely, then, that metacoverage will occur in conjunction

Table 7.1   Classification of Topics in Campaign 2000 Coverage

Topic Class	Specific Topics	Topic Description
Politics and Process	Electioneering/ Campaigning	Campaign tactics and techniques and organizations, political marketing and advertising, targeting and maneuvering, efforts of winning and risk of losing, traveling, speeches.
	Voters/Public Opinion	Polls, surveys, focus groups conducted by media or campaign teams; reference to public attitudes and public opinion; voter segments and voter support.
	Electoral/ Political System	Portrayals of political parties (fringe and mainstream) and institutions (House, Senate, electoral college); explanation of voting procedures and regulations, of debate commission and procedures, of political culture, of state of democracy and parties.
Ideas	Issues/Plans	Substantial information about public policy matters, programs, platforms, issue stances, problems and proposals for solutions.
	Prospective/ Retrospective Evaluation	Candidate's past competence, former accomplishments, political track record, experience—and likely future actions, decisions, course, focus, performance.
	Ideology/ Political Worldview	Election as a choice between different worldviews, different sets of ideas, different ideological positions, different political beliefs or philosophies.
Personality	Personal Character	Candidate's personality, character traits, psyche, trustworthiness, integrity, honesty—often dwelling on problematic aspects.
	Nonissues/ Misdemeanor	Negative revelations and handling of them, public blunders, gaffes, and exaggerations, character difficulties and youthful indiscretions, or unsubstantiated rumors, or political jokes as news.

with topics related to politics and process and much less so in conjunction with topics related to policy issues.

However, since media politics has brought about candidate-centered elections, candidates are required to communicate that they have the strength of character and requisite personality traits to be president (Troy, 1991). In addition, candidates must meaningfully meld their character messages with issue positions (Arterton, 1984). Character-related coverage is therefore ingrained in election news (Robinson & Lichter, 1991), prompting critics to contend that at times character coverage devolves into an attempt on the part of the press to police the campaign via coverage of candidate indiscretions, past or present (Sabato, 1991). When that happens, it triggers coverage of external criticisms about the behavior and role of the press as well as coverage of internal criticisms from within the press corps that serve to demonstrate accountability (D'Angelo, 2002).

Because it is unclear the extent to which metacoverage occurs within the topical structure of individual campaign stories, the following research question is posed:

RQ$_2$: Which campaign topics are more likely to contain press and publicity frames in Campaign 2000 network news?

METHOD

This study examined metacoverage in Campaign 2000 news through a content analysis of network news stories that aired on ABC's *World News Tonight* and NBC's *Nightly News* between Labor Day (September 4, 2000) and the day before the election (November 6, 2000). All stories about the presidential race were included in the analysis, even if that topic was incidental to other topics in the story. The content analysis yielded 284 stories, 145 of which appeared on ABC and 139 on NBC. Stories about congressional and gubernatorial races that did not mention the presidential race were excluded from the analysis. With an average audience share of 10.5 million and 10.7 million viewers every weeknight, respectively, ABC and NBC were the two most-watched newscasts in the election year 2000. Although the networks' influence over the news agenda has diminished over the decades, their combined audience is still higher than the combined readership of the nation's fifty largest newspapers.

Coders were instructed to determine if either or both dimensions of metacoverage were a topic in each story by observing sentence-level propositions or shot-level visuals about the press or publicity. Propositions indicating the presence of press metacoverage in a story contained the following words or images: journalists, reporters, commentators, us, we, press, television, news, news media, news reports, interviews, stories, editorials, investigation, media effects, and names of media outlets or programs. Propositions indicating the presence of publicity metacoverage in a story contained the following words or images: staging, public appearance, ads, on/off message, picture of the day, line of the day, press secretary, media consultants, aides, crafted, rehearsed, orchestrated campaign, and marketing. If propositions about the press or publicity designators occupied more then 50% of a story, the respective dimension of metacoverage was coded as having a primary presence in that story. If propositions about the press or publicity occupied 10–50% of a story, the respective dimension was coded as having a secondary presence. If press or publicity propositions totaled less than 10%, the respective dimension was coded as having a peripheral presence.

In addition to observing Campaign 2000 network news for the salience of metacoverage, coders also observed how propositions are embedded in syntactical structures that convey scripts about media politics. Following the procedure of Esser and D'Angelo (2003), five press scripts were identified (e.g., news media as technical transmitter of campaign events, news media as consequential actor in a strategic game of politics) and six publicity scripts (e.g., political publicity and PR are manipulative; publicity requires tactical expertise). These scripts are structurally linked to the six frames of metacoverage (see D'Angelo, 2002; Esser & D'Angelo, 2003). Therefore, each story was coded for the presence of three press frames (news media as *conduit* of information; as autonomous actor in a *strategy*-oriented game; or as demonstrating *accountability* for democratic functioning by self-critically analyzing the news media's own role) and three publicity frames (mass media as *conveyor* of publicity acts; the candidate as a *strategy*-oriented user of advertising, communication personnel, or image management strategies, etc.; or the news media demonstrating *accountability* by providing a platform from which to discuss the democratic value of publicity efforts).

Two coders examined content. A consensus approach was employed to assess the reliability of all variables. The coding procedure followed that of Kerbel et al. (2000). Specifically, coders worked together and watched every story multiple times. Agreement was required of both, with discrepancies resolved through discussion. If, despite repeated viewing, no agreement could be reached on a specific variable, that variable was not coded.

RESULTS

The first research question inquired about the extent to which press and publicity topics are present in the same story in Campaign 2000 network news. To answer this question, only Campaign 2000 stories coded as having a secondary or primary presence of press and publicity propositions were analyzed. This decision is based on the framing analyses of D'Angelo (2002) and Esser and D'Angelo (2003), in which it is argued that campaign stories must have "enough" of either a press or publicity topic to warrant the claim that a press frame or a publicity frame exists in the story's narrative structure. Similarly, for the present analysis, a story must have enough of a press or publicity topic, operationalized as a secondary or primary amount of publicity propositions, to warrant comparison of their topical structures. A total of 116 (41%) of the 284 election stories satisfied this criterion.

To answer this first question, stories containing a press topic (i.e., a secondary or primary presence of press propositions) were cross tabulated with stories containing a publicity topic. Table 7.2 shows a negative correlation, Kendall's tau-c (4) = −.547, $p < .001$, which indicates that these dimensions of metacoverage occur highly independently of each other. Table 7.2 reveals that 41 stories (35% of 116) contain a salient amount of propositions that are mainly about the press and 61 stories (53% of 116) contain a salient amount of propositions that are mainly about publicity. Only 14 stories (12%) contain a salient amount of both press and publicity propositions (i.e., both topics have a primary or secondary presence in the story). Thus, there is compelling empirical evidence supporting the analytical distinction between the two dimensions of metacoverage.

It is worth examining the 14 stories that contain salient amounts of press and publicity dimensions because those stories arguably constitute the most complex narratives about media politics. Of those 14 stories, 11 occurred primarily within the topical field of electioneering/ campaigning, and 3 occurred primarily within the topical field of personal character and nonissues/misdemeanor. Most of these stories are about the direct and antagonistic confrontation between the news media and the candidate's publicity efforts. For example, 4 of the stories are about reactions by the Bush and Gore camps to news coverage of Bush's 1976 arrest for driving under the influence (DUI) and whether this raises the question of a cover-up to the press by Bush or whether it raises the question of dirty tricks and strategic leaks to the press by Gore sympathizers. Another story is about Bush's reaction to accusations by a news report that the Republican National Committee used subliminal messages in a TV ad ("RATS"). Still another story is about Bush using an obscenity to describe a veteran *New York Times* reporter who had apparently fallen out of favor with the Bush team. Two stories are about how correspondents on the campaign trail see Bush's relationship with the news media and his problems with his publicity efforts. Along these lines, one story discusses Dick Cheney's criticism of his press coverage and how advisers are retooling his campaign image. Against this backdrop it is not surprising that these stories contained strategy press and strategy publicity frames (see Esser & D'Angelo, 2003). In fact, strategy frames make up 75% of all frames in

Table 7.2   Co-occurrence of Press and Publicity Propositions

	Publicity designators		
Press designators	Primary presence (propositions >50%)	Secondary presence (propositions 10–50%)	Peripheral presence (propositions <10%)
Primary presence (propositions > 50%)	4% (n = 5)	3% (n = 3)	23% (n = 27)
Secondary presence (propositions 10–50%)	1% (n = 1)	4% (n = 5)	12% (n = 14)
Peripheral presence (propositions < 10%)	21% (n = 24)	32% (n = 37)	—

Kendall's tau-c = − .547, df = 4 , p < .001.
Note: Based on 116 stories that have at least a secondary presence of either press or publicity coverage

those 14 stories, compared with 16% of conduit frames, and 9% of accountability frames.

The press or publicity is never the sole topic in a campaign story, even if it contains enough verbal or visual references to the news media or to publicity efforts to warrant the claim that the story is "about" the news media or publicity. The theoretical grounds for this stipulation lie in the relational nature of media politics (Arterton, 1984). As Blumler and Gurevitch (1981) state, the instrumental goals of candidates and the news media are mingled to such an extent that news stories about electoral politics "may virtually be said to constitute a subtly composite entity" (p. 469). Thus, the press and publicity are always covered in conjunction with other topics of media politics. The first row in table 7.3 presents the topic profile of ABC and NBC news—excluding press and/or publicity topics—by presenting frequencies and percentages for the eight campaign topics as found in all 284 network stories on the 2000 campaign. In order to observe the rich topical architecture of campaign coverage (see Esser & D'Angelo, 2003), each story was coded for up to three topics. Table 7.3 shows that a total of 472 salient topics suffused our sample of stories. Because Research Question 2 inquires about which campaign topics are more likely to contain press and publicity frames, the analysis that follows treats topic, not story, as the unit of analysis.

The closeness of the race between Governor Bush and Vice President Gore generated extensive focus on the topic of electioneering/campaigning. Specifically, the subtopics of campaign tactics and traveling, political marketing and targeting, as well as efforts of winning and risks of losing were found in 161 of the 284 stories (57%). Another effect of the down-to-the-wire race was that the media commissioned more surveys and daily tracking polls than ever before in a presidential contest. As a result, the topic of voters/public opinion was a major theme in more than a third of all stories ($n = 98$). Interestingly, coverage of policy ideas, defined as news about public policy, programs, platforms, problems, and proposals, was about as frequent as coverage of voters/public opinion, being prominent in 36% of ABC and NBC network news. However, other issue-oriented coverage received considerably less media attention: News items offering prospective and retrospective evaluations of the candidates (22 stories = 8%) or stories putting events in a larger context of ideology/political worldview (7 stories = 2%) were not prevalent on network news. Neither were background stories on the electoral/political system (18 stories = 6%). In contrast, topics related to personality received more coverage. Personal character was of primary or secondary salience in 54 stories, and nonissues/misdemeanors in 10 stories. Such stories, with a combined share of 23%, either examined the candidate's personality and character traits or delved into negative revelations, public blunders, character difficulties, and youthful indiscretions.

In answering the second research question ("Which campaign topics are more likely to contain press and publicity frames in Campaign 2000 network news?"),

Table 7.3 Press and Publicity Frames by Campaign Topics

	Personality		Politics & Process				Ideas	
	Nonissues/ Misdemeanor	Personal Character	Electioneering/ Campaigning	Voters/Public Opinion	Electoral/ Political System	Issues/ Plans	Prospective/ Retrospective Evaluations	Ideology/ Political Worldview
Frequency of salient topic in each category; N = 472 topics[a]	n = 10 (2%)	n = 54 (11%)	n = 161 (34%)	n = 98 (21%)	n = 18 (4%)	n = 102 (22%)	n = 22 (5%)	n = 7 (1%)
Percentage of 284 stories with salient topic[b]	4%	19%	57%	35%	6%	36%	8%	2%
Topic with press conduit frame	10%	4%	6%	30%	5.5%	3%	—	—
Topic with press strategy frame	50%	11%	4%	—	—	—	—	—
Topic with press accountability frame	20%	—	1%	1%	—	—	—	—
Topic with publicity conduit frame	—	4%	8%	1%	—	—	4.5%	—
Topic with publicity strategy frame	20%	39%	24%	3%	—	3%	4.5%	—
Topic with publicity accountability frame	—	—	8%	3%	5.5%	7%	—	—
Frequency of frames within story topic; N = 178 frames	n = 10	n = 31	n = 82	n = 37	n = 2	n = 14	n = 2	n = 0
Ratio: % of topic with frame/ without frame	100:0	57:43	51:49	38:62	11:89	14:86	9:91	0:100
Rank order of co-occurrence of story topic and frame	1	2	3	4	6	5	7	8

Note: Based on all 284 ABC and NBC network stories on the 2000 presidential election.

[a] A topic was coded as being salient if it had either primary prominence (occupying more than 50% of story content) or secondary prominence (occupying 10–50% of story content).

[b] Percentage total for row is greater than 100% because stories were coded for up to three topics.

table 7.3 reveals that some topics are much more prone than others to coinciding with press and publicity topics. Press and publicity frames cannot occupy a story unless enough of its topical architecture includes propositions about the press and/or publicity. Also, the conceptual basis for identifying different press and publicity frames rests on how propositions express various scripts about the press and publicity (see Esser & D'Angelo, 2003, for a more extensive discussion).

Table 7.3 reveals that the topic cluster associated with the category personality is by far the most likely to serve as the pretext for journalists to cover the press and publicity, even though there were relatively few stories specifically about personality in our sample of Campaign 2000 network news. In particular, whenever a story contained nonissues/misdemeanors as a salient topic, either press or publicity frames were discursively intertwined with the topic. Thus, press and publicity frames always occurred in nonissue stories in the 2000 presidential campaign. Those stories included a report about rumors behind the search for a "mole" in George W. Bush's media consulting firm, Maverick Media, who allegedly mailed Bush's confidential debate materials to a Gore adviser. Two other nonissue stories were about Bush's profane comments over an open microphone about a reporter at a rally, including reporters' reactions to these comments. Still other nonissue stories were about the leaking of information about Bush's 1976 DUI arrest to a local FOX-TV reporter and the kind of media frenzy and spin-control response it generated.

The existence of a press frame in a personality story is often indicated by phrases such as "breaking news," "latest story," or "media revelation." In the case of nonissue/misdemeanors, this was not often done with a conduit press frame (10%), which stressed the press's sheer connectivity function, and only rarely with a press accountability frame (20%), which depicted an awareness on the part of journalists about their standards, behavior, effects, and responsibilities in the course of covering such incidents. Rather, as table 7.3 shows, most prevalent was a press strategy frame (50%) that accentuated the news media's role as a consequential actor that compels a candidate to adapt his strategies to press coverage. In some cases, these stories contained a publicity strategy frame (20%). Such stories highlighted the campaign's concern to preserve the carefully crafted public image and the use of professional consultants and special strategies, though without direct reference to the news media.

Similarly, metacoverage is likely to be found in stories about personal character, which is the other topic in the personality cluster. Just over half of the time (57%), the topic of personal character was accompanied by a press or publicity frame. This seems to be a logical outgrowth of the fact that in mass media elections the press and publicity operations are the main channels through which candidates create, develop, soften, or sharpen a public image. In Campaign 2000, personal character stories with press or publicity frames were either about candidates' behaviors and style during debates, on the stump, or their manner of coping with scandal. Most personal character stories focused on the debates, namely, on the candidates' individual debating styles, images they tried to convey, how media critics or the opposition mocked a candidate's debating style, or how professional observers and focus groups perceived the personality of candidates during the debates. When these topics were covered with accompanying metacoverage, they were most often done so with a publicity strategy frame (39%) that emphasized the impression and image management techniques by the candidates and how they tried to make use of their allotted time on millions of TV screens to their best advantage. A smaller percentage (11%) of personal character topics were accompanied by a press strategy frame, as when news journalists commented on these tactics or candidates complained about their press coverage. Because these reports all involved the consequential role of the news media, they contained a press strategy frame.

Contrary to research on metacoverage by Kerbel (1997, 1998), politics and process topics are, in relative terms, less likely to occur in conjunction with coverage of the press or publicity than personality topics. As table 7.3 shows, 51% of the time that electioneering/campaigning was a salient topic and 38% of the time that voters/public opinion topic was a salient topic, a press or publicity frame was intertwined with that coverage. A publicity strategy frame most frequently occurred in conjunction with the electioneering/campaigning topic (24%), being found in stories that dealt with candidates' tactical considerations behind ad blitzes in battleground states, their predebate strategies, or their image-, event-, and issue-management strategies around campaign appearances. The bulk of stories with voters/public opinion as a major topic contained a conduit press frame (30%). Those stories merely mentioned the results of media-sponsored polls. Even though the pretext of those polls may have been to generate (or stage) exclusive news, the press frame stressed the connective function of the news media by simply conveying those results.

In answering Research Question 2, it can be concluded that when nonissue/misdemeanor or personal character was a salient topic within a campaign story, press and publicity frames were most likely to occur, as compared to the other topics. The reason, in part, is that nonissues are in many cases reflexively constituted by coverage of them, as when coverage of revelations are fought with publicity exercises by the candidate, which then engender more coverage (see D'Angelo, 2002). The topic of personal character is closely linked to the topics of press and publicity, too, because news reports as well as appearances in debates, ads, and entertainment programs are important avenues to build a public image. When nonissues and personal character are examined through the lens of the press or publicity, the strategic aspect is often prevalent whereas conduit and accountability frames are the exception.

Different frame and topic configurations accompany the topic cluster of ideas, including the specific topics of issues/plans, prospective/retrospective evaluations, and ideology/political worldviews, which seem almost resistant to metacoverage. The narrative quality of these topics is not complementary with press or publicity frames. Worth mentioning are those few cases where issue topics are conveyed via an accompanying *publicity accountability frame* (7%, see table 7.3). These rare (and valuable) examples show the news networks as performing the role of truth squad by analyzing evidence of issue-related claims or promises made by candidates in ads or debates.

DISCUSSION

This study builds on the framing model of metacoverage developed by D'Angelo (2002) and utilized by Esser and D'Angelo (2003). That model shows that coverage of the press and publicity dimensions of campaign reality—or metacoverage—occurs within the broader topical architecture of campaign news and that from metacoverage emerge press and publicity frames. Rather than delve deeply into the mechanics of the framing model, this study attempts to precisely locate the co-occurrence of press and publicity topics—and by extension, press and publicity frames—within the topics of campaign news. At the same time, it shows that press and publicity dimensions of metacoverage are distinct. Whereas previous content analyses have tended to merge categories of press and publicity, this analysis shows that in practical terms journalists tend to compose stories that for the most part contain either the press or publicity as the topic.

Normative implications of the findings deserve discussion. Alexander (1981) notes that in societies with differentiated political institutions such as the United States, the press flexibly integrates an array of propositions about politics into its coverage, thereby assuming an active integrative voice in political life while at the same time appearing to undermine the norms of those core political institutions. Arguably, the sheer presence of press and publicity propositions in campaign news undermines the electoral process because, as Kerbel (1998, chap. 3) notes, metacoverage tends to displace issue coverage, which he argues is more amenable to the democratic role of elections. However, as Esser and D'Angelo (2003) note, some press propositions indicate an effort on the part of the press corps to "test" hypotheses that do not manifestly communicate that candidates mistrust the press or are mistrusted by the press, which is the so-called strategy frame that Kerbel (1997) says suffuses campaign metacoverage. Rather, the integrative function of the campaign press to forge propositions into scripts (i.e., hypotheses and value assessments) about key political actors, including the press, appears flexible enough to generate scripts—and frames—that do not express a patently cynical view of media politics. Those "better" frames are the accountability frames, as opposed to strategy frames, which are built from propositions that support scripts about the antagonistic relationship between the press and politicians and are, therefore, cynical portrayals of the press and the publicity process.

That being said, it is evident that press strategy frames and the publicity strategy frames far outnumber their counterpart accountability frames. Therefore, coverage containing these frames is reasonably conceived to contribute to the cynical tenor of campaign news in general and Campaign 2000 news in particular. However, while it may be appropriate to bemoan the relative paucity of accountability frames in Campaign 2000 coverage, it should be pointed out that accountability frames mainly arise in coverage when norms have been breached by political scandals (e.g., negative information about a candidate leaked to the media) or media mistakes (e.g., after the incorrect election night predictions). Thus, the relative lack of accountability frames could be interpreted as a sign that Campaign 2000 progressed smoothly in its final stage.

REFERENCES

Agranoff, R. (1976). *The management of electoral campaigns*. Boston, MA: Holbrook Press.

Alexander, J. C. (1981). The mass media in systemic, historical, and comparative perspective. In E. Katz & T. Szecsko (Eds.), *Mass media and social change* (pp. 17–52). London: Sage.

Ansolabehere, S., Behr, R., & Iyengar, S. (1991). Mass media and elections: An overview. *American Politics Quarterly, 19* (1), 109–139.

Arterton, C. F. (1984). *Media politics*. Boston: Lexington Books.

Blumler, J. G., & Gurevitch, M. (1981). Politicians and the press: An essay on role relationships. In D. D. Nimmo & K. R. Sanders (Eds.), *Handbook of political communication* (pp. 467–493). Beverly Hills, CA: Sage.

Blumler, J. G., & Kavanagh, D. (1999). The third age of political communication: Influences and features. *Political Communication, 16* (3), 209–230.

Cappella, J. N., & Jamieson, K. H. (1997). *The spiral of cynicism: The press and the public good*. New York: Oxford University Press.

D'Angelo, P. (1999, May). *Framing the press: A new approach to assessing the cynical nature of press self-coverage and its implications for information processing*. Paper presented at the International Communication Association, San Francisco.

D'Angelo, P. (2002). *Framing the press: A new model for observing press frames in presidential campaign news*. Unpublished doctoral dissertation. Temple University, Philadelphia, PA.

Davis, R. (1992). *The press and American politics: The new mediator*. New York: Longman.

Esser, F., & D'Angelo, P. (2003). Framing the press and the publicity process: A content analysis of metacoverage in Campaign 2000 network news. *American Behavioral Scientist, 46*, 617–641.

Esser, F., Reinemann, C., & Fan, D. (2001). Spin doctors in the United States, Great Britain, and Germany: Metacommunication about media manipulation. *Harvard International Journal of Press/Politics, 6* (1), 16–45.

Graber, D. (1997). *Mass media and American politics* (5th ed.). Washington, DC: Congressional Quarterly Press.

Johnson, T. J., Boudreau, T., with Glowaki, C. (1996). Turning the spotlight inward: How leading news organizations covered the media in the 1992 presidential election. *Journalism & Mass Communication Quarterly, 73* (3), 657–671.

Joslyn, R. (1984). *Mass media and elections*. Reading, MA: Addison-Wesley.

Kerbel, M. R. (1997). The media: Viewing the campaign through a strategic haze. In M. Nelson (Ed.), *The elections of 1996* (pp. 81–105). Washington, DC: Congressional Quarterly Press.

Kerbel, M. R. (1998). *Edited for television: CNN, ABC, and American presidential politics* (2nd ed.). Boulder, CO: Westview Press.

Kerbel, M. R., Apee, S., & Ross, M. (2000). PBS ain't so different: Public broadcasting, election frames, and democratic empowerment. *Harvard International Journal of Press/ Politics, 5* (4), 8–32.

Patterson, T. E. (1980). *The mass media election.* New York: Praeger.

Patterson, T. E. (1993). *Out of order.* New York: Knopf.

Polsby, N. W. (1983). *Consequences of party reform.* Oxford: Oxford University Press.

Robinson, M. J., & Lichter, S. R. (1991). "The more things change . . .": Network news coverage of the 1988 presidential nomination races. In E. H. Buell, Jr. & L. Sigelman (Eds.), *Nominating the president* (pp. 196–212). Knoxville: University of Tennessee Press.

Sabato, L. (1981). *The rise of political consultants: New ways of winning elections.* New York: Basic Books.

Sabato, L. (1991). *Feeding frenzy: How attack journalism has transformed American politics.* New York: Free Press.

Stempel, G. H., & Windhauser, J. W. (1991). Newspaper coverage of the 1984 and 1988 campaigns. In G. H. Stempel III & J. W. Windhauser (Eds.), *The media in the 1984 and 1988 presidential campaigns* (pp. 13–66). Westport, CT: Greenwood Press.

Tankard, J., & Sumpter, R. (1993, August). *Media awareness of media manipulation: The use of the term "spin doctor."* Paper delivered at the annual meeting of the Association for Education in Journalism and Mass Communication, Kansas City, MO.

Troy, G. (1991). *See how they ran: The changing role of the presidential candidate.* New York: Free Press.

Wattenberg, M. P. (1994). *The decline of American political parties 1952–1992.* Cambridge: Harvard University Press.

8

Representations of the Public and Public Opinion in National Television Election News

Stephanie Greco Larson

Since democratic elections are inherently about the public, what prospective voters say, think, and do during campaigns is important. Yet media coverage focuses primarily on the candidates and their strategies using sports analogies and game metaphors that treat voters as spectators rather than important political actors (Hart, 1994; Patterson, 1993). One way that the public is included in coverage is through the use of polls. However, poll coverage focuses narrowly on candidate preference to report the horse race (who is ahead and behind) rather than substantive concerns of voters (Broh, 1980; Keenan, 1986; Lavrakas & Holley, 1991; Patterson, 1993). However, polls are only part of how the media covers public opinion.

Television news also covers the public by talking to them on camera. These "people-on-the-street" interviews are consistent with the way journalists are trained to collect information (Hess, 1981). They conform to the medium's need for visuals and the narrative structure of television news, which personalizes events (Bennett, 1996; Iyengar, 1991). Matthew Kerbel (1994) was among the first to document the extent of this coverage. He found that 18% of ABC news coverage of the 1992 election treated "members of the mass public" as the subject or object of the story, second only to the candidates and their aides. Citizen involvement in presidential campaign news was purposely increased by the networks in 1996 (Just, 1997) with additional reliance on focus groups (Just et al., 1996). In network news coverage of the 1996 general election campaign, there were forty-two stories including 145 different people on the street (Larson, 1999a). Not only was this coverage prevalent, but also the range of topics discussed by people on the street was vast compared to the narrow and superficial use of polls (Larson, 1999a).

The purpose of this chapter is to examine how the public and public opinion were covered on national television news during the 2000 general election by looking at both people on the street and poll coverage. This descriptive analysis looks at the breadth and focus of public opinion coverage, highlighting similarities and differences between poll reports and people-on-the-street coverage. This coverage was assessed using a quantitative content analysis that analyzed who was covered, what they said, and how they were used in the stories.

METHOD

First, the population of national evening news segments about the presidential election from Labor Day to Election Day 2000 was identified for ABC, CBS, and NBC. Next, these stories were examined for coverage of public opinion (either through poll use or inclusion of people on the street). People on the street were defined here as "members of the general public." They excluded candidates, paid members of their staff, spokespeople of interest groups, and individuals identified as experts (such as pollsters, journalists, academics, and representatives of think tanks). Poll stories included those that referred to poll findings either explicitly (specific polls by name) or implicitly (either as unidentified polls or as "the public").

The poll stories were coded for the origin of the poll information (network poll, clearly identified nonnetwork poll, unidentified poll, or public opinion generally), the inclusion of certain types of poll questions (candidate preference, candidate evaluation, issue positions, status quo evaluations, campaign event evaluations, or knowledge assessments), inclusion of sound bites from academic experts or pollsters, and focus on particular subgroups or subgroup comparisons (the undecided or particular age, gender, geographic, or racial groups).

People on the street who appeared in the stories were coded for their sex, race, age, and state of residence and for their party identification and voting intent when these were explicitly identified. To get a better sense of why certain individuals were selected and how people on the street were used in the story, story characteristics were examined. The stories were coded for subject and collapsed into the topics of *the public, issues,* or *campaigning.*[1] In addition, stories were coded for the use of polls or pollsters' commentary, the centrality of the public in the story (major, medium, or minor), and how the person seemed to be selected (at random, at a candidate's event, or to represent a type discussed in the story). It was also noted if the individual was part of a network focus group.[2]

Statements made by people on the street were coded for topic and direction of comments about candidates. Topics included *horse race, candidate evaluation, issues, campaign evaluations,* and *status quo evaluations. Horse-race* statements included statements people made about their own or others' voting preferences or lack of preferences. Comments by undecided voters about how or when they might decide were also included here. *Issue* statements included any policy statements, general or specific. These comments either conveyed the person's issue position, the saliency of an issue to them, or their desire for the government to fix something they identify as a problem. *Candidate evaluations* included statements made about the candidates' personal or professional characteristics. These needed to be more general than an evaluation of how candidates performed at certain events. For example, the statement "Bush didn't answer the question about affirmative action in the debate" would be coded as a campaign evaluation rather than as a candidate evaluation. *Campaign evaluations* included comments about the candidates' strategies or their performance in campaign settings. It also included general comments about the campaign or electoral process. *Status quo evaluations* included statements about personal circumstances (e.g., "I lost my job") or the nation's (e.g., "the economy stinks").

RESULTS

Poll Coverage

There were 192 stories that included poll reports. Of these, 60 (31%) were from network-sponsored polls, 18 (9%) were from polls whose sources were clearly identified as other than network, 62 (32%) referred to unidentified polls, and 52 (27%) did not specifically refer to polls or a poll but seemed to rely on poll data to talk about public opinion. NBC ran a greater number of poll stories (75) than ABC (61) or CBS (56).

Most of the poll stories (149, 78%) included attention to respondents' vote preferences in order to assess the horse race. Reporters talked about which candidate had a lead overall and among particular groups (e.g., certain states, age groups, or sexes). Attention to candidate preference was also present in the second most frequent type of survey question included in stories. These asked respondents which candidate would do a better job dealing with certain issues or situations. These questions were included in 21 stories (11%).

Fifteen stories (8%) included issue positions or issue priorities of the public. The issues covered were size of government, school vouchers, Social Security privatization, and prescription drug costs. The issue priorities identified were education, health care, Medicare, family values (including entertainment violence), the economy, and taxes. Fourteen stories (7%) included poll results for questions having to do with campaign events (such as the debates, use of a particular commercial, and Bush's arrest for driving under the influence being revealed). Other types of questions received substantially less coverage. Nine stories (5%) included findings from questions that dealt with candidate likability or favorability. Two stories (1%) included polls that asked which candidate would make a better leader. Evaluations of the status quo (such as assessments of the economy or the health care system) were found in six stories (3%). Three stories (2%) covered an MTV poll that tested candidate name recall and recognition among eighteen- to twenty-four-year-olds.[3]

Overall, this analysis indicates that while poll coverage was extensive, it did not provide a comprehensive picture of what was on the public's mind. This superficiality was reinforced by the lack of expert analysis of what poll findings meant. Most stories (167, 87%) did not include experts (academics or pollsters). In fact, only 16 stories included sound bites from pollsters. ABC was less likely to include such experts than the other two networks, Cramer's $V = .231$, $p \leq$ .01. ABC included experts in only 2% of its poll stories compared to 18% of CBS's and 19% of NBC's.[4]

Attention was paid to subgroups of the population either by making comparisons between categories of respondents (such as men and women) or by looking exclusively at one group (such as Florida voters). These distinctions were most commonly made in terms of geographic groups. Sixty-three stories (33%) included information from polls done in states. The results of these tended to be summarized on maps that identified who was ahead in each state. Additional attention was paid to polls from Arkansas, California, Connecticut, Florida, Michigan, Minnesota, Pennsylvania, Tennessee, and Washington. These states were chosen either because the race there was considered close enough for additional scrutiny or because they were relevant for telling stories about particular individuals. For example, the story using a Connecticut poll (NBC, September 25) focused on Gore's running mate, Joe Lieberman. The amount of attention residents of particular states got differed by network. Forty-three percent of NBC poll reports included a geographic focus compared to 30% at ABC and 23% at CBS, Cramer's $V = .176$, $p \leq .05$.[5]

Twenty poll stories (10%) focused on gender of respondents. This coverage documented the extent of the gender gap (women's preference for Gore and men's preference for Bush), speculated as to the reason for the gap, and discussed what Bush was doing to appeal to women. The reasons offered for the gap were heavily speculative with no direct use of poll data to make sense of the gap or changes in it. In other words, polls might have informed some of the reporting or expert commentary, but they were not used explicitly to demonstrate differences in the issue positions, issue priorities, or candidate evaluations between women and men. Most speculation for why there was a gender gap focused on Gore's issue positions (including stories that talked about his "anti-Hollywood" position on violence in entertainment); however, one story introduced a "personality breakthrough" and "The Kiss" at the Democratic convention as possible explanations (ABC, September 18). Other stories talked about Bush's campaign strategies as contributing to his problem appealing to women and to his efforts to close the gap. These included appearing on *Oprah*, talking more about certain issues, and having his wife and mother campaign more in battleground states. No analysis was offered of why Bush was more popular with men or what Gore might be doing about it.

Although voter preference divided more starkly along racial than gender lines (Ceaser & Busch, 2001), only a few poll stories mentioned race and none provided poll data on a "race gap." Most of these references were simply to Gore's need for a high turnout among blacks and what he was doing to try to get it. Two reports that mentioned race and candidate evaluations were contradictory. One said that Gore was doing well among "union, minority, and city dwellers" (ABC, November 6), and the other asserted (without documentation) that "blacks have been slow to warm to Gore" (ABC, November 5). One report dismissed the importance of race by noting that in Florida, Republican Cubans and Democratic blacks "cancel each other out" (CBS, October 25).

Other subgroups given particular attention in poll stories were the elderly and the young. Nineteen poll stories (10%) talked about public opinion in terms of respondents' age. NBC was significantly more likely to analyze these subgroups than the other two networks. Sixteen percent of NBC's stories looked at age compared to 9% of CBS's and 3% of ABC's, Cramer's V = .18, $p \le .05$. Rather than looking at "age gaps," these stories tended to focus on young or old voters. Of the two groups, the elderly's public opinions were more clearly explained and presented as important. Voters sixty-five and older were said to be abundant in key states, an important undecided group, and "courted" by the candidates. The horse race was assessed for older voters nationally (NBC, October 4) and in Florida (CBS, October 25). Poll numbers on Florida's senior citizens' opinions on Social Security privatization and prescription drugs were offered to explain Gore's lead among the elderly in that state. On the other hand, poll stories that included attention to young voters emphasized how uninformed, undecided, and uninterested they were in the campaign. All three networks covered the MTV poll that showed their lack of familiarity with the candidates' names. Only NBC (October 19) used this poll as a peg for a more extensive discussion of why young people are not more politically active. References to young people were also made in stories about Ralph Nader's campaign. No attention was paid to polls measuring the issue preferences of young voters.[6]

Twenty-two stories (12%) looked at undecided voters. Undecided voters (or "holdouts," as ABC sometimes called them) were talked about in a variety of ways. Sometimes these were at odds with each other. There was some effort to quantify the number of undecided voters without explicitly discussing the methodology used to identify them. They were said to make up 2% of the public, 10% of the public, 6 million people, and 8.5 million people. They were described as being young, suburban, middle class, fiscally conservative, and elderly. They were said to care about health care, violence in entertainment, fiscal responsibility, and morality issues. They supposedly thought that Social Security privatization was a bad idea and that Bill Clinton was not trustworthy or ethical. Much attention was paid to what candidates were doing to gain their support. The following points were made to address this concern: Bush switched from attacking Gore to issues; Bush got an "image makeover"; Bush changed his issue agenda to emphasize tax cuts, health care, morals, and education; Bush began campaigning more aggressively; Gore started talking about the environment. Although a few stories mentioned in passing that undecided voters might not vote, this did not stop the stories from treating undecided voters as the most important members of the public. The extensive attention to undecided likely voters focused on asserting their importance to the outcome of the race rather than systematically assessing the reasons for their fence-sitting. Of course, this attention to candidate preferences, rather than the reasons for the preferences, was not unique to stories about the undecideds.

People-on-the-Street Characteristics

One hundred and fifty people on the street appeared on the news in 58 stories. Fifty percent were women, 84% were white, and there were slightly more elderly people than young people (19% compared to 13% with the rest middle-aged). While individuals were not identified as representing their racial group and rarely identified as representing their sex, many old and young people were presented as speaking for their age group. People on the street came from fifteen states. Most were selected from the battleground states of Pennsylvania (28), Michigan (25), Missouri (24), and Florida (12). Only ten individuals had their party identifications specified in the stories: three Republicans, three Democrats, and four independents. Twenty-one people (14%) were said to have decided for whom they were voting. More than twice as many (46, 31%) were identified as undecided.

Some of these characteristics of the people on the street differed by network. ABC news had proportionately more men than the other networks (61%, compared to 44% on CBS and 41% on NBC). This difference (between ABC and the other two networks combined) was statistically significant, Cramer's V $= .189$, $p \leq .05$. CBS had more elderly people on the street (31%) than ABC (19%) and NBC (11%). ABC and NBC combined had 15% elderly, significantly fewer than CBS, Cramer's V $= .168$, $p \leq .05$. This difference does not conform to the network differences in poll coverage, in which NBC paid more attention to age. All three networks covered undecided voters, but NBC was the most committed to covering this group and ABC was the least committed. The majority of people on the street on NBC were undecideds (54%) compared to 47% on CBS and only 8% on ABC, Cramer's V $= .35$, $p \leq .001$.

People-on-the-Street Statements

The statements made by these people also showed a diversity beyond that found in poll reporting. The distribution of subjects commented on by people on the street can be seen in table 8.1. Rather than mirroring the horse-race focus of polls, the most frequent category for people-on-the-street statements was "issues," followed by "candidate evaluations." "Voter preference" (the equivalent of horse-race reporting of polls for people on the street) was a distant fourth. The statement topics differed significantly by network. More than half of ABC's people-on-the-street comments were about issues. This is a far greater percentage than for the other networks. CBS emphasized campaign evaluations. Sixty percent of the statements made about the campaign and 56% of those that evaluated the candidates were found in stories where people on the street played a major role compared to only 19% for statements about the horse race and 9% for issues and status quo stories combined, Cramer's V = .37, $p \le .001$.

The fifty-one people-on-the-street issue statements varied in terms of their generality. Only a few of these statements identified an issue without giving some sense of what the interviewee wanted done about it. For example, one person said that the "moral issues" Bush talked about were appealing to her (NBC, November 5). What these issues were and what she liked about Bush's positions on them was unclear. Other statements shared clearer goals but no definite plan for how to achieve them (e.g., "getting oil prices under control"—NBC, September 22). Issue positions related to education illustrate the ways that a topic was talked about. Of the seventeen statements made about education, nine were on the school voucher issue. The other eight education statements indicated that we should not cut taxes because that would hurt schools; a proposed tuition tax credit was a good idea; schools were overcrowded and more needed to be built; teachers needed a pay raise; and more mandatory testing would not solve problems in the schools. The other frequently discussed issues were the cost of prescription drugs, which was sometimes talked about in terms of inadequate Medicare coverage (10 statements), taxes (9), gun control (6), and Social Security privatization (6).[7] Since attitudes toward school vouchers, prescription drug plans, and Social Security privatization were among the few issues included in

Table 8.1   Subject of People-on-the-Street Comments by Network and Year

	Network, 2000				
	ABC	*CBS*	*NBC*	*Total 2000*	*Total 1996*
n	58	32	52	142	178
Subject					
Horse race	12%	13%	19%	15%	16%
Issues	52%	19%	29%	36%	39%
Candidate	9%	22%	29%	19%	19%
Campaign	19%	31%	17%	21%	15%
Status quo	9%	16%	6%	9%	11%

For 2000 Network Differences, Cramer's V = .26, $p \le .001$.
For 1996 data see Larson, 1999a.

poll stories, it appears that some of these interviews were used to put "flesh on the statistical bones" of polls (Hart, 1994, p. 107).

People-on-the-Street Stories and Selection

Looking at the how people on the street were used in stories might provide additional evidence that individuals were used to illustrate public opinion trends. A majority of the people on the street (63%) were included in stories that also mentioned polls or had experts talking about polls. CBS did this less frequently than the other networks. Only 34% of CBS's people on the street were in stories with polls/poll experts compared to 59% for ABC and 63% for NBC, Cramer's V = .38, $p \leq .001$.[8]

People-on-the-street interviews also appear to have been used to put a face on abstractions. Seventy-eight percent of the people in stories seemed to be selected to illustrate an idea, group, or problem identified by the reporter. For example, old people were used to talk about Social Security, prescription drugs, and concerns of the elderly. Teachers, principals, students, and parents were interviewed when the topic was education. Members of the National Rifle Association spoke in the gun control story. All but one of the people included in stories in which people on the street played a major role were used in this way.

Only 11% of the members of the public seemed to be randomly selected and asked to comment without the reporter using the statement as evidence of something he or she was noting in the story. These included people in diners and restaurants and people (literally) on the street who were asked "What do you think character is?" (ABC, November 3). Another 9% of the people were talking at campaign events and their statements were used on the news. For example, an Iowa senior citizen told Gore in a town hall meeting that she had to pick up cans along the roadside to pay for her medication (ABC and CBS, September 27). Although reporters did not find Winifred Skinner on their own to put an elderly face on the Medicare/prescription drug issue, her sound bites were used to personalize an issue that the candidates were talking about and that the news gave ample coverage.

The topics of the stories that people on the street appeared in can also reveal what purpose the interview served. Stories were coded as being primarily about the public, issues, or campaigning. The greatest percentage were about issues (39%), the fewest about the public (25%) with campaign stories in between (35%). However, people on the street played a greater role in stories that were about the public and only a minor role in those about campaigning (see table 8.2). This differs from poll stories, which were primarily used to evaluate the candidates and their campaigns.

The networks differed significantly in the types of stories in which their interviews were included (see table 8.3). ABC was the most distinctive, with 58% of its people on the street being included in issue stories. CBS used the interviews

Table 8.2   The Relationship between Centrality of People on the Street and Story Type

| | Centrality of People on the Street in News Segments | | | |
	Minor	Medium	Major	Total
n	25	80	45	150
Story Type				
Issues	24%	63%	7%	39%
Public	8%	18%	49%	25%
Campaigning	68%	20%	44%	35%

Cramer's V = .42, $p \leq$ .001.

in campaign stories the most (44%). NBC was somewhat balanced with stories about the public containing the greatest percentage of their people on the street (39%).

The importance of public voices can be seen in the centrality that people on the street had in stories. More stories used people on the street in a major role than in a minor one (30% compared to 17%). This centrality varied by network. In only 7% of the NBC stories with members of the public talking did they play a minor role in the story (compared to 22% for both ABC and CBS). ABC gave the least centrality to people on the street; only 6% of their people played a major role in stories. NBC's more extensive attention to the public is consistent with the "populist news" approach they took in 1996 (Larson, 2000; Tucher, 1997).

The extensive attention to undecided voters seen in the analysis of poll stories can also be seen in people-on-the-street coverage. Members of the public were frequently found talking in stories about undecided voters. A full 20% of the people on the street were included in the eight stories specifically about undecided voters.[9] The networks differed significantly in their attention to undecided people on the street, Cramer's V = .351, $p \leq$ .01. NBC provided the most extensive coverage of this group with 54% of their people on the street identified as undecided. A far smaller proportion of ABC's (8%) and CBS's (8%) people on the street were in this category.

Many of the undecided individuals were found in NBC's special continuing

Table 8.3   The Relationship between Story Characteristics and Network

| | Network | | | |
	ABC	CBS	NBC	Total
n	64	32	54	150
Story Type				
Issues	58%	25%	26%	39%
Public	11%	31%	39%	25%
Campaigning	31%	42%	35%	35%

Cramer's V = .26, $p \leq$ .001.

feature called "The Undecided." Some of these stories looked at particular types of undecideds (women, young, those in swing states), others looked at campaign appeals to these voters (plans for curbing prescription drug prices and for tax relief) or how campaign strategies were being perceived by this group. Other stories grappled with who the undecideds were and what might get them off the fence. Twelve of the fifteen undecideds interviewed by CBS were from a focus group intentionally put together to talk to people who had not made up their minds before the first debate. ABC also focused most of its attention on undecideds in two stories on "holdouts" that aired before and after the first debate. Three of the four undecided voters on ABC were part of a Pennsylvania group assembled by the network to watch the debates together. Overall, this extensive attention to the undecideds in people-on-the-street coverage reinforced their prominence in poll stories.

CONCLUSION

As in 1996, the networks gave much election coverage to the general public in their 2000 evening news shows. The topical breakdown of the two types of public opinion coverage was also similar to that in 1996 when people-on-the-street comments were rich in issues and poll coverage focused on the horse race. Networks continued to differ from each other. In 1996 NBC used more people on the street and special segments that highlighted voters than their competitors did (Larson, 2000; Tucher, 1997). In 2000, ABC edged out NBC for the greatest number of people on the street; however, NBC continued to emphasize people on the street by making them more central in stories and dedicating a continuing special feature to them.

The diversity of the people on the street was also similar to previous years' coverage. People of various sexes, races, ages, states, and attitudinal positions appeared (Larson, 1999a, 1999b). Unlike 1992, when selection of interviews was guided by concerns over the economy and unemployment, and unlike 1996, when the issue of education guided selection (Larson, 1999b), in 2000 the closeness of the race pushed selection toward undecided voters.

Undecideds played major roles in people-on-the-street stories. They were analyzed separately in 12% of the poll stories and were the implicit focus of horse-race poll coverage. The relentless attention to undecided voters distorted their prevalence in the electorate and usually avoided the question of whether "undecided voters" were actually going to be "undecided nonvoters." Not only did the coverage exaggerate the extent of indecision in the electorate, but also it conveyed the impression that politicians and the public had little in common. By giving attention to members of the public who were the least involved, the news made the public look ambivalent, nonpartisan, and uninvolved compared to the polarized, partisan, and combative politicians. The networks *could* have provided coverage of voters who identified with a party, knew whom they were voting for, and could have articulated a rationale for both. Since the vast majority of likely voters could have done these things, giving them coverage would have better represented the public and might have provided useful information to the unde-cided voters in the audience who were trying to make up their minds.

NOTES

1. Originally there were fifteen attributes for this variable. They included prescription drugs, education, energy, Social Security, gun control, taxes, economics, debate, character, undecided voters, elderly voters, young voters, women voters, "get out the vote" efforts, and campaigning.

2. The term *focus group* is used here to connote instances when people were brought together by the news organization or reporter for a discussion. Sometimes this was done more formally than at other times. An example of a formal focus group is CBS's use of political consultant Linda DeVall. An example of an informal one is when ABC brought three Allentown, Pennsylvania, residents together to watch a debate.

3. These percentages total more than 100% because some stories included more than one type of question.

4. These differences are even greater when the fifty-two stories that did not explicitly mention polls are excluded. In the remaining stories, ABC used no experts, CBS included them in 12% of the stories, and NBC in 22%, Cramer's V = .283, $p \leq .01$.

5. These differences are even greater when the fifty-two stories that did not explicitly mention polls are excluded. In the remaining stories 19% of CBS's stories focused on states, as did 23% of ABC's and 43% of NBC's, Cramer's V = .234, $p \leq .05$.

6. Young, suburban families in Florida fared better. They were referred to as an impor-tant undecided group for which candidates were making certain issue appeals. However, it does not seem that this "young" group is a subset of the eighteen- to twenty-five-year-olds in the other stories.

7. The 51 issue statements made were: prescription drug costs/Medicare (10), school vouchers (9), Social Security privatization (6), gun control (6), tax cuts (for or against without specifics) (5), desire to increase taxes for education and/or health care (3), energy policy/oil prices (2), "pay down the debt" (2), school crowding/build schools (2), health care generally (1), tuition tax credits (1), school testing (1), increase teachers' pay (1), moral issues (1), and environment (1).

8. To some extent this reflects the relative extent of poll usage among the networks discussed earlier.

9. Furthermore, the undecideds were likely to be found in stories where the public played a major role—56% of the undecideds were in these stories compared to 24% of decideds and 18% of those who were not clearly identified, Cramer's V = 27, $p \leq .001$.

REFERENCES

Bennett, W. L. (1996). *News: The politics of visibility* (3rd ed.). New York: Longman.

Broh, C. A. (1980). Horse-race journalism: Reporting the polls in the 1976 presidential election. *Public Opinion Quarterly, 44*, 514–529.

Ceaser, J. W., & Busch, A. E. (2001). *The perfect tie: The true story of the 2000 presidential election*. Lanham, MD: Rowman & Littlefield.

Hart, R. P. (1994). *Seducing America: How television charms the modern voter*. New York: Oxford University Press.

Hess, S. (1981). *The Washington Reporters*. Washington, DC: Brookings Institution.

Iyengar, S. (1991). *Is anyone responsible? How television frames political issues*. Chicago: University of Chicago Press.

Just, M. R. (1997). Candidate strategies and the media campaign. In G. M. Pomper (Ed.), *The elections of 1996: Reports and interpretations* (pp. 77–106). Chatham, NJ: Chatham House Publishers.

Just, M. R., Crigler, A. N., Alger, D. E., Cook, T. E., Kern, M. (1996). *Crosstalk: Citizens, candidates, and the media in a presidential campaign*. Chicago: University of Chicago Press.

Keenan, K. (1986). Polls in network newscasts in the 1984 presidential race. *Journalism Quarterly, 63*, 617–630.

Kerbel, M.R. (1994). *Edited for television: CNN, ABC, and the 1992 presidential campaign*. Boulder, CO: Westview.

Larson, S. G. (1999a). Public opinion in television election news: Beyond polls. *Political Communication, 16*, 133–145.

Larson, S. G. (1999b). Who are 'we' and what do 'we' want? Representations of the public in election news. In P. E. Scheele (Ed.) *We get what we vote for . . . or do we? The impact of elections on governing* (pp. 68–81). Westport, CT: Praeger.

Larson, S. G. (2000). Network differences in public opinion coverage during the 1996 presidential campaign. *Journal of Broadcasting & Electronic Media, 44*, 16–26.

Lavrakas, P. J., & Holley, J. K. (1991). *Polling and presidential election coverage*. Newbury Park, CA: Sage.

Patterson, T. E. (1993). *Out of order*. New York: Knopf.

Tucher, A. (1997, May/June). You news. *Columbia Journalism Review*, pp. 26–31.

9

Watching the Adwatchers

Examination of Adwatch Stories from the 2000 Election

Kimberly C. Gaddie and Lori Melton McKinnon

Political advertising has long been a staple of American campaigns. Most scholars agree that not only does political advertising help today's candidates to reach
voters, but it also can impact voter learning and decision formation. However,
some, usually in the public arena, express concerns about political advertising.
They argue that it is too costly, too negative, and too likely to diminish the quality of political discourse.

In response many journalists have come forward as watchdogs over campaign
ads, creating a journalistic tool known as the adwatch. In adwatches, the media
assess the content and accuracy of claims made by the candidates (Kaid, Tedesco, & McKinnon, 1996). Thus, the ads themselves become a campaign issue.

Seib (1994) contends that as candidates have a right to purchase political ads,
journalists have both a right and a responsibility to monitor political advertising
in the same way they cover other campaign experiences. He explains, "If a candidate's speech to a thousand people merits a news story, so does a candidate's ad
that reaches a million people" (Seib, 1994, p. 94). In fact, many journalists feel
that it is their Fourth Estate duty to serve as a check on the political campaign
process. By doing so, journalists may be helping to shape American voters' perceptions of candidate advertising and their political realities. However, these
political realities may differ depending on where the voter sits.

FRAMING

In preparing the daily news, gatekeepers select from numerous framing strategies. The tone, context, and placement of the news story may affect the way vot-

ers interpret its meaning. Scholars and journalists agree that adwatch coverage may help voters understand a candidate's political messages. However, as Jamieson (1992) points out, only if reporters question the legitimacy of ad claims can a watchdog role actually aid the political process.

According to Jamieson (1992), during 1988, 17% of newspaper coverage focused on advertising content while only 1.7% dealt with the accuracy of advertising claims. A study of 1992 televised political adwatches revealed that the media attempted some form of ad analysis only in about half of the total news stories (Kaid, McKinnon, & Tedesco, 1996). Jamieson (1992) explains that when reporters fail to reframe political advertisements, the power of the ad's messages may be enhanced (Jamieson, 1992).

Likewise, McKinnon et al. (1996) found that few newspaper adwatches analyze ethically suspect video techniques. Cappella and Jamieson (1994) warn that simple visual distinctions made by journalists may not be enough. Because adwatches focus on ads that are likely to be both emotionally and cognitively involving, Cappella and Jamieson suggest interrupting the ad. According to Jamieson (1992), ways for journalists to help lessen the ads' effects include separating accuracy/fairness from strategy effectiveness and labeling advertisement reviews.

For example, many newspapers have placed advertisement reviews in "truth boxes" or labeled reviews as "adwatches." Likewise, television stations have taken similar approaches to separate the ad review from the ad itself. In many cases, advertisements have been downsized and placed in a box or television-set graphic on the screen. According to West, Kern, and Alger (1992), "This downsizing of video in the Ad Watch is an important advance because it undercuts the visual impact of the advertisements" (p. 22). Additionally, some stations have used graphic overlays to indicate that the image being shown is merely a review of an ad. CNN reporters have placed text across the commercial such as "falsehood," "misleading," or "unfair," and NBC political analysts have attached "false" labels or put a red X over the ad. Other newscasters have warned viewers that they were about to review an advertisement by declaring a "time out" (Kern, West, & Alger, 1993). Such practices attempt to reduce the political advertisement's credibility by interrupting voters' short-term memory.

Additionally, research on "videostyle" suggests that the way candidates are presented in ads may impact ad effects (Kaid & Davidson, 1986). Indeed, visual images can often be more powerful than verbal content. In an experimental study by McKinnon and Kaid (1999), they found that the content of a broadcast ad that appeared in an NBC evening newscast may have been more powerful than the media commentary that accompanied it. In fact, subjects were more likely to recall claims made in the ad itself. Moreover, channel differences existed, as the broadcast adwatch appeared more powerful than the black-and-white still frames provided by the print adwatch version. Thus, images in the broadcast adwatch may have formed stronger impressions than the verbal analysis. However, visuals accompanying the print adwatch may not have created such strong impressions.

According to Jamieson (1992), journalists give the most attention to ads that are evocative, humorous, and controversial. Indeed, such spots often contain elements that emphasize candidates' "videostyle." Wicks and Kern (1993) explain, "These advertisements provide news directors with ready-made images containing strong visuals and drama—elements that have historically attracted television news" (p. 252). Likewise, content analyses show that adwatches focus on more negative ads than positive ones (Jamieson, 1992; Kaid et al., 1993; Kaid et al., 1996; McKinnon et al., 1996; Tedesco, McKinnon, & Kaid, 1996; West, 1993). Emphasizing negative spots enhances the widespread belief that American political campaigns are overly negative.

Indeed, journalists can and do serve a very influential role, providing much of the background for Americans' political realities. Reporters teach us about candidates' backgrounds, personalities, strategies, and goals (West, 1993). In response to Bowen's (1994) exit-poll study, the author writes, "The amount of press coverage given to the 'attack' commercials obviously contributed to their high recall and mitigated their impact. In this case, the press acted as 'spin' doctors commenting and elaborating on the content of the spots and turning them from their intended purpose" (p. 673).

Some scholars warn that adverse effects may occur when journalists provide a negative slant to political stories. Kaid et al.'s (1993) content analysis of coverage of televised political ads appearing between 1972 and 1988 revealed that network news coverage was often slanted negatively by media commentators. However, a study of newspaper adwatches found that most news stories were neutral in their focus (McKinnon et al., 1996). Interestingly, later content analyses on televised political adwatches revealed that although most coverage of political ads was neutral, when a slant was provided, that slant was largely negative (Kaid et al., 1996; Tedesco et al., 1996). Cappella and Jamieson (1994) caution that how a reporter frames a political adwatch may affect voters' attitudes toward the ad itself, the perceived fairness of the ad, and the perceived importance of the ad.

However, adwatch coverage is not always harmful to the candidate sponsoring the ad under investigation. Experimental research indicates that adwatch coverage may benefit the campaign in two major ways. First, news coverage enhances the campaign by providing unpaid access to millions of voters. Not only do such strategies assure that candidates receive free coverage, but they also increase the likelihood that candidates' ads will receive priority treatment. Content analyses on newspaper (McKinnon et al., 1996) and television adwatches (Kaid et al., 1993; Kaid et al., 1996; Tedesco et al., 1996) indicate that adwatches often are placed as priority agenda items. In fact, most newspaper adwatches appeared in the first section of the paper, and most television adwatches aired in the first ten minutes of the newscast. According to Roger Ailes, "You get a 30% to 40% bump out of an ad by getting it in the news. You get more viewers, you get more credibility, you get it in a framework" (quoted in Runkel, 1989, p. 136).

Second, news coverage may legitimize false or misleading claims by airing candidates' messages in a credible news environment (Jamieson, 1992; West, 1993). Experimental research by Pfau and Louden (1994) reveals that some adwatches may produce a boomerang effect, further enhancing the ad itself. Possible boomerang effects also were found in McKinnon and Kaid's (1999) experimental study, which investigated the effects of adwatches on voters' evaluations of political candidates and their ads. Surprisingly, results revealed that no significant differences existed between treatment formats (ad, adwatch, combination). Moreover, gender and party identification did not affect evaluations. In fact, the ad that appeared as an adwatch (in a credible news environment) produced more powerful evaluations of the sponsoring candidate than the ad alone. The researchers concluded that placement of ads in the news without careful analysis may do more to "magnify advertising effects than to mediate political mudslinging" (p. 105). Likewise, Jamieson (1992) found that viewers in focus groups recalled the ad itself better than the corrections made by the media commentator. Indeed, a single media critique cannot compare to an advertisement that has been repeated time and time again (Hinerfeld, 1990; Wolinsky et al., 1991). Thus, this study investigates broadcast-station coverage of political advertising during the 2000 election cycle. In addition to frequency of coverage by other major networks, researchers wanted to know how the adwatchers were covering 2000 political advertisements.

DOES MEDIUM OR MEDIA OUTLET MATTER?

Another major question for this study was whether the medium or media outlet a voter turns to for political information makes a difference in understanding of political advertising claims. Using a case study approach, researchers focus on the advertisement as the unit of analysis, tracing such variables as number of ads covered, what networks engaged in adwatch stories, slant of the coverage, the type of ad covered (e.g., negative ads versus positive ads), commentary provided by the reporter or journalist. Indeed, previous research suggests that print and broadcast adwatch coverage differs by the nature of each medium. For example, broadcast adwatches often reair all or part of the ad itself and often offer little critical analysis of the advertisement's claims. On the other hand, print adwatches often provide no visuals or only several still-frame images from the political spot but have space to provide more thorough analysis (Tedesco et al., 1996).

The 2000 presidential campaign offered a number of options for voters to receive and interpret political information. In addition to traditional print and broadcast outlets, voters turned to the Internet for up-to-date political information. Candidates for almost any and every level of office maintained websites to stay connected with voters. Nonprofit groups and sites like www.freedomchannel.com covered everything from candidates' advertisements and press conference briefings in attempts to help hold candidates accountable for their comments. These are only a portion of the breadth of information made available during the 2000 election.

Adwatch stories, like many other pieces of political information, were also covered in many different formats. The major networks at times covered televised advertisements by the candidates, websites like www.adcritic.com addressed the content of candidate advertising, and traditional print sources such as major newspapers covered these ads in both their print and online versions. The diversity of such formats for adwatch stories prompts the question: Are all of these different media responding to or covering the content of the candidates' advertisements in a similar manner? Or are their interpretations of the ads all very different?

This paper uses a case-study approach to trace candidate advertising and its presentation as a political adwatch across and within media and attempts to assess the consistency and/or validity of competing types of media and news sources when evaluating advertising content. The overriding question for this study is: Could what medium or media outlet a voter turns to for political information make a difference in his or her understanding of political advertisement claims?

METHODS

In an attempt to examine the frequency and type of coverage political advertising received during the 2000 election season, this chapter presents content analysis data. Specifically, all broadcast adwatch coverage on ABC, CBS, and NBC during the general election period (Labor Day to Election Day) was analyzed. Trained coders used a code sheet and codebook to examine source; story length; advertising as a main feature/supplement to story; type of story (campaign report, advertising feature, candidate profile, issue report, other); placement; experts used; ad/ads shown; candidate/party affiliation; slant of story; ethically suspect techniques identified; ad claims identified as suspect or misleading; whether the ad was shown full screen or reduced. The frequency results from that analysis are presented first.

Additionally, for an in-depth look at how multiple media outlets covered the same ad content, a selection of ads was chosen, and the adwatch story was utilized as the unit of analysis and traced through multiple media outlets. Six televised campaign advertisements from the 2000 presidential election were selected for the study. In making the selection, the researchers were looking for advertisements that were available among a set of media outlets that would be consistent for all ads. To this end, the researchers selected a set of media, or sources, that had all carried adwatch stories during the election and then determined a set of televised campaign advertisements from the presidential election covered by each of the media. The media used in this study are the *New York Times,* the *Los Angeles Times,* the *Milwaukee Journal-Sentinel,* CBS.com, and *Slate Magazine.* The *New York Times, Los Angeles Times,* and *Milwaukee Journal-Sentinel* represent the traditional print sources. CBS.com and *Slate* are both online, Internet sources; the former obviously is the online site for CBS television network, and the latter is an online magazine.

The televised campaign advertisements selected for analysis among these media are "Notebook," sponsored by the Republican National Committee; "Judge," sponsored by the Democratic National Committee; "Compare," sponsored by the Bush campaign; "Really," sponsored by the Republican Party; and "Nonsense," sponsored by the Bush campaign. Each of these advertisements, which represent diverse sponsorships, was covered in at least five of the six media selected. For the purposes of this study the advertisement itself is the unit of analysis as it is discussed in each of the above-mentioned media. Both the visual and the verbal content of the advertisement are traced through these media looking for patterns of consistency, or inconsistency, between the media and how they "cover" the advertisement.

RESULTS

Frequency analysis of the broadcast adwatch stories examined here reinforces findings of previous research on adwatch stories. A total of fifty broadcast adwatch stories were identified and coded. Of this total, eighteen (36%) aired on ABC, fourteen (28%) aired on CBS, and eighteen (36%) on NBC. In breaking the adwatch stories down further, coders marked whether the ad was the primary feature of the story. In only thirteen of the fifty stories (26%) was the political ad(s) the dominant feature of the story. For the other thirty-seven stories (74%), the coverage of the ad(s) was part of a larger story such as a campaign or issue report. In fact, thirty-one stories (62%) were campaign report pieces with seven stories (14%) airing as issue reports.

One of the trends discussed earlier, and an advantage of broadcast adwatch stories, is to show portions of the actual ad in the story. In this analysis, all but one story (98%) included at least a portion of the ad in the story itself. Usually it was only a small portion; the average length of the ad clip totaled ten to fifteen seconds of the entire story. Looking at party affiliation for the candidate in the ads, sixteen of the fifty adwatch stories (32%) were for Republicans, and twelve (24%) were for Democratic candidates. Two stories were for candidates labeled "other" by the coding. Seventeen stories (34%), however, were done as combinations with multiple candidates and ads shown.

One of the major trends in adwatch stories uncovered by prior research is to focus primarily on negative advertising. This was certainly the case in this project as well. Of the fifty stories coded, thirty-seven (74%) focused on negative ads. Also, the coverage of those stories remained primarily neutral with thirty-eight (76%) having no slant by the reporter. The other trend, unfortunately also seen in prior research and reinforced by this study, is that virtually no analysis was provided by reporters in these stories (90%). This statistic is particularly alarming when the goal of these stories is to help provide voters with an understanding of political advertising that can contain misleading or false claims by a candidate. These simple frequency reports offer one look at how the broadcast media covered political advertising in the 2000 election. The other important question asked by this project was, How do different media cover the same ad? The results of tracing those six advertisements identified earlier is presented in a series of tables to help facilitate side-by-side comparison.

Table 9.1 provides an overview of the elements present for each adwatch story. As this table indicates, all five of the media included in this study provided the complete, original text of advertisement, the producer for the ad, some description of the visual elements in the advertisement, and some analysis of the verbal content. For the traditional print sources, retrieved through the Lexis-Nexis database, a location of where the story appeared in the paper was also provided. For at least four of the five sources, a distinct section was also provided in the story that focused on interpretations about the strategies behind the ad or used as a "scorecard" for how each campaign might be benefiting. For *Slate*, which tended to be more editorial in its approach, "strategy" comments were incorporated into the body of the article.

Table 9.2 contains a breakdown of the visual elements in each advertisement, listed for each medium. This facilitates a side-by-side comparison of the similarities and differences in how each medium and media outlet treated the visual components of the advertisements.

To minimize any confusion, discussion for the results of this study are grouped by advertisement with a "walk-through" of how each of the media covered that particular ad. For reference purposes, a comparison listing has been created for each of the advertisements and broken down by media.

Republican National Committee Ad: "Notebook"

For this advertisement sponsored by the Republican National Committee, the *New York Times* and the *Milwaukee Journal-Sentinel* reported the most depth in their description of visual elements from the ad, while CBS.com provided the least detail, as shown in table 9.3. The *New York Times* provided a detailed account of the computer-generated graphic of the notebook used as well as specific reference to what text appears and when. Both the *New York Times* and the *Milwaukee Journal-Sentinel* go so far as to re-create for the reader the closing

Table 9.1 Elements Present in Each Adwatch Story Listed by Medium

	Text of ad	Description of visual elements	Analysis attempted	Producer of ad	Location of story (for print sources)	Other elements provided in adwatch
New York Times	√	√	Accuracy	√	√	• Scorecard
Los Angeles Times	√	√	Accuracy	√	√	• Scorecard
Milwaukee Journal-Sentinel	√	√	Accuracy	√	√	• Scorecard
CBS.com	√	√	Fact check	√	N/A	• The Strategy • List states where airing
Slate (online magazine)	Link to text given	Some in text references	√	√	N/A	• This is more editorial in nature • Discussion between 2 writers

Table 9.2 Comparison of Visual and/or Graphical Aspects in Ads by Media

	New York Times	Los Angeles Times	Milwaukee Journal-Sentinel	CBS.com	Slate magazine
Notebook (RNC)	No picture or still shot is shown. **ON THE SCREEN:** The advertisement features a notebook that is ostensibly comparing the Bush and Gore prescription drug plans. Under the Gore column, are words like "Charges Seniors $600 Big Government Access Fee Annually." Under the Bush column, words appear like "Seniors Choose Coverage". The advertisement summarizes all its charges against Gore, then cuts to the Democratic candidate himself in a television set, while the words appear "Gore's Rx Plan? PrescriptionFor Disaster.com." As the advertisement ends, Gore is speaking with the sound turned off, but he appears to be saying, "For you."	No picture or still shot is shown. **THE PICTURES:** The backdrop is a graphic of a yellow spiral notebook, broken down into two side-by-side columns, one for Bush and one for Gore. Short phrases such as "Age 64, Forced to Join Drug HMO" appear and disappear to track the announcer's words. Ends with a closeup of a television on a kitchen counter, with Gore speaking on the screen.	No picture or still shot is shown. **ON THE SCREEN:** The advertisement features a notebook that is ostensibly comparing the Bush and Gore prescription drug plans. Under the Gore column, are words like "Charges Seniors $600 Big Government Access Fee Annually." Under the Bush column, words appear like "Seniors Choose Coverage". The advertisement summarizes all its charges against Gore, then cuts to the Democratic candidate himself in a television set, while the words appear "Gore's Rx Plan? PrescriptionFor Disaster.com." As the advertisement ends, Gore is speaking with the sound turned off, but he appears to be saying, "For you."	No picture or still shot is shown. **VISUAL:** The ad features a computer-generated image of a notebook with the announcer's key text typed on the pages. It ends with a shot of Gore on a TV with prescriptionfordisaster.com on the screen.	

| Judge (DNC) | Frame from the ad shown w/ story. ON THE SCREEN: Video footage of Mr. Bush appears and dissolves. Cut to the faces of several young children. Then a gavel comes down and the words "corrective action" are superimposed on the screen. More shots of children are seen, followed by a final, scowling portrait of the governor. | No picture or still shot is shown. THE PICTURES: Opens with a shot of Bush speaking. Cuts to a shot of a little girl looking up at her mother. A gavel comes down. A little boy is shown standing in a doorway. Closes with a shot of Bush. | No picture or still shot is shown. VISUALS: The ad begins with a screen-sized picture of Bush—the GOP presidential candidate—woefully looking downward, as the narrator recounts Texas' below standard record on providing health coverage to needy, low-income children. Subsequent scenes provide glimpses of the children reportedly neglected by Gov. Bush. The ad then shows a magnified headline from the New York Daily News, "Texas Kids Robbed of Benefits," to verify the ad's claims. The ad concludes with another sorrowful image of Bush, possibly meant to lament his health care record as governor. | No picture or still shot is shown. ON THE SCREEN: Video footage of Bush appears and dissolves. Cut to faces of several young children. Then a gavel comes down and the words "corrective action" are superimposed on the screen. More shots of children are seen, followed by a final, scowling portrait of the governor. | Frame from the ad shown w/ story. In the text of the article they use the descriptions—"the image of a falling gavel"; "the words 'Judge's findings' hang over the screen as the ad recites the court's harsh findings"; "below 'Judge's findings' the screen displays a banner newspaper headline: 'Texas kids robbed of health benefits'" |

(continues)

Table 9.2 Continued

	New York Times	Los Angeles Times	Milwaukee Journal-Sentinel	CBS.com	Slate magazine
Compare (Bush)	Frame from ad shown w/ story. **ON THE SCREEN:** The 30-sec. ad features statements about Gore's proposals in black on a stark white background, counterposed with color pictures of Bush. It then show pictures in color of Americans of different ethnicity, as it speaks of people who will not get a tax cut under Gore's plan for tax relief.	No picture or still shot shown. **THE PICTURES:** Bush speaking to a group of supporters outdoors. Bush & his wife, Laura, sitting on a school stairway w/a group of children. A rapid-fire sequence of scenes from daily life, such as woman sitting on a porch swing, young woman in a classroom. Shots of an elderly black woman. Bush speaking to a large crowd. Bush wearing a hard hat speaking to workers.	No picture or still shot shown. **ON THE SCREEN:** The 30-sec. ad features statements about Gore's proposals in black on a stark white background, counterposed with color pictures of Bush. It then shows pictures in color of Americans of different ethnicity, as it speaks of people who will not get a tax cut under Gore's plan for tax relief.	No picture or still shot shown. **VISUAL:** Lots of shots of Bush campaigning & key text against a white background. Compare also shows lots of people of varying ethnicity & age.	

Really
(Rep. Party)

No picture or still shot is shown. **THE PICTURES:** Opens with the camera zooming in on a television sitting on a kitchen counter. On the screen, Al Gore appears with Buddhist monks. The screen cuts to Gore speaking from the podium at the Democratic convention. The TV screen goes fuzzy. Then Gore is shown being interviewed by CNN. Then the camera shows the full kitchen scene again, slowly zooming in to the television, where Gore is speaking at low volume.	No picture or still shot is shown. **KEY IMAGES:** Al Gore on someone's television in a kitchen; Gore with Buddhist monks; Gore at the 2000 Democratic convention and Gore in a television interview.	No picture or still shot is shown. **VISUAL:** Opens with a view of a kitchen with Al Gore playing on the TV set. Next, a TV set with a scene from the Democrat's 1996 fund-raiser at a Buddhist temple—Al Gore mixing with the monks. Then a set showing Gore's 2000 convention address followed by a snippet from a Gore interview. Then back to the TV in the kitchen.	Frame from ad shown with story. In the text of the article they use the descriptions—"rather than deliver images directly to your screen, they put them on a television in a staged kitchen-set within your set".

Table 9.2 Continued

	New York Times	Los Angeles Times	Milwaukee Journal-Sentinel	CBS.com	Slate magazine
Nonsense (Bush)	Frame from ad of Gore w/ word "nonsense" shown. **ON THE SCREEN:** Framed by a television screen within a screen, Gore is seen in video footage greeting a pharmacist in his store. The scene freezes and an article from The Washington Times, headlined "Aides concede Gore Made Up Story" is superimposed. Cut to another shot of the vice-president and the word "nonsense". Scene shifts to Gov. George W. Bush in a hard hat, talking to factory workers, and finally, back to Mr. Gore, in mid-debate with Bradley.	No picture or still shot shown. **THE PICTURES:** Opens with a shot of a TV screen, with a shaky footage of Gore at a pharmacy. A newspaper clip floats in one corner. On the TV screen, Gore is shown speaking at the Dem. National Convention. Bush is shown wearing a hard hat & shaking the hand of a worker. On the TV screen, Gore is shown at a podium debating former opponent Bradley. Closeup of Gore at the debate.	No picture or still shot shown. **KEY IMAGES:** Gore at pharmacy, then headline "Aides concede Gore made up story". Goes to white screen with text "Now Al Gore is bending the truth again" giving the script extra punch. Gore shown speaking with the word "nonsense" floating next to him. Images of Bush & factory workers, all in hard hats, while Bush's plan is discussed. Ends with Gore in debate with primary opponent Bradley. The story also comments that this ad uses no music, only voice-over, and the announcer's voice is sharp and that rather than images of everyday life, it uses words on a blank screen and newspaper headlines.		

Down (Gore)			
No picture or still is shown. THE PICTURES: A $100 bill fills the screen as the camera slowly pulls back. Benjamin Franklin's face and the rest of the bill start to dissolve, melting into a row of coins. Gore is shown speaking in front of a crowd with an American flag behind him. Gore is shown looking solemn in front of a window. A man is shown working at home. Three graduates are shown smiling at each other.	No picture or still is shown. KEY IMAGES: A large $100 bill fills the screen and then visually melts away as drops of water fall onto it. A line of coins adding up to 62 cents stand on their edges in a row. As the announcer begins talking about Gore's plan, the images are of Gore speaking and of regular Americans with their doctors, at work and graduating from school.	No picture or still is shown. VISUAL: Begins with a shot of a $100 bill with drops of water slowly dissolving it. After it fully dissolves, two quarters, two nickels, and two pennies appear (62 cents). That's followed by shots of Gore, families, students, seniors and doctors.	No picture or still is shown. There is a discussion of a $100 bill on screen which dissolves, "amid the trickling sound of water to reveal 62 measly cents." Mentions shots of family eating dinner, a doctor with a patient, and college graduates celebrating. The story also mentions that the negative comments about Bush are followed by an "ominous hum" and the nice words about Gore are "followed by a dynamic melody."

Note: All text describing the visual content of the advertisements is taken directly from the story as it is written, except for the pieces taken out of the Slate magazine descriptions, where some condensing has been done to isolate the discussion about the visual elements, and then the direct text appears in quotations.

scenes of the ad, recounting that "as the advertisement ends, Gore is speaking with the sound turned off, but he appears to be saying 'for you.'" CBS.com, however, merely refers to a computer-generated notebook and "key text" typed onto the screen. One of the key elements from this ad is a closing line that appears on screen reading "Gore's Rx plan? Prescriptionfordisaster.com." All media included in this study, except the *Los Angeles Times,* make a reference to that closing line.

In the discussion of verbal content in these advertisements and the accuracy of the assertions made, more of the differences start emerging. Nowhere is this more evident than with the advertisement "Notebook." This advertisement centers around the differences between Gore's and Bush's plans for prescription drugs. The *New York Times* takes the claim that the "access fee" that Gore would charge is really a premium that "is based on an estimate for 2009—eight years out." However, CBS.com takes the discussion of this same point and comments that "the access fee won't reach that level for 10 years." Here is a direct example of the inconsistencies in covering the straight facts presented by the candidates in these advertisements. The adwatch does clarify for readers and viewers that Gore's plan is voluntary and that seniors do still get to choose their doctors. So again there are mixed interpretations: for some basic facts the media do not seem to be in agreement, but for other points of fact they all seem to be able to clarify assertions from the advertisements for readers.

Democratic National Committee Ad: "Judge"

This advertisement includes several visual elements worth noting, such as a falling gavel that strikes a desk and newspaper headlines that target Bush's record on health coverage for children in Texas. While only the *Milwaukee Journal-Sentinel* provides a detailed account of the newspaper headlines included in the ad, each of the media discusses the visual of the gavel. What is most interesting in the coverage of the visual elements here, as shown in table 9.4, is the journalists' use of varying adjectives to describe the scenes. For example, the *New York Times* refers to one of the closing scenes and states that on screen are "more shots of children followed by a final, scowling portrait of the governor." While the *Milwaukee Journal-Sentinel* describes the same scene by reporting that "the ad concludes with another sorrowful image of Bush, possibly meant to lament his health care record as governor." The *Los Angeles Times,* however, simply reports that the "ad closes with a shot of Bush."

For the accusations made in this advertisement sponsored by the Democratic National Committee, all of the adwatch stories explain where the "judge's ruling" came from and that the lawsuit it was based on was part of an earlier class-action lawsuit when Bush was not even in office. However, there are inconsistencies in other areas. For example, the Consumer Health Information Program and Services (CHIPS) plan that was instituted in Texas to help provide health care for

Table 9.3 Comparison for "Notebook" on Verbal Content and Analysis Listed by Media

	Accuracy / Analysis	Scorecard / Strategy Commentary
New York Times	• Points out that Gore's plan is "voluntary" and seniors are not "forced" to join an HMO. • Says drug benefit in Gore's plan is provided through Medicare. • Discussion about "access fee" is the estimated premium for 2009—eight years out—and that it is only $300/year or $25/month. • Mentions it is hard to draw comparisons to Bush's plan since he gives little details but offers the comments that analysts believe Bush's plan might end up relying more heavily on HMO's & other private plans. • Explains that the reference to the "government HMO" is apparently the pharmaceutical benefit managers.	• Points to the ad appealing to two powerful fears: "big government" intruding into private health care decisions and "the fear of HMO's doing the same thing." • References the notion that "big government" is a traditional line of attack used against Democrats, although "Medicare is a big government plan" but a popular one. • Comments that the attack against "big government HMO's" of the Gore plan may be an attempt at inoculation because Bush's plan envisions a greater role by HMO's and other private plans and that Republicans are "bracing for a Democratic assault against it."
Los Angeles Times	• Mentions that this misleads viewers because Gore's plan is voluntary and that only seniors who join plan would pay additional premiums. • Explains about the "access fee" being the projected premium for 2010 long after plan takes effect. • Says Bush's plan does not give specifics about premiums and would rely heavily on private HMO's to devise own plans—and premiums.	• Discusses the strategy of the notebook style comparison and how this method "in effect blurs the line between the two candidates' plans." • Mentions that the repeated use by the GOP of ads on this issue is critical to Gore's lead in polls.

Milwaukee Journal-Sentinel

- Points out that Gore's plan is "voluntary" and seniors are not "forced" to join an HMO.
- Says drug benefit in Gore's plan is provided through Medicare.
- Discussion about "access fee" is the estimated premium for 2009—8 years out—and that it is only $300/year or $25/mo. the 1st year.
- Mentions that it is hard to draw comparisons to Bush's plan since he gives little details but offers the comment that analysts believe Bush's plan might rely more heavily on HMO's; other private plans.
- Explains that the reference to the "government HMO" is apparently the pharmaceutical benefit managers.

- Points to the ad appealing to two powerful fears: "big government" intruding into private health care decisions and "the fear of HMO's doing the same thing."
- References the notion that "big government" is a traditional line of attack used against Democrats, although "Medicare is a big government plan" but a popular one.
- Comments that the attack against "big government HMO's" of the Gore plan may be an attempt at inoculation because Bush's plan envisions a greater role by HMO's and other private plans and that Republicans are "bracing for a Democratic assault against it."

CBS.com

- Points out that Gore's plan does not involve an HMO, but runs through Medicare where Seniors can choose doctors.
- Drug benefit portion of Gore's plan—handled by independent group.
- $600 "access fee"—won't reach that level for 10 years and is only $300/year (or $25/mo).
- Bush claim on opposing fee is unclear since he has not released details.

- Discussion of the need for both candidates to "sell" seniors on their plan for prescription drugs.
- Mention of recent CBS News poll showing the 61% of seniors favor Gore's plan & believe it would lower cost as opposed to the 47% who support Bush's plan.

Slate magazine

Note: Text of ad was run in its entirety in the New York Times, Los Angeles Times, Milwaukee Journal-Sentinel, and CBS.com, as follows:

Announcer: On prescription medicines, compare: Al Gore will charge seniors a new $600-a-year government access fee. George Bush opposes Gore's $600 fee. Gore's plan: When seniors turn 64, they must join a drug HMO—selected by Washington—or they are on their own. Bush's plan: Seniors choose and it covers all catastrophic health care costs. Gore's plan doesn't. And has a government HMO. And a $600 fee. A prescription for disaster.

Table 9.4 Comparison for "Judge" on Verbal Content and Analysis Listed by Media

	Accuracy / Analysis	Scorecard / Strategy Commentary
New York Times	• Starts with the central accusation in the spot—the judge's ruling and says that yes, Judge William Wayne Justice, did rule that the state had failed to abide by a 1996 decree and provide appropriate health care for more than 1.5 million children in Texas not eligible for Medicaid. Goes on to explain that what is not said in the ad is that this was part of a class-action lawsuit filed on behalf of Texas children in 1993—two years before Bush took office. • Claim of Texas ranking 49th in the nation is shown to have come from Texas newspaper articles in 1999 that put Arizona as the only state with a higher percentage of children without health insurance. • Cites Bush's campaign as calling the ad a "serious distortion" and noting that the governor "supported and signed" a bill last year giving health insurance to 423,000 Texas children.	• This adwatch points more to the overall tone of the ad and comments that the "closing line hints at more commercials of this kind to come." • The story also states that the "effort in this spot is to take Bush on the issues, a form of attack that those who study political advertising say is often effective."
Los Angeles Times	• The story states that it is true that Texas ranks 2nd to last in the percentage of kids without health insurance, ahead only of Arizona, but also points out that this is according to 1995–1997 census population surveys, the most recent available. • Points out the class-action lawsuit that led to the judge's ruling and that was filed while Gov. Ann Richards was in office. • Gives Bush credit that he did sign the decree in 1996, that stated the "state would make improvements in its program to provide care for 1.5 million children eligible for Medicaid but receiving benefits." • Points out that the judge's ruling was only issued last month (August) and that they were in violation of the decree and had 60 days to file a plan to fix the problem.	• In their "Scorecard" area the story refers to Democrats wanting to keep a focus on health care because "they believe that this is where Gore can draw swing voters." • Comments about the original plans to release the spot the prior week but holding off because the GOP had released an ad attacking Gore's credibility and they wanted to make sure there was no backlash. • The story mentions that this is the sixth ad to attack Bush's record in Texas. • Talks about this being a successful strategy for Bush's father in 1998 against Dukakis, but working poorly against Clinton in 1992.

(continues)

Table 9.4 Continued

	Accuracy / Analysis	Scorecard / Strategy Commentary
Milwaukee Journal-Sentinel	• Starts with the central accusation in the spot—the judge's ruling and says that yes Judge William Wayne Justice, did rule that the state had failed to abide by a 1996 decree and provide appropriate health care for more than 1.5 million children in Texas not eligible for Medicaid. Goes on to explain that what is not said in the ad is that this was part of a class-action lawsuit filed on behalf of Texas children in 1993—two years before Bush took office. • Claim of Texas ranking 49th in the nation is shown to have come from Texas newspaper articles in 1999 that put Arizona as the only state with a higher percentage of children without health insurance. • Cites Bush's campaign as calling the ad a "serious distortion" and noting that the governor "supported and signed" a bill last year giving health insurance to 423,000 Texas children.	• This adwatch points more to the overall tone of the ad and comments that the "closing line hints at more commercial of the kind to come." • The story also states that the "effort in this spot is to take Bush on the issues, a form of attack that those who study political advertising say is often effective."
CBS.com	• Begins its analysis of the ad by saying that the "content of the ad is true." • Asserts that Texas has the "2nd largest number of uninsured children in country—1.4 million." • Additionally states that even though Texas no longer rates the worst in the country, it does "have more uninsured children now than in 1995 when Bush assumed office." • In challenging the content, the adwatch refers to a comment by Bush that CHIPS has only been available for about three years and that Texas, like other states, is still in the initial stages of implementing it. They do not explain what CHIPS stands for.	• In discussing the strategy of the ad they refer to the closing line of the ad, which says "Bush's record. It's becoming an issue." • The adwatch points to the "DNC and Gore campaign goal" to make Bush's record on children's health care "a dominant campaign issue and thereby diminishing his credibility as a candidate capable of providing health care coverage to the millions of Americans without coverage." • The adwatch also points out that the ad was released on the same day that the Bush campaign unveiled its Medicare prescription drug plan. • In closing, the story points out that the "Gore camp hopes that by hammering Bush on his record in Texas, they can maintain Gore's lead among voters as the candidate most qualified to manage the nation's health care programs."

Slate magazine

- In parts of the story, the authors do try to focus on objective criteria from the ad by referring to specific ad content like the ranking of Texas as 49th out of 50.
- They also point out that there are problems in Texas that "Bush can be reasonably blamed for and those he cannot."
- Furthermore, they draw on the data that Texas is a state "with a large population of poor people, many of them Mexican immigrants, and a long tradition of not spending very much on its government" and that this was also true when Ann Richards was governor.
- The adwatch does explain about the CHIPS program.
- In clarifying what Bush has tried to do while in office about children without health care, the story refers to Bush signing the plan to provide more health care to children but also notes that the measure covered families with incomes up to 200% of the poverty line and mentions that Bush "preferred" a plan that would have only covered families at 150% above the poverty line.

- This story comments that the strategy of this ad may not have been a good idea and that because Gore had made an "Adam Clymer of himself with that snarky attack ad last week," he might have been better off to postpone the spot indefinitely, leaving Bush to take all the heat for running purely negative ads.
- The story does point out that if Democrats are going to attack Bush, they have done it in smart fashion by attacking issues.
- Additionally, the adwatch points to the attempt of the Gore campaign to distance itself from the attack by relying on these statistics and court rulings.
- This story takes much greater editorial license in the comparisons it draws and its opinions of Gore and Bush with comments like "here we don't even have a closing line that's an imperative. It just says, 'the Bush record is becoming an issue.' Who's making it an issue? Not us, say the DNC. Objective forces—the courts and the press—are making Bush's health care record an issue and thereby giving the DNC a breakthrough in issue advertising, replacing the bogus imperative with the bogus nonimperative."

Note: *Slate* magazine included a link to the text of the ad in its story. The text was run in its entirety in the *New York Times*, *Los Angeles Times*, *Milwaukee Journal-Sentinel*, and CBS.com, as follows:

Narrator: George Bush says he has a plan to improve children's health care. But why hasn't he done it in Texas? Texas ranks 49th out of 50 in providing health coverage to kids. It's so bad, a federal judge just ruled Texas must take immediate "corrective action." The judge's findings: Bush's administration broke a promise to improve health care for kids. Texas failed to inform families of health coverage available to a million children. Bush's record—it's becoming an issue.

children is explained in the adwatch by the *Los Angeles Times*, but the adwatch in *Slate Magazine* refers to this same program with no clarification about what it is or what it is supposed to do.

Bush Ad: "Compare"

The discussion of this advertisement's visual content remains fairly constant across media. Each media outlet refers in some manner to the images of a white background and black text about Gore's tax plan, while color shots of Bush are alternated among the frames shown (table 9.5). In the closing portions of the advertisement, the viewer sees a mixture of color pictures such as a woman in a porch swing, an elderly black woman, and a young woman in a classroom. The treatment of these images in the reporting of visual images by the media is primarily condensed to wording such as "pictures of Americans of different ethnicity and age" (*New York Times*).

Republican National Committee Ad: "Really"

Table 9.6 shows that, again with this advertisement, sponsored by the Republican Party, the adwatch stories report either significant detail about all of the images and how they appear on screen or very little detail at all. One of the key elements from this ad is the depiction of Al Gore speaking, but he is doing so from scenes of himself on a television set that sits on a kitchen counter during the advertisement itself. Each of the media discussed here references this point, giving the reader the opportunity to know the "setting" for the ad.

The "Really" ad is the only advertisement for which the adwatch stories are consistent and direct in explaining the verbal content. All of the media point to the "misstatement by Gore" about taking credit for the Internet and try to clarify where the comment came from and explain that Gore has already spoken out about how this statement was taken out of context. In the strategy, or scorecard, section of these adwatches we do see some inconsistencies. CBS.com goes to great lengths in trying to create for the reader the "rationale" behind this advertisement and what the Republican National Committee is hoping to accomplish. The *New York Times*, however, only mentions that this is the first direct attack by the Republicans on Gore.

Bush Ad: "Nonsense"

Here the analysis of the adwatch story shows more similarities than differences across media. The adwatch stories all discuss the mixture of scenes including Bush and Gore and the settings of those pictures, as table 9.7 shows. As for the verbal content and accuracy of the claims, the adwatch stories are similar. They all point to Bush's claim about setting aside the $2.4 trillion for Social Security,

Table 9.5 Comparison for "Compare" on Verbal Content and Analysis Listed by Media

	Accuracy / Analysis	Scorecard / Strategy Commentary
New York Times	• The adwatch points out that to try and link Gore's plan to HMO's in the ad requires that "Bush has to stretch the facts." • It clarifies that Gore's plan is voluntary and that Medicare recipients can stay in traditional plans where they choose their own doctors. • Additionally, the story explains that Gore's plan does rely on private benefit managers to manage the program—but that this is just like private insurers, who would also encourage the use of generic drugs but are not HMO's. • On the school testing issue, the story clarifies that Bush's and Gore's plans both call for testing but Bush's plan calls for more frequent testing and would cover more grades. • The story calls Bush's claim about his 10-year tax-cut plan giving a tax reduction to every income bracket "true."	• The story interprets the closing line of the ad ("Governor Bush has real plans that work for real people") as "suggesting that Gore is not credible and neither are his programs." • Also in the "scorecard" section of the story is the point that "Bush has his work cut out for him because many polls show that voters trust the Democratic candidate more on health care and education." • Finally, the story mentions that while Bush may have the traditional Republican advantage on tax cutting, "tax cuts are not one of the top concerns of voters."
Los Angeles Times	• On the accusation about Gore's plan forcing seniors into a federal insurance company, the story calls the ad "incorrect." • The story also calls the claim about education "a subjective claim" and clarifies the claim by explaining that Gore's plan would require states to administer a national test to a "sample of students" or risk losing federal funding but Bush's plan would require the same sampling plan but administered more often and also have state-level testing for grades 3–8. • The adwatch calls the claims made about taxes in the ad "essentially correct" but adds that contrary to the suggestion in the ad, almost no taxpayers currently pay more than one-third of their income in taxes.	• The story calls this ad "the first attempt by the [Bush] campaign to promote Bush's tax cut plan in a general election advertisement while also contrasting his policies with Gore's on health care." • The story also points out that up until now most of the harshest attacks have come from the Republican Party and that this is the first time that a Bush campaign ad has directly criticized the vice president.

Milwaukee Journal-Sentinel	• The adwatch points out that to try and link Gore's plan to HMO's in the ad requires that "Bush has to stretch the facts." • It clarifies that Gore's plan is voluntary and that Medicare recipients can stay in traditional plans where they choose their own doctors. • Additionally, the story explains that Gore's plan does rely on private benefit managers to manage the program—but that this is just like private insurers, who would also encourage the use of generic drugs but are not HMO's. • On the school testing issue, the story clarifies that Bush's and Gore's plans both call for testing but Bush's plan calls for more frequent testing and would cover more grades. • The story calls Bush's claim about his 10-year tax-cut plan giving a tax reduction to every income bracket "true."	• The story goes on to interpret the closing line of the ad ("Governor Bush has real plans that work for real people") as "suggesting that Gore is not credible and neither are his programs." • Also makes the point that "Bush has his work cut out for him because polls show voters trust the Democrats more on health care and education." • Finally, the story mentions that while Bush may have the traditional advantage for Republicans on tax cutting, right now "tax cuts are not one of the top concerns of voters."
CBS.com	This adwatch applies its "fact check" to several elements presented in the ad. The story argues: • Gore's drug plan is voluntary and would allow seniors to get coverage through Medicare, and this is not an HMO. • Gore does require student testing—just not as often as Bush. • Gore doesn't make funding contingent upon testing results. • Under Gore's economic plan, the wealthy do not receive a tax cut, but only low-income Americans and those paying college tuition and day care receive a refund.	• The story calls this ad a "classic contrast ad portraying Gore's proposals in inflammatory terms and Bush's in glowing terms." • It also provides a listing of the states where the ad is running.

Slate magazine

Note: Text of ad was run in its entirety in the *New York Times, Los Angeles Times, Milwaukee Journal-Sentinel,* and CBS.com, as follows:

Announcer: Al Gore's prescription plan forces seniors into a government-run HMO. Gov. Bush gives seniors a choice. Gore says he's for school accountability, but requires no real testing. Gov. Bush requires tests and holds schools accountable for results. Gore's targeted tax cuts leave out 50 million people—half of all taxpayers. Under Bush, every taxpayer gets a tax cut and no family pays more than a third of their income to Washington. Gov. Bush has real plans that work for real people.

Table 9.6 Comparison for "Really" on Verbal Content and Analysis Listed by Media

	Accuracy / Analysis	Scorecard / Strategy Commentary
New York Times		
Los Angeles Times	• Story points out that it is true that Gore attended a fund-raiser luncheon in 1996 at the Hsi Lai Buddhist Temple in Hacienda Heights, California, which prompted a federal inquiry. • Also discussed is the fact that it is true that "Gore has said the first bill he would send to Congress if elected is a campaign finance reform package." • The adwatch states that while it is true that Gore once took credit for creating the Internet, it is attributed to "an awkward comment made that was supposed to describe his support of funding for scientists involved in the early days of the computer network."	• Points out that this is the first direct attack of the general election by the Republicans on Gore. • The story also elaborates that the ad has a "humorous tone at a time when campaigns face a potential voter backlash if they appear to be too negative." • Commentary in this area states that "Republicans hope the ad will raise questions about Gore's credibility and truthfulness, linking him to some of the negative qualities attributed to the Clinton White House."
Milwaukee Journal-Sentinel	• The adwatch points out that the Republican National Committee is "returning" to a prior theme in its targets of Al Gore and that is to use Gore moments where he "reintroduces himself" but overstates his accomplishments. • The only aspect of the ad's content that is directly addressed is the idea that Gore claims credit for things he didn't do; the story says Gore has "admitted using awkward language to note his early support for the Internet while in Congress."	No Scorecard section given with this story.

(continues)

Table 9.6 Continued

	Accuracy / Analysis	Scorecard / Strategy Commentary
CBS.com	• The story points to "no inaccuracies" in the ad but also notes that Gore has claimed he didn't know the Buddhist temple event was a fund-raiser but will admit he knew it was "finance-related."	• The commentary here admits that Bush and Republicans have often "pegged Gore as the candidate who is always reinventing himself." • The story points out that while this attack is "tongue-in-cheek" in nature, voters may not find this so funny. • The story points out that the ad is airing at a time when Gore is ahead in the polls and moving ahead in key battleground states and that this explains why "the RNC is running such a negative ad especially at a time when political waters are usually so calm." • Additionally, the story points out that the Democrats have usually been matching ad buys and had planned to release a new ad attacking Bush's record on health care for children, but now they may try to take the high road and hold off.

Slate magazine

Note: Text of ad was run as follows in the *Los Angeles Times, Milwaukee Journal-Sentinel, CBS.com,* and *Slate* magazine:

Woman (voice-over): There's Al Gore . . . reinventing himself on television again. Like I'm not going to notice. Who's he gonna be today? The Al Gore who raises campaign money at a Buddhist temple? Or the one who promises campaign finance reform? Really, Al Gore . . . claiming credit for things he didn't even do.

Gore: I took the initiative in creating the Internet.

Woman (voice-over): Yeah, and I invented the remote control, too. Another round of this and I'll sell my television.

but they do so in the context of how this will probably not be enough to keep the fund solvent in the long term. Again, as with the advertisement "Really," the big discrepancies are in the conclusions drawn about motive and strategy behind the ad. The *Milwaukee Journal-Sentinel* comments only that "this ad is far more negative than many of Bush's previous ads." On the other hand, the *Los Angeles Times* states that "the ad is the toughest commercial Bush has released" and that "it seeks to reinforce the Republican charge that Gore is untrustworthy."

DISCUSSION

In performing the case-study analysis of these advertisements, the researchers find some common and important elements. The first of these elements is the inclusion in each story of the complete text of the advertisement. Each of the media included here also provided an Internet link to video of the advertisement. Whether or not viewers or readers were able to access and play the video, the fact that the option is available is worth noting. Also of note is the labeling or other specific identification of these stories as "adwatches" or articles that attempt to break down the content for a reader or viewer (if using the online version).

In spite of the similarities, these media also have some stark contrasts in their treatment of the visual content, verbal content, or actual "fact check" about what is said and in their "interpretations" for strategy. It is in these contrasts that there arises a greater concern about how media cover televised campaign advertisements. While some variation among the visual components of the advertisement may not be critical, we found evidence that for any single advertisement, the media may report differing "facts" related to content, as seen with the analysis for the "Notebook" and "Judge" advertisements where use of confusing numbers and statistics is being reported.

If journalists are going to continue performing this watchdog role over televised candidate advertising, then readers need to feel confident that they are in fact being presented with the correct interpretations. In looking through these few adwatches, it is evident that with no prior knowledge about the advertisement itself, a reader of any one story might come away with a very different picture of the ad than someone else reading another media interpretation.

This study focused only on print or online stories and does not include broadcast adwatch stories, which have increased over the years during election years. Further research might include these stories and compare the depth and type of coverage provided by broadcast networks versus print sources. While the data presented here is limited, the findings are enough to warrant further investigation if adwatches are to continue as a true information source for voters.

Table 9.7 Comparison for "Nonsense" on Verbal Content and Analysis Listed by Media

	Accuracy / Analysis	Scorecard / Strategy Commentary
New York Times	• This story clarifies the comparisons made between medicine costs for Gore's mother and costs for his dog by reminding readers that Gore has already acknowledged that it was a poor comparison. • On the Social Security claim, the story only points out that Bush has been promising to set aside the $2.4 trillion from the budget surplus to protect Social Security in the future.	• The story calls the ad "funny, devastating—and clearly intended to zing Mr. Gore more than to defend Mr. Bush." • The story points out that the ad is an "indirect criticism" of Gore's earlier ads, especially one citing conclusions drawn by "eight Nobel laureates" that Bush's plan promises the same $1 trillion to young people and the elderly, but this ad switches the earlier claim to the interpretation that Gore is simply stretching the truth again. • The author claims that the "spot's payoff" is the "mocking clip in which Mr. Gore asserts that 'there has never been a time' when he uttered an untruth" followed by the "announcer's cynical comeback."
Los Angeles Times	The only attempts to clarify any points of accuracy in this story deal with Gore's comments about medicine costs and where that statement originated.	• The strategy comments in this story call the ad "the toughest commercial the Bush camp has released." • It is argued that the ad "seeks to reinforce the Republican charge that Gore is untrustworthy." • The story says that the "tone of this ad is especially noteworthy given the [Bush] campaign's decision to pull an earlier GOP ad because it would contradict Bush's pledge to 'change the tone' in Washington."

(continues)

Table 9.7 Continued

	Accuracy / Analysis	Scorecard / Strategy Commentary
Milwaukee Journal-Sentinel	• The story reiterates that Gore has acknowledged he was wrong to say an arthritis medicine cost his mother three times as much as medicine for his dog, as the figures came from a study "not from his family finances." • Some discussion is given to the claim in the ad and that Bush sets aside $2.4 trillion to strengthen Social Security and pay all benefits and that this claim does not acknowledge the fact that even that isn't enough to pay for the baby boomers' pending retirement and draining $1 trillion will only exacerbate the program's long-term solvency problem.	• The only real "strategy" comment made about this ad is that it is far more negative than many of Bush's previous ads. • The adwatch also points out that the spot is trying to imply that because Gore "has stretched the details about his dog's medicine" his claims about Bush's Social Security plan is also exaggerated.
CBS.com		
Slate magazine	All of the comments made in this story go more to strategy interpretation, and there is no real "checking" of the facts. It is a highly "editorial"-type piece.	• The story labels this the "big nasty ad" everyone has been waiting for. • The story claims that what the ad is really trying to say is that "you can't believe anything Gore says because he is a liar." • The authors believe that the rationale for the ad is that for two weeks Gore has been attacking Bush on Social Security. • The story also says that "the ad does a terrific job of reminding you about what you don't like about Gore, but does a lousy job of refuting Gore's charge." However, "Bush's rebuttal doesn't contradict Gore's charge."

Note: Text of ad was run in its entirety in the New York Times, Los Angeles Times, Milwaukee Journal-Sentinel, and Slate magazine, as follows:

Announcer: Remember when Al Gore said his mother-in-law's prescription cost more than his dog's? His own aides said the story was made up. Now Al Gore is bending the truth again. The press calls Gore's Social Security attacks "nonsense." Gov. Bush sets aside $2.4 trillion to strengthen Social Security and pay all benefits.

Al Gore: There has never been a time in this campaign when I have said something that I know to be untrue. There has never been a time when I have said something untrue.

Announcer: Really?

REFERENCES

Bowen, L. (1994). Time of voting decision and the use of political advertising: The Slade Gorton–Brock Adams senatorial campaign. *Journalism Quarterly, 71,* 665–675.

Cappella, J. N., & Jamieson, K. H. (1994). Broadcast adwatch effects: A field experiment. *Communication Research, 2,* 342–365.

Hinerfeld, D. S. (1990, May). How political ads subtract: It's not the negative ads that are perverting democracy, it's the deceptive ones. *Washington Monthly,* pp. 12–22.

Jamieson, K. H. (1992). *Dirty politics: Deception, distraction, and democracy.* New York: Oxford University Press.

Kaid, L. L., & Davidson, D. (1986). Elements of videostyle. In L. L. Kaid, D. Nimmo, & K. R. Sanders (Eds.), *New perspectives on political advertising* (pp. 184–209). Carbondale: Southern Illinois University Press.

Kaid, L. L., Gobetz, R. H., Garner, J., Leland, C. M., & Scott, D. K. (1993). Television news and presidential campaigns: The legitimization of televised political advertising. *Social Science Quarterly, 74,* 274–285.

Kaid, L. L., Tedesco, J. C., & McKinnon, L. M. (1996). Presidential ads as nightly news: A content analysis of 1988 and 1992 televised adwatches. *Journal of Broadcasting and Electronic Media, 40,* 279–303.

Kern, M., West, D., & Alger, D. (1993, August). Ad-watch journalism. Paper presented at the annual meeting of the American Political Science Association, Washington, DC.

McKinnon, L. M., & Kaid, L. L. (1999). Exposing negative campaigning or enhancing advertising effects: An experimental study of adwatch effects on voters' evaluations of candidates and their ads. *Journal of Applied Communication Research, 27,* 217–236.

McKinnon, L. M., Kaid, L. L., Acree, C. K., & Mays, J. (1996). Policing political ads: An analysis of five leading newspapers' responses to 1992 political advertisements. *Journalism and Mass Communication Quarterly, 73,* 66–76.

Pfau, M., & Louden, A. (1994). Effectiveness of adwatch formats in deflecting political attack ads. *Communication Research, 21,* 325–341.

Runkel, D. (Ed.) (1989). *Campaign for president: The managers look at '88.* Dover, MA: Auburn House.

Seib, P. (1994). *Campaigns and conscience: The ethics of political journalism.* Westport, CT: Praeger.

Tedesco, J. C., McKinnon, L. M., & Kaid, L. L. (1996). Advertising watchdogs: A content analysis of print and broadcast adwatches from the 1992 presidential campaign. *Harvard International Journal of Press/Politics, 1* (4), 76–93.

West, D. M. (1993). *Air wars: Television advertising in election campaigns, 1952–1992.* Washington, DC: Congressional Quarterly Press.

West, D. M., Kern, M., & Alger, D. (1992). Political advertising and ad watches in the 1992 presidential nominating campaign. Paper presented at the American Political Science Association Convention, Chicago.

Wicks, R. H., and Kern, M. (1993). Cautious optimism: A new proactive role for local television news departments in local election coverage? *American Behavioral Scientist, 37,* 262–271.

Wolinsky, L. C., Sparks, J., Funk, J., Rooney, E., Lyon, G., & Sweet, L. (1991). Refereeing the TV campaign. *Washington Journalism Review, 13* (1), 22–29.

10

Issue Agendas in Candidate Messages versus Media Coverage

Are Women and Men on the Same Page?

Mary Christine Banwart, Dianne G. Bystrom,
Terry Robertson, and Jerry Miller

Studies analyzing the newspaper coverage of women gubernatorial and U.S. Senate candidates (Banwart, Bystrom, & Robertson, 2003; Bystrom, Robertson, & Banwart, 2001; Devitt, 1999; Kahn, 1991, 1992, 1994a, 1994b, 1996; Kahn & Goldenberg, 1991; Robertson et al., 2002; Serini, Powers, & Johnston, 1998; Smith, 1997) who ran for office in the 1980s, 1990s, and the 2000 election as well as Elizabeth Dole's bid for the Republican nomination for president in 1999 (Aday & Devitt, 2001; Bystrom, forthcoming; Heldman, Carroll, & Olson, 2000) have documented that women and men are treated differently by the media. However, some of the more recent studies (Banwart et al., 2003; Bystrom et al., 2001; Devitt, 1999; Robertson et al., 2002; Smith, 1997) show that the media coverage of women and men candidates has become more equitable over time, particularly in terms of quantity.

One area of media coverage in which inequities persist is in the issue coverage of female and male candidates. Studies (Aday & Devitt, 2001; Bystrom, forthcoming; Devitt, 1999; Heldman et al., 2000; Kahn, 1991, 1992, 1994a, 1994b; Kahn & Goldenberg, 1991; Miller, 2001; Serini et al., 1998) continue to show that women receive less issue-related coverage than men do. Women also are more likely to be stereotyped through their association with "feminine" issues, particularly in the earlier studies (Kahn, 1991, 1992, 1994a, 1994b; Kahn & Goldenberg, 1991). Although more recent studies (Banwart et al., 2003;

Bystrom, forthcoming; Bystrom et al., 2001; Heldman et al., 2000; Robertson et al., 2002) show some balance in the issue association of female and male candidates, it is the men who appear to be treated most equitably by the media in their coverage on both "masculine" and "feminine" issues.

However, one question that remains largely unexplored in the literature is whether these differences in issue coverage emanate from media bias or from differences in the candidate messages. That is, perhaps female and male candidates are emphasizing different issues in their campaigns, and this is reflected in their media coverage.

This study seeks to answer that question by comparing the issue messages of female and male candidates running in mixed-gender campaigns for the U.S. Senate and governor in the 2000 general election with the issue content of newspaper articles covering those campaigns. Specifically, the issue content of these candidates' television political advertisements is compared with the issue content of newspaper articles covering their campaigns. To set the foundation for this examination and comparison, we begin with a review of previous research on the issue content of female and male political ads as well as the issue coverage of women and men candidates by the media.

ISSUE CONTENT IN FEMALE VERSUS MALE POLITICAL COMMERCIALS

Early studies have found some stereotypical gender differences in the issues emphasized by female and male candidates in their political commercials. For example, Kahn (1993) and Trent and Sabourin (1993) found that women were more likely to emphasize social issues, such as education and health care, whereas men were more likely to focus on economic issues, such as taxes, in their political spots. However, Benze and Declercq (1985) found no gender differences in the issues stressed by female and male candidates in their political spots. Williams (1998) also found more gender balance in the issue emphasis of women and men candidates. Both men and women talked about social programs (10% compared to 12%) and economic issues (25% to 22%) with about the same frequency in their ads; however, men were more likely to address social issues—which included crime—than women (41% to 29%).

In their comprehensive study analyzing the "videostyle"—verbal, nonverbal, and production content—of the political ads of women and men running against each other for the U.S. Senate in 1990 through 1998, Bystrom and Kaid (2002) concluded that the issues mentioned by female and male candidates seemed to be more attributable to the "context of the election year" than the gendered videostyle of the candidate. For example, both women and men focused on education, the environment, and senior citizen issues in 1990; the economy, health care, and taxes in 1992–1993; taxes and crime in 1994; taxes, senior citizen issues, and education in 1996; and taxes, the economy, and senior citizen issues in 1998.

In her study of candidates running in mixed-gender races for governor, U.S. House, and U.S. Senate, Banwart (2002) found that while women discussed almost all issues more frequently than men, both women and men discussed the same four issues most frequently: education, health care, senior citizen issues, and taxes. Thus, if women and men are discussing the same issues in their television commercials, it would seem that their media coverage would reflect the same issue balance. Next, we look at the issue coverage of female versus male candidates by the media.

ISSUE COVERAGE OF FEMALE VERSUS MALE CANDIDATES BY THE MEDIA

Studies (Kahn, 1991, 1992, 1994a, 1994b; Kahn & Goldenberg, 1991) examining the newspaper coverage of women candidates running for election in the 1980s found that this medium not only stereotypes female candidates by emphasizing "feminine traits" and "feminine issues" but also questions their viability as candidates. Studies conducted since Kahn's work (1992, 1994a, 1994b, 1996) on the media coverage of women running for governor and the U.S. Senate have both confirmed many of her findings and given some hope that media coverage of women candidates—including their issue coverage—might be improving in the 1990s and the twenty-first century.

For example, a study (Serini et al., 1998) examining the coverage of a gubernatorial campaign by two major newspapers confirmed many of Kahn's (1992, 1994a, 1994b, 1996) findings that women receive less issue coverage and more negative assessments of their viability as candidates. A study examining media coverage of the 1996 races for the Illinois House of Representatives (Miller, 2001) also found some differences in the issue coverage of female and male candidates, but to a lesser degree.

In his study of 1998 gubernatorial candidates, Devitt (1999) found that while male and female candidates for governor received about the same amount of coverage, women received less issue-related coverage than men did. Three studies (Aday & Devitt, 2001; Bystrom, forthcoming; Heldman et al., 2000) examining the newspaper coverage of Elizabeth Dole during the seven months she sought the Republican nomination for president in 1999 found that she received less-equitable coverage in terms of quality and, especially, quantity as compared to her male opponents. All three studies found that Dole received less issue coverage than George W. Bush, Steve Forbes, or John McCain. However, according to the two studies (Bystrom, forthcoming; Heldman et al., 2000) that considered the types of issues mentioned, Dole's issue coverage was balanced between such stereotypically masculine issues as taxes, foreign policy, and the economy and such stereotypically feminine issues as education, drugs, and gun control.

A study of newspaper coverage of women and men running for U.S. Senate and governor in the 2000 primary (Bystrom et al., 2001) and general election (Robertson et al., 2002) races found that these women received more coverage than men in terms of quantity, and that the quality of their coverage—slant of the story and discussion of their viability, appearance, and personality—was mostly equitable. Still, these women candidates were much more likely to be discussed in terms of their role as mothers and their marital status, which can affect their viability with voters.

Perhaps surprisingly, Robertson et al. (2002) found that men were much more associated with the feminine issue of education in the general election than women, with 32% of male-candidate-focused articles and 11% of female-candidate-focused articles discussing the issue. And in their comparison of the media coverage of women and men in the 2000 primary and general elections, Banwart et al. (2003) found that male candidates in 2000 were associated at significantly higher percentages in their general election coverage (32%) than in their primary coverage (9%) with education/schools—a traditionally feminine issue—while still being associated with the traditionally masculine issues of taxes and the economy in both the general (43%, 41%) and the primary (22%, 11%) election. Women candidates, on the other hand, were twice as likely to be associated with the feminine issue of health care in the general (17%) than in the primary (8%) election, while their association with issues concerning the budget, unemployment/jobs, and immigration—traditionally masculine issues—decreased or became nonexistent in their general election coverage (Banwart et al., 2003).

Although such studies still show that differences exist in the media coverage of female and male candidates, including in the amount and type of their issue coverage, they do not provide evidence for the source of such disparities. Is media coverage merely reflecting the differences in the candidates' messages, or is the difference in news coverage the result of media bias and stereotypes? Very few studies address this question.

ISSUE CONTENT OF POLITICAL SPOTS VERSUS MEDIA COVERAGE OF FEMALE AND MALE CANDIDATES

Very few researchers have compared the media coverage of male and female candidates to the content of their political commercials. Such studies would help determine whether media coverage is consistent with the messages of candidates in their political commercials, whether the media and candidates have separate agendas, and whether gender biases exist.

In general, it can be inferred by comparing the results of studies analyzing the content of female and male candidates' political commercials to research on the media coverage of women and men candidates that newspaper articles do not always reflect the messages of the candidates. That is, while most studies (Banwart, 2003; Benze & Declercq, 1985; Bystrom & Kaid, 2002; Williams, 1998) show few or no differences between women and men candidates in the issue content of their political ads, many studies (Devitt, 1999; Kahn, 1991, 1992, 1994a, 1994b; Kahn & Goldenberg, 1991; Miller, 2001; Serini et al., 1998) have noted a difference in their issue coverage by the media, in both the amount of issue coverage and the types of issues covered.

Two recent studies (Miller, 1996; Robertson, 2000) have specifically compared the content of political candidates' commercials to the content of their media coverage. Using Spearman rho (ρ) rank-order correlations, Miller (1996) found that the media are more responsive to the issue agendas set by the male candidates than those set by the female candidates. Even though there were no differences between the issue agendas produced by female and male political candidates in their advertisements in the gubernatorial races studied, there were differences in their issue coverage by the media.

Robertson (2000) also found differences between the issue agendas of female and male candidates and their media coverage. In his study, female candidates were significantly more likely than male candidates to discuss education, health care, youth violence, and "women's issues," (e.g., choice, sexual harassment, women's rights) in their political commercials. Men were significantly more likely to discuss taxes in their ads. However, in their media coverage, the male candidates were significantly more likely to be linked with a number of issues, including taxes, the budget, crime, dissatisfaction with government, and defense. Only women's issues were significantly more likely to be associated with female candidates by the media.

The review of the literature on the issue content of female and male candidates' messages in their political ads, the issue content of newspaper articles covering the campaigns of women and men candidates, and the few studies that have tried to compare the two suggests that more comparative analysis is needed. Thus, our study is designed to answer the following research question:

RQ: Do the print media associate the same issues in their newspaper articles with female and male candidates as the candidates emphasize in their advertising messages?

METHOD

Reliability for this study was achieved by establishing criteria for the selection of televised political advertisements and print media reports. Only those advertisements for candidates in mixed-gender campaigns for U.S. Senate and governor in 2000 were selected, and only the newspaper articles discussing these races were analyzed. The purpose of this study was to determine whether the media covering these campaigns emphasized the same issues in their stories as the candidates discussed in their political ads during the 2000 election cycle. A difference in the media coverage of male and female U.S. Senate and gubernatorial candidates may reflect explicit strategies employed by the candidates themselves or an institutional bias; a comparison of the ads' issue content and media coverage of candidate issues will promote a discussion on this issue.

Content analysis has been described as a "multipurpose research method developed specifically for investigating any problem in which the content of communication serves as the basis of inference" (Holsti, 1968, p. 2) and as a research technique employed for replicating and validating inferences from the data in context (Krippendorff, 1980). Using content analysis, a code sheet and codebook were developed on the basis of similar studies investigating the content of political advertisements from previous elections (e.g., Bystrom, 1995; Bystrom & Miller, 1999; Kaid & Davidson, 1986; Kaid & Johnston, 1991; Miller, 1996; Robertson, 2000). A code sheet and codebook were developed for the newspaper analysis on the basis of studies investigating potential media bias when reporting on campaign news (e.g., Bystrom et al., 2001; Miller, 1996; Robertson, 2000).

The instrument used to analyze campaigns spot ads coded for general commercial categories, such as campaign year, candidate gender, political status (i.e., incumbent, challenger, open race), and commercial sponsor, and for specific political issues discussed in the candidate ad. The instrument used to analyze the print news articles coded for variables encompassing demographic and general data (i.e., candidate name, gender, publication date, page number, paragraph length), the focus of the article (i.e., whether the article predominantly focused on the male or the female candidate), and specific political issues associated with the candidate. Both instruments coded for issues such as taxes, the economy, reproductive choice, the environment, poverty, gun control, health care, government ethics, education, crime, youth violence, and defense. The issue categories were adopted from prior research on candidate videostyles (e.g., Bystrom, 1995; Bystrom & Kaid, 2002; Kaid & Johnston, 1991).

Sample

Prior research on videostyle (e.g., Bystrom, 1995; Bystrom & Kaid, 2002; Bystrom & Miller, 1999; Kaid & Johnston, 1991; Kaid & Tedesco, 1999) has typically relied on the resources of the University of Oklahoma's Political Commercial Archive. Previously considered the world's largest collection of political spot ads (Kaid & Haynes, 1995), the Political Commercial Archive commonly has been used because of the extensive nature of its collection. However, only a minimal number of ads were available in the archive from the 2000 election cycle.

Therefore, using a listing of candidates in mixed-gender races for the U.S. Senate and governorships in 2000, the study relied on correspondence with the identified campaigns and media agencies. Although the universe of spot ads was not acquired for all mixed-gender races in 2000, 163 spot ads were gathered and analyzed, 84 (52%) of which were female-candidate spot ads and 79 (48%) of which were male-candidate spot ads. Of those, 17 (20%) were female gubernatorial ads and 67 (80%) were female Senate candidate ads; 20 (25%) were male gubernatorial ads and 59 (75%) were male Senate candidate ads.

Articles pertaining to mixed-gender general election races for the U.S. Senate and governor were gathered from twelve newspapers. Newspapers were chosen on the basis of large circulation and their availability online. The newspaper articles were initially researched through an online computer search, and the names of candidates were used to conduct the search. A total of 578 general election articles from September 1, 2000, through November 6, 2000, were gathered. However, for the sake of comparison with the candidate commercials collected, only those articles with a specific, dominant focus on either the female or the male candidates were selected for this analysis. Articles that equally focused on both candidates and those covering candidates for which this study was unable to secure campaign spot ads were excluded from this analysis. Thus, a total of 36 articles dominantly focusing on male candidates and 166 articles dominantly focusing on female candidates made up the final sample of newspaper articles used in this study.

Training of Coders

Three coders were recruited and trained to code the advertising sample in this study. The training of coders included one ninety-minute session that familiarized the coders with the coding instrument, codebook, and the procedures for coding. The coders then coded a political spot ad from the sample to discuss and clarify any areas in question. At the conclusion of the training session, the coders were assigned additional spot ads from the sample (7% of the total sample) to be coded and analyzed for intercoder reliability. To test for intercoder reliability on the political spot ads and appropriateness of the training session and coding instrument, Holsti's formula (North et al., 1963) was used.[1] The intercoder reliability across all categories was calculated at +.91. Following the calculation of intercoder reliability in each set of the advertising sample, the coders were assigned random sets of the political spot ads to code.

Four different coders were recruited to evaluate the newspaper content of articles collected from the general election races. The coders were trained during a four-hour session that included a reading of the coding instrument and the coding of five articles with like content. During the coding sessions, the categories on the coding instrument were reviewed and defined by visual or literary examples. To ensure that coders comprehended the definitions of each category and use of the coding instrument, each coded several examples of the artifacts under investigation and their responses were compared. Retraining of the coders occurred until all coders fully understood the procedures.

Ten percent of the print media articles were used in the intercoder reliability test. Intercoder reliability on the news articles, calculated using the formula suggested by Holsti (North et al., 1963), averaged +.88.

Data Analysis

The unit of analysis in this study consisted of a commercial in its entirety and a print news article in its entirety. Based on the method of data collection, this study used descriptive statistics to record frequencies, the presence/absence of data in the defined categories, and the rank order of the frequency of issues associated with either ads or articles. To compare issue association between candidate advertising messages and news article coverage, the Spearman rank order correlation coefficient (ρ) was calculated on the rankings. For all calculations, a significance level of $\le .05$ was set.

RESULTS

To compare issue association between candidates' advertising messages and news articles covering their campaigns, frequencies of issue mentions were calculated across all candidate ads and across all articles associated with the candidates. Then, the issue mentions in the candidate spot ads and the issue mentions in the newspaper articles were rank ordered by frequency of mentions and analyzed through Spearman's ρ.

When considering all nineteen issues coded, a significant Spearman's ρ was found for both female and male candidates in the issues discussed in their ads and newspaper coverage, indicating a positive association of candidate and media agendas (see table 10.1). Specifically, the issue agendas in male-candidate advertising and news coverage had a stronger relationship ($\rho = .684$, p $= .001$) than the issue agendas in female-candidate advertising and news coverage ($\rho = .583$, p $= .022$).

However, when the "top" issues were identified in each medium for the candidates, differing results emerged (see table 10.2). Of the nineteen issues coded, the most frequently discussed issues—those capturing a majority of mentions when combined—in female-candidate spot ads included education (39 ads, 46%), health care (34 ads, 40%), senior citizen issues (32 ads, 38%), taxes (19 ads, 23%), and women's issues (13 ads, 15%). Female candidates discussed sixteen of the nineteen issues coded in this study at least once, although they did not discuss topics that included poverty, welfare, or international issues. The issues most frequently associated with female candidates in their newspaper article cov-

Table 10.1   Issues Associated with Candidates in 2000 by Gender

Issue	Freq	(%)	Issue	Freq	(%)	r_s
Female Candidates: Ads (n = 84)			*Female Candidates: Articles (n = 166)*			.583*
1. Education	39	46	1. Taxes	26	167	
2. Health Care	34	41	2. Education	22	13	
3. Senior Citizen Issues	32	38	3. Health Care	21	13	
4. Taxes	19	23	4. International issues	16	10	
5. Women's Issues	13	16	5. Economy	14	8	
6. Economy	8	10	6. Environment	12	7	
7. Budget	6	7	7. Women's Issues	10	6	
8. Unemployment	6	7	8. Dissatisfaction w/Gov.	8	5	
9. Environment	4	5	9. Senior Citizen Issues	8	5	
10. Crime	3	4	10. Defense	4	2	
11. Cost of Living	2	2	11. Drugs/Drug Abuse	2	1	
12. Defense	1	1	12. Crime	2	1	
13. Dissatisfaction w/Gov.	1	1	13. Unemployment	2	1	
14. Drugs/Drug Abuse	1	1	14. Cost of Living	1	1	
15. Ethics/Ethical issues	1	1	15. Welfare	1	1	
16. Youth Violence	1	1	16. Budget	0	0	
17. International Issues	0	0	17. Ethics/Ethical Issues	0	0	
18. Poverty	0	0	18. Poverty	0	0	
19. Welfare	0	0	19. Youth Violence	0	0	

Issue	Freq	(%)	Issue	Freq	(%)	r_s
Male Candidates: Ads (n = 79)			*Male Candidates: Articles (n = 36)*			.684**
1. Taxes	23	29	1. Taxes	22	61	
2. Education	22	28	2. Education	18	50	
3. Senior Citizen Issues	18	23	3. Economy	14	39	
4. Health Care	10	13	4. Health Care	12	33	
5. Environment	6	8	5. International Issues	4	11	
6. Economy	6	8	6. Budget	2	6	
7. Dissatisfaction w/Gov.	5	6	7. Crime	2	6	
8. Budget	3	4	8. Defense	2	6	
9. Crime	3	4	9. Drugs/Drug Abuse	2	6	
10. Drugs/Drug Abuse	3	4	10. Environment	2	6	
11. International Issues	3	4	11. Poverty	2	6	
12. Women's Issues	3	4	12. Senior Citizen Issues	2	6	
13. Unemployment	1	1	13. Unemployment	2	6	
14. Cost of Living	0	0	14. Women's Issues	2	6	
15. Defense	0	0	15. Cost of Living	1	3	
16. Ethical issues	0	0	16. Dissatisfaction w/Gov.	0	0	
17. Poverty	0	0	17. Ethics/Ethical Issues	0	0	
18. Welfare	0	0	18. Welfare	0	0	
19. Youth Violence	0	0	19. Youth Violence	0	0	

*p ≤ .05
**p ≤ .001

erage were taxes (26 articles, 15.7%), education (22 articles, 13.3%), health care (21 articles, 12.7%), international issues (16 articles, 9.6%), the economy (14 articles, 8.4%), the environment (12 articles, 7.2%) and women's issues (10 articles, 6.0%). Newspaper articles associated female candidates with fifteen of the nineteen coded issues yet chose not to mention the budget, poverty, ethics/moral decline, or youth violence. Notably, when the top issues in female-candidate advertising were compared with the top issues associated with female candidates in the news articles using Spearman's ρ, there was no association between the two agendas (ρ = .310, n.s.).

When the male-candidate spot ads were further analyzed, the most frequently discussed issues included taxes (23 ads, 29%), education (22 ads, 28%), senior citizen issues (18 ads, 23%), health care (10 ads, 13%), and the environment (6 ads, 8%). Male-candidate spot ads mentioned thirteen of the nineteen coded issues yet did not mention the cost of living, poverty, welfare, ethics/moral decline, defense, or youth violence. The most frequently discussed issues in newspaper articles associated with male candidates included taxes (22 articles, 61.1%), education (18 articles, 50%), the economy (14 articles, 38.9%), health care (12 articles, 33.3%), and international issues (4 articles, 11.1%). Welfare, dissatisfaction with the government, ethics/moral decline, and youth violence were not discussed in those articles dominantly focusing on male candidates, although fifteen of the nineteen total coded issues were mentioned. When the top issues in male-candidate advertising were compared with the top issues associated with male candidates in the news articles using Spearman's ρ, there was no association between the two agendas (ρ = .505, n.s.).

Table 10.2   Issues Most Frequently Associated with Candidates in 2000 by Gender

Issue	Freq	(%)	Issue	Freq	(%)	r_s
Female Candidates: Ads (n = 84)			*Female Candidates: Articles (n = 166)*			.310 n.s.
1. Education	39	46	1. Taxes	26	16	
2. Health Care	34	41	2. Education	22	13	
3. Senior Citizen Issues	32	38	3. Health Care	21	13	
4. Taxes	19	23	4. International Issues	16	10	
5. Women's Issues	13	16	5. Economy	14	8	
			6. Environment	12	7	
			7. Women's Issues	10	6	

Issue	Freq	(%)	Issue	Freq	(%)	r_s
Male Candidates: Ads (n = 79)			*Male Candidates: Articles (n = 36)*			.505 n.s.
1. Taxes	23	29	1. Taxes	22	61	
2. Education	22	28	2. Education	18	50	
3. Senior Citizen Issues	18	23	3. Economy	14	39	
4. Health Care	10	13	4. Health Care	12	33	
5. Environment	6	8	5. International Issues	4	11	

*p ≤ .05
**p ≤ .001

Although the Spearman's ρ was not strong enough to reject the null hypothesis regarding the association of top issues in female and male ads and newspaper coverage, the correlation was stronger for men than women.

To further explore and perhaps provide more insight into the agendas at work, we compared the issues discussed by the female and male candidates within their advertising and the issues associated with female and male candidates within the news articles. Our findings indicated that a significant association emerged in the comparison of female and male advertising issue agendas (ρ = .744, p = .001) when all nineteen issues were compared and analyzed. A significant association also emerged in the comparison of news issue agendas (ρ = .839, p = .001) when all nineteen issues were compared between articles dominantly focused on male and female candidates. When the top issues in candidate advertising were compared, no association emerged between the female- and male-candidate advertising agendas, (ρ = .543, n.s.). However, a significant positive association emerged between the top issues discussed in the news issue agendas associated with female and male candidates (ρ = .883, p = .008).

DISCUSSION

The initial purpose of this study was to determine whether the media associated the same issues in their newspaper coverage of female and male candidates as the candidates emphasized in their advertising messages in the 2000 general election. Prior research suggests that female and male candidates have discussed similar issues in their televised advertising (e.g., Banwart, 2002; Benze & Declercq, 1985; Bystrom & Kaid, 2002; Williams, 1998). However, prior research on the media coverage of male and female candidates also suggests that the media may ascribe differing issues agendas on the basis of the gender of the candidates (e.g., Devitt, 1999; Kahn, 1991, 1992, 1994a, 1994b; Kahn & Goldenberg, 1991; Miller, 2001; Serini et al., 1998).

The findings of this current study are mixed. When considering all nineteen issues coded, we found significant correlations between the issues discussed by female and male candidates in their television commercials with the issues mentioned in their newspaper coverage. However, when focusing on the top issues discussed in the ads and in the newspaper articles, we found no significant association between the issue agendas of female and male candidates with the issue agendas in their newspaper coverage.

Specifically, using a rank-order comparison of all issues discussed by female and male U.S. Senate and gubernatorial candidates in their television advertising with all issues discussed in newspaper articles dominantly focusing on these female and male candidates, respectively, our results concluded that the candidates' issue agendas as expressed in their television advertising were similarly associated with those agendas ascribed to the candidates by the media. For instance, male candidates talked most frequently about taxes in their televised ads, followed by education; newspaper articles also emphasized these issues most heavily when focusing on male candidates. Other issues similarly ranked between male candidate ads and articles focusing on male candidates included health care, the budget, crime, drugs/drug abuse, women's issues, and unemployment.

Female candidates discussed education most frequently in their advertising, yet the issue ranked second in frequency mentions within news articles dominantly focusing on their campaigns. Health care ranked second in frequency mentions among female-candidate ads and third in issues associated with female candidates in news articles. Taxes ranked fourth in frequency mentions in female-candidate ads, yet first in their news coverage. Other issues similarly ranked between female-candidate ads and articles included women's issues, the economy, crime, drugs/drug abuse, cost of living, and defense.

We also were interested in responding to our research question by analyzing those issues most frequently discussed in candidate ads and in news articles. Those issues identified as top issues in both candidate ads and news articles—a total of eight issues overall—constituted more than 80% of the issue mentions in each respective medium. Since such issues constituted the top five issue mentions in both male-candidate ads and in news articles focusing on male candidates, as well as the top five issue mentions in female-candidate ads and the top seven mentions in news articles focusing on female candidates, we propose that we clearly isolated those issues that established an "issue agenda" in either medium. Our evaluation of the top issues discussed in candidate ads and in candidate news coverage illustrated that while there was no statistically significant association between the two media for either male or female candidates, a lower correlation between the two agendas existed for female candidates than for male candidates.

This low correlation is obvious from a glance at the issues discussed in female-candidate ads and in the news articles focusing on female candidates. For example, whereas female candidates discussed education prominently in their advertising, the news media were more likely to associate female candidates with the issue of taxes. While education did emerge as the second issue most frequently associated with female candidates in news articles, followed by health care, female-candidate ads emphasized health care and senior citizen issues second and third in terms of frequency mentions. Senior citizen issues offered a more distinct difference, however, as it was not even a top issue discussed in the news coverage of female candidates. Issues such as international affairs and the economy rated much higher among news articles covering female candidates, although they were not among the top issues discussed in female-candidate ads.

Yet, there is cause for a closer analysis of the female candidates' messages and news coverage. The fact that more issues achieved top issue status as defined by this study suggests that, in fact, female candidates might be associated with more issues than male candidates in news coverage and/or that a broader issue agenda is associated with female candidates. Such a finding could prove promising for female candidates, as they may achieve a fuller media portrayal on a variety of issues of interest to voters; or it could be detrimental, in the case where a concise and consistent message is rewarded by voters. Nonetheless, such a finding invites future research.

The comparison of top issues between male-candidate ads and articles dominantly focusing on male candidates also resulted in no association, although the relationship between the two agendas yielded a higher correlation for male candidates than that identified for female candidates. For example, both the advertising issue agenda of male candidates and the issue agenda of news articles covering the men mentioned taxes most frequently, followed by education. Senior citizen issues were mentioned third in frequency on the male candidate advertising agenda, while the economy was third on the news media's agenda for male candidates. The frequency of mentions for health care placed it in a consistent fourth across both agendas. And, while the environment was mentioned often enough in male-candidate ads to appear fifth on their top issues list, international issues emerged as fifth on the media's top issues list for male candidates.

So, when we considered all nineteen issue mentions, a significant correlation was found between the female and male candidates' advertising messages and their newspaper coverage. Some of this correlation, however, could be attributed to the correlation between issues not frequently mentioned (20% of the issues overall) rather than those (80%) frequently mentioned.

When the agendas of the candidate advertising versus the media were further reviewed through a comparison of male-candidate ads to female-candidate ads and male-candidate articles to female-candidate articles, our study found that certain associations within the two media emerged. Such a finding is not entirely surprising when all nineteen issues were compared. Beyond the top issue mentions that constituted 80% of all issue mentions, the remaining issues were talked about at similar—low—frequencies or not at all. As such, beyond any differential in the top five to seven issues mentioned, the remaining twelve to seventeen received the same consistent attention. Based on this majority finding when coding all nineteen issues, we were not at all surprised to find an association within medium of the two agendas.

When the top issues—or those issues garnering more than 80% of the issue mentions in candidate advertising and news articles—were isolated and compared, the differential that occurred deserves further attention. In fact, the top issue agendas in female- and male-candidate advertising respectively illustrated no association. Such a finding contradicts prior research (e.g., Banwart, 2002; Benze and Declercq, 1985; Bystrom & Kaid, 2002; Williams, 1998) showing that women and men discuss the same issues in their television ads. Perhaps this is because prior research did not use the same methodology to determine similarity, e.g. the Spearman rank-order correlation coefficient. In this study, five issues in both female- and male-candidate advertising agendas made up a large majority of issue mentions, although they resulted in differing ranks within each agenda based on frequency mentions.

For example, the top issue for female candidates—education—ranked second within the male-candidate agenda and the top issue for male candidates—taxes—ranked fourth within the female-candidate agenda. Health care ranked second in frequency of mentions on the female-candidate ad agenda and fourth in the male-candidate ad agenda. Senior citizen issues ranked third within both female- and male-candidate advertising agendas. However, the environment emerged as a top issue for male candidates, but not for female candidates; and women's issues ranked as a "top issue" for female candidates, but not for male candidates.

Conversely, when the top issues were analyzed for news articles about female and male candidates, our results identified a significant relationship between the two news media agendas. The relationship is evidenced by the emergence of taxes as the most frequently mentioned issue in articles focusing on female and male candidates, followed by education as the second most frequently mentioned issue. Further, health care mentions ranked third on the female news article agenda and fourth on the male news article agenda. International issues received the fourth and fifth most frequent mentions in female candidate and male candidate news articles, respectively.

Although we believe the results of this study offer interesting insights as to the competing agendas at work during political campaigns, certain limitations must be considered within our analysis. As indicated previously, an attempt was made to at least capture a representative sample of television commercials from each race. Although a majority of mixed-gender Senate and gubernatorial races are represented in the collection of spot ads, we were able to capture neither the universe of ads from all races nor ads from all the candidates in each race. To maintain consistency, we narrowed the news article sample to include only those articles corresponding to the candidate ads collected. Thus, this study serves as an analysis of the spot ad and newspaper samples in a broader context only, with no attempt to draw distinctions between races or specific candidates.

Overall, this study provides another indication that the media are treating female and male political candidates more equitably. In an examination of all nineteen issues coded, media coverage of female and male candidates correlated with the issue agendas espoused by men and women in their political ads. However, when focusing the analysis on the top issues in the candidate ads and in their news coverage, we found no significant correlation for either female or male candidates. Still, though the difference was not significant, the media were more likely to cover the top issues discussed by male candidates in their political ads than the top issues addressed by female candidates in their commercials in their news stories focusing on men and women, respectively.

The fact that the media might have a different agenda—for both women and men candidates—in their campaign coverage may be a cause for concern. But perhaps the media may be more interested in reporting on issues they believe their readers are interested in hearing about than in echoing the candidate messages. For example, senior citizen issues ranked third among the issue mentions of both female and male candidates in their political ads and were not among the top issues mentioned by the news media in their campaign coverage. This may be a reflection of the fact that all candidates were targeting a specific group of citizens more likely to vote, rather than of the overall importance of senior citizen issues to all voters. Similarly, female candidates may have directed their messages on women's issues, and male candidates on the environment, to specific voters deemed important to their campaign strategies. And the fact that the media were more interested in the economy and international issues than the candidates in 2000 might demonstrate the importance of these issues to the public overall.

NOTE

1. The formula used to calculate intercoder reliability is that given in North et al. (1963). It is given for two coders and can be modified for any number of coders.

$$R = \frac{2(C_{1,2})}{C_1 + C_2}$$

$C_{1,2}$ = number of category assignments both coders agree on
$C_1 + C_2$ = total category assignments made by both coders

REFERENCES

Aday, S., & Devitt, J. (2001). Style over substance: Newspaper coverage of Elizabeth Dole's presidential bid. *Harvard International Journal of Press/Politics, 6,* 52–73.

Banwart, M. C. (2002). *Videostyle and webstyle in 2000: Comparing the gender differences of candidate presentations in political advertising and on the Internet.* Unpublished doctoral dissertation, University of Oklahoma, Norman.

Banwart, M. C., Bystrom, D. G., & Robertson, T. (2003). From the primary to the general election: A comparative analysis of media coverage of candidates in mixed-gender races for governor and U.S. Senate in 2000. *American Behavioral Scientist, 46,* 658–676.

Benze, J. G., & Declercq, E. R. (1985). Content of television political spot ads for female candidates. *Journalism Quarterly, 62,* 278–286.

Bystrom, D. G. (1995). *Candidate gender and the presentation of self: The videostyles of men and women in U.S. Senate campaigns.* Unpublished doctoral dissertation, University of Oklahoma, Norman.

Bystrom, D. G. (forthcoming). Media content and candidate viability: The case of Elizabeth Dole. In M. S. McKinney, D. G. Bystrom, L. L. Kaid, and D. B. Carlin (Eds.), *Communicating politics: Engaging the public in democratic life.* New York: Peter Lang.

Bystrom, D. G., & Kaid, L. L. (2002). Are women candidates transforming campaign communication? A comparison of advertising videostyles in the 1990s. In C. S. Rosenthal (Ed.), *Women transforming Congress* (pp. 146–169). Norman: University of Oklahoma Press.

Bystrom, D. G., & Miller, J. L. (1999). Gendered communication styles and strategies in campaign 1996: The videostyles of women and men candidates. In L. L. Kaid and D. G. Bystrom (Eds.), *The electronic election: Perspectives on the 1996 campaign communication* (pp. 293–302). Mahwah, NJ: Lawrence Erlbaum Associates.

Bystrom, D., Robertson, T., and Banwart, M. (2001). Framing the fight: An analysis of media coverage of female and male candidates in primary races for governor and U.S. Senate. *American Behavioral Scientist* 44: 1999–2013.

Devitt, J. (1999). *Framing gender on the campaign trail: Women's executive leadership and the press.* Washington, DC: Women's Leadership Fund.

Heldman, C., Carroll, S. J., & Olson, S. (2000, August). Gender differences in print media coverage of presidential candidates: Elizabeth Dole's bid for the Republican nomination. Paper presented at the annual meeting of the American Political Science Association, Washington, DC.

Holsti, O. R. (1968). Content analysis. In G. Lindzey and E. Aronson (Eds.), *The handbook of social psychology* (Vol. 1) (pp. 596–692). Reading, MA: Addison-Wesley.

Kahn, K. F. (1991). Senate elections in the news: Examining campaign coverage. *Legislative Studies Quarterly, 16,* 349–374.

Kahn, K. F. (1992). Does being male help? An investigation of the effects of candidate gender and campaign coverage on evaluations of U.S. Senate candidates. *Journal of Politics, 54,* 497–512.

Kahn, K. F. (1993). Gender differences in campaign messages: The political advertisements of men and women candidates for U.S. Senate. *Political Research Quarterly, 46,* 481–502.

Kahn, K. F. (1994a). The distorted mirror: Press coverage of women candidates for statewide office. *Journal of Politics, 56,* 154–173.

Kahn, K. F. (1994b). Does gender make a difference? An experimental examination of sex stereotypes and press patterns in statewide campaigns. *American Journal of Political Science, 38,* 162–195.

Kahn, K. F. (1996). *The political consequences of being a woman: How stereotypes influence the conduct and consequences of political campaigns.* New York: Columbia University Press.

Kahn, K. F., & Goldenberg, E. N. (1991). Women candidates in the news: An examination of gender differences in U.S. Senate campaign coverage. *Public Opinion Quarterly, 55,* 180–199.

Kaid, L. L., & Davidson, D. K. (1986). Elements of videostyle: Candidate presentations through television advertising. In L. L. Kaid, D. Nimmo, & K. R. Sanders (Eds.), *New perspectives on political advertising* (pp. 184–209). Carbondale: Southern Illinois University Press.

Kaid, L. L., and Haynes, K. J. (1995). *Political Communication Center: A catalog and guide to the archival collections.* Norman, OK: Political Communication Center.

Kaid, L. L., & Johnston, A. (1991). Negative versus positive television advertising in presidential campaigns. *Journal of Communication, 41,* 53–64.

Kaid, L. L., & Tedesco, J. C. (1999). Presidential candidate presentation: Videostyle in the 1996 presidential spots. In L. L. Kaid & D. Bystrom (Eds.), *The electronic election: Perspectives on the 1996 campaign communication* (pp. 209–221). Mahwah, NJ: Lawrence Erlbaum Associates.

Krippendorff, K. (1980). *Content analysis: An introduction to its methodology.* Newbury Park, CA: Sage.

Miller, G. (2001). Newspaper coverage and candidate gender: An analysis of the 1996 Illinois state legislative house district races. *Women and Politics, 22* (3), 83–100.

Miller, J. L. (1996). *Dynamics of political advertisements, news coverage, and candidate gender: A content analysis of the campaign messages of the 1990 and 1994 California and Texas Gubernatorial elections.* Unpublished doctoral dissertation, University of Oklahoma.

North, R. C., Holsti, O., Zaninovich, M. G., & Zinnes, D. A. (1963). *Content analysis: A handbook with applications for the study of international crisis.* Evanston, IL: Northwestern University Press.

Robertson, T. (2000). *Sex and the political process: An analysis of sex stereotypes in 1998 senatorial and gubernatorial campaigns.* Unpublished doctoral dissertation, University of Oklahoma, Norman.

Robertson, T., Conley, A., Szymcynska, K., & Thompson, A. (2002). Gender and the media: An investigation of gender, media, and politics in the 2000 election. *New Jersey Journal of Communication, 10,* 104–117.

Serini, S., Powers, A., & Johnston, S. (1998). Of horse race and policy issues: A study of gender in coverage of a gubernatorial election by two major metropolitan newspapers. *Journalism Quarterly, 75* (1), 194–204.

Smith, K. B. (1997). When all's fair: Signs of parity in media coverage of female candidates. *Political Communication, 14,* 71–81.

Trent, J. S., & Sabourin, T. (1993). Sex still counts: Women's use of televised advertising during the decade of the 80s. *Journal of Applied Communication Research, 33,* 21–40.

Williams, L. (1998). Political advertising in the year of the woman: Did X mark the spot? In E. A. Cook, S. Thomas, & C. Wilcox (Eds.), *The year of the woman: Myths and realities* (pp. 197–215). Boulder, CO: Westview Press.

11

Candidates as Comedy

Political Presidential Humor on Late-Night Television Shows

Michael Nitz, Alyson Cypher, Tom Reichert, and James E. Mueller

"What did you think of the debates? I'll let you know after watching *Saturday Night Live.*"

(Jenkins, 1994)

The presidential election of 2000 will go down in history as one of the closest ever. It was one of only three elections (along with those of 1876 and 1888) in which the popular-vote winner did not receive an electoral college majority. Wayne (2001) states that the presidential campaign was the most expensive, one of the longest, highly concentrated, and highly competitive. These latter two factors were exhibited particularly in the media.

This chapter attempts to determine how the entertainment media, specifically late-night comedy shows, may have helped or hindered the electorate in Election 2000. In other words, how did we get into this mess? The quotation that introduces this chapter (Jenkins, 1994) suggests not only a communication form that television comedians use for their amusement—presidential debates—but also a communication form that could provide illuminating, informative insights into an important way voters evaluate candidates—through the use of political humor (Hollihan, 2001). This chapter offers a brief description of late-night television comedy, reviews the literature on political humor, and attempts to integrate this literature with extant work on the effects of humor, political information, and media coverage of political campaigns. In essence, the chapter proposes that late-night television comedy is an increasingly popular form of mediated political information. Several late-night comedy shows are content analyzed to determine the nature of their political humor. Finally, implications for future political campaigns are discussed.

165

POLITICAL HUMOR

Much humor is inherently political (Paletz, 1999). Yet, most research on political discourse adopts a more sober tone. Scholars of campaign discourse lament a trivialization or simplification of political information and rhetoric (Hart, 1982, 2000). Hart notes that political discourse is commonly criticized for emphasizing image over issue. Hollihan (2001) cites critics of campaign communication who assert that image-based communication overly simplifies and is unhelpful to the process.

Yet humor can highlight the positive features of a situation. As a pervasive facet of American life, humor is liberating and helps us detach ourselves from everyday worries (Lefcourt, 2001; Purdie, 1993). Paletz (1999) notes that it both sublimates aggression and eases tension. Laughter has often been an effective political weapon to distinguish oneself from another (Boller, 1984; Udall, 1988). For example, Ostrom and Simon (1989) note that voters respond more favorably to a candidate who has a sense of humor.

Humor is also a way of understanding political issues. Markiewicz (1974) suggests that humor often enhances the effectiveness of political messages. Hollihan (2001) notes how popular culture and knowledge have transformed American television by arguing that official journalism contains "little that is of much use to the people" (p. 10). Humor and other forms of "popular knowledge" can help the people argue or question an official line. Politicians are now risking their dignity for laughs by appearing on TV talk shows. David Letterman's mother urges Donald Rumsfeld to "put the hammer" on Osama bin Laden. First Lady Laura Bush, appearing on Jay Leno's *Tonight Show*, jokes that her husband practices "safe snacks." On *Politically Incorrect*, Gov. Jesse Ventura and James Brown debate the merits of allowing females to serve in combat roles in the navy.

Swanson (2001) argues that the institutions of political communication are undergoing rapid change and that these changes are leading to new forms and opportunities and new and altered forms of information and communication (p. 200). Little research, however, has been conducted on the images of humor and its effects within the political arena. One key exception is Paletz (1990, 1999), whose conceptualization asserts that political humor can be arranged along a continuum from supportive and benign to undermining and subversive. Where humor gets placed on this continuum depends on several different features. Targets of humor can be individuals, policies, authority positions, institutions, and the political system as a whole. More specifically, humor can focus on certain idiosyncrasies of its targets. These can include physical appearance, mannerisms, rhetoric, and a politician's stance on an issue. Also, according to Paletz, presentation of the humor is important in determining placement. Presentation refers to the medium, production values, and the humorist's body language and delivery.

One of the most popular venues for the presentation of this humor is the media. Popular culture is highly media based (Zelizer, 2001). Election 2000 saw yet another definition of "news" (Barney, 2001; Rosen & Taylor, 1992; Wayne, 2001) as candidates bypassed the traditional news and made appearances on late-night comedy shows. Hollihan (2001) cites the increasing use of emotionally intense narrative styles that emphasize images at the expense of official commentary and fact-based objectivism. Hollihan argues that late-night comedy on television ("non-news") has a strong ability to define and influence these images more than the traditional evening news shows (p. 67). For example, Hillary Clinton presented a Top Ten list on David Letterman, and major 2000 presidential candidates appeared on David Letterman and Jay Leno in the course of the fall campaign. Candidates also appeared on several other talk shows, including *Live with Regis and Kelly* and *Oprah*. The "mainstream" networks joined in with clips of the previous night's monologues and Top Ten lists.

Of particular interest to this chapter is Sears's (1987) argument that the media can make certain symbols salient. Political socialization is a process of people acquiring and using a vocabulary of political symbols embedded with meaning. Images are not constructed from a blank slate but come from the social construction of reality (Hollihan, 2001). The humor in Election 2000 focused (using words, satires, and skits) on certain idiosyncrasies of Bush (competence) and Gore (woodenness) that were already salient in voters' mental images. In addition, framing theory provides a useful tool for explaining humor effects. For example, the media can select, define, interpret, and frame campaign messages as they deliver news (Entman, 1993; Iyengar, 1991). The candidates' idiosyncrasies could have been transformed and framed by television comedians into an image that solidified itself in the electorate's minds. These images would then serve as an informational tool for voters to make decisions.

POLITICAL INFORMATION

A key impact of mass media is their ability to inform (Graber, 2000). The obligation to be politically informed has been an essential theme in democratic theory and practice (Bennett, 1996). Delli Carpini and Keeter (1996) believe that the quality of the public debate on issues depends critically on the nature of information brought to the information marketplace and the ability of citizens to use that information to discern and articulate their interests (p. ix). Political communication scholars have buttressed this claim that citizens lack information and have searched for ways to help them become more informed (Doppelt & Shearer, 1999).

Many scholars have lamented a deterioration in political discourse, arguing that the available information is often vapid, foolish, and harmfully false (Hart, 1982, p. 378). Many voters, especially young voters (Kat, 1992), argue that conventional journalism is almost as guilty of such vapidness. Rosen and Taylor (1992) believe the "New News" is mimicking the "Old News" habit of trivialization and scandal stories. Barney (2001) points to a political media culture of conspiracy, entertainment, and celebrity.

Americans are less informed politically today than in recent decades, primarily because they are less interested (Moy & Pfau, 2000). News coverage, when it is paid attention to, can lead to disaffection and disgust. Bennett (1996) is very prescient when he notes that if knowledge about public affairs is to be increased, communicators will have to find ways to increase lukewarm political interest.

Humor as a Burgeoning Form of Political Information

One potential way to provoke this type of voter interest is humor. Jamieson (2000) argues that most people learn about politics from the mass media. Opinions are thus shaped by information sources. Of particular relevance for the current chapter is that the political reality of these opinions is transformed, or mediated, into a "fantasy," and "reality" disappears. One could assume here that the fantasy of humor should remain removed from politics. However, the nature of what constitutes "valid" or "good" political information is becoming blurred.

This blurring may be due partly to the confusion over images versus issues (Edwards, 2001; Hollihan, 2001; Jamieson, 2000). Bennett (1996) argues that much of the information in political campaigns is image based. Myers (2001) argues that the line between politics and entertainment is fuzzier than ever. Sella (2000) twists the *New York Times* newspaper slogan, "The most trusted source for campaign news—well almost," and puts a picture of Jay Leno on the cover of the *New York Times Magazine*. Both issues and image are critical in evaluation of a candidate. Since the distinction is so hard to draw, Hollihan (2001) argues that scholars of political communication must blend the two in order to get a more accurate picture of how voters view and evaluate candidates. Relatedly, emotional images are critical in enabling citizens to access and process political information (Schudson, 2000; Trent et al., 2001). Information may thus remain inaccessible unless an emotional stimulant such as humor provokes it. Humor, therefore, can be thought of as a key component in the formation and shaping of a voter's mental image of a candidate. These emotional images potentially created by the mediated realities of late-night television can become salient symbols in voters' evaluations of political candidates.

Therefore, this chapter argues that humor can be a reliable, and potentially useful, source of political information. A recent survey by the Pew Research Center for the People and the Press showed that 47 percent of Americans between eighteen and twenty-nine obtained information about presidential campaigns from late-night comedy shows (Sella, 2000). The appeal goes well beyond young people as the survey indicated that one-quarter of all American adults get campaign news from these late-night shows.

Humor is an integral part of campaign talk (Boller, 1984; Hart, 2000). As such, it is a form of political communication. Communication is all about the exchange and transfer of symbols to arrive at shared meaning. Humor can serve as an excellent device for people to understand issues (Jenkins, 1994; Lefcourt, 2001; Purdie, 1993). Humor in the media could be highly salient in that emotional images help voters personalize candidates via a process of homophily (seeking out likable politicians). Additionally, humor could be important since images make political information easier to process (Hollihan, 2001).

Humor can also be effective at stimulating interest and actual involvement. Smith and Ferguson (1992) found that voters, especially political independents, use political television to seek out political information. If one takes into account that many political independents are nonvoters and represent a high proportion of adults aged eighteen to thirty-four (Doppelt & Shearer, 1999), then political television plays an important role in the information process. Further, if adults in this younger age group get a large amount of their information from late-night television comedy, then it is important to study humor. Eliasoph (1998) talks about a need for more public-spirited political conversation. Humor certainly provides spirit and may stimulate political conversation. At the very minimum, humor grabs attention (Perry et al., 1997; Unger, 1995), a prerequisite to obtaining interest and subsequent attitude and behavior change.

RESEARCH QUESTIONS

This chapter attempts to examine the nature of humor in late-night television shows and to explore the nature of the "information" and "images" present to determine the potential utility for voters in the 2000 campaign. Specifically, the chapter addresses the following research questions:

RQ₁: How does humor frame political issues?
RQ₂: What is the nature of humor on late-night television comedy shows?
RQ₃: What are the foci of humor in late-night television comedy shows?

METHOD

Late-night television comedy shows (*The Daily Show, Late Night with David Letterman, Politically Incorrect, Saturday Night Live,* and *The Tonight Show with Jay Leno*) were recorded during the 2000 presidential campaign. Only the Top Ten segments from *Late Night with David Letterman* were analyzed, including the two shows on which Al Gore and George W. Bush appeared. A random sample of 115 segments (defined as a skit, monologue, or conversation focusing on one distinct issue or personal feature) was coded. Owing to coder error and technical misfunctions, some segments were missing.

Paletz's (1990, 1999) conceptualization of humor and Iyengar's (1991) work on framing served as the bases for the coding scheme. Framing was examined for its thematic (humor with general background information and context) and episodic (isolated, anecdotal humor) content. An example of thematic humor would be relating a gaffe from the campaign trail to a common theme (Bush and alleged incompetence, or Gore and alleged dishonesty). An example of episodic humor would be where comedians joked about a candidate's stance on an issue and moved on to another issue. Framing also examined the overall tone or bias of the humor to see whether it was positive (Bob Hope joking about astronauts wearing Gucci suits) or negative (cynical and potentially subversive Don Imus calling President Bill Clinton a pot-smoking weasel).

The nature of humor was examined using Paletz's continuum of supportive and subversive humor. Supportive humor would be akin to Jenkins's (1994) use of Johnny Carson as an example of one who does not defiantly mock injustice but uses detachment. Thus, there is no cause for alarm among voters. Subversive humor is comedy that is cynical and scorns figures and institutions and does so in a way that verges on the unacceptable (Powell & Paton, 1988). Humor content was thus coded on a continuum from very supportive to very unsupportive.

Building on this definition, Paletz (1999) argues that the nature of the forums and the mannerisms in which humor is presented are intimately related. Therefore, this study also examined how late-night television comedy shows presented humor. Delivery was coded for the presence of animation or control and the rawness or slickness of humor. In addition, the humor was coded as being daring, conventional, or self-deprecating. Finally, the forum of humor (skit, monologue, or conversation) was analyzed.

In terms of foci, this study divided humor into two categories: individuals and issues. If the humor primarily focused on individuals, coders analyzed humor content to determine whether the humor focused on physical traits/appearance (Gore's woodenness), personal qualities (Bush's malapropisms), and actual words as they related to stances on issues and events (jokes about Bush's comments about reporters). If the humor focused on issues, coders recorded the actual issue(s) discussed and focused on the potential utility of the information embedded in humor. Coders rated the humor for its sophistication (did the humor present several different angles?), its truthfulness (did the humor generally represent consensus about what was said, or done or was there distortion or embellishment of a trait or issue stance?), and its overall utility (did the humor seem to be used to illuminate an issue or show how a trait was relevant to evaluating a political entity, or was the humor merely "piling on"?).

RESULTS

The present investigation attempted to ascertain the content and tone of political humor in late-night television shows. Overall, 115 instances of political humor were coded. A total of 74 segments from *Politically Incorrect*, 9 from *The Daily Show*, 17 from *Saturday Night Live*, and 15 from *Late Night with David Letterman* were coded. To determine whether coders reliably identified the instances of political humor, two individuals independently coded a random sample of 10% of the total instances. The intercoder agreement was acceptable, with an agreement rate of 72% and a Kappa coefficient of .65.

The first research question attempted to ascertain how humor framed political issues. Extremely surprising was the large thematic focus (44%). Episodic stories represented 36% of the focus, while 20% of the segments were coded as mixed thematic-episodic. Comedians continued to relate the day's events to the common themes or images of the presidential candidates.

In terms of tone or bias, humor presented some interesting dimensions. Many of the comedians on late-night television were negative in tone (68%). Nearly every joke or skit made fun of something a candidate did or said, and an unflattering frame was usually attached to this. Daring and outrageous humor was prominent (44%), with smaller amounts of conventional (9%) or self-deprecating humor (6%). There was still, however, a substantial percentage (31%) of humor that was positive or mixed.

The second research question looked at the nature of humor. Overall, the humor on late-night television comedy shows was mostly or somewhat unsupportive of its targets (64%). There was also a good percentage (23%) of humor that mixed supportive and unsupportive elements. Very little, if any, humor was very supportive (5%) or very unsupportive (5%).

The presentation of humor was also examined. Nearly all (88%) of the instances of humor were controlled as opposed to animated (7%). On the other hand, most of the presentations were raw in nature (89%). Humor was mostly daring (37%), with a mixture of conventional (18%) and self-deprecating (24%). The formats were nearly equally divided between monologues (47%) and conversational format (48%).

The third research question asked about the focus of humor. The focus of late-night television humor was predominantly individual traits. Only 14% (16 segments) focused on a candidate's stance on the issues. In targeting individual traits, the late-night television shows mainly targeted the individuals themselves (75%). Additional foci included policies of individuals (13%), institutions (5%), authority position itself (1%), and the political system in general (5%). Late-night comedians were quite flexible in their targeting of individuals. Targets were separated into three categories: physical appearance/characteristics, personal qualities, and something said or done. All three categories were the combined focus of 23% of the late-night comedy. In approximately 25% of the humor, two of the three were a combined focus. This was more likely the case for the latter two categories (20%) than for the first two (4%). Separately, humor was concentrated on something said or done by the candidate 19% of the time. Examples of this would be making fun of Gore's "invention" of the Internet or Bush's anatomical characterization of a *New York Times* reporter. Personal qualities were the second-highest separate focus (16%). Examples of this would be Gore's lack of honesty and Bush's lack of intelligence. Finally, physical traits were the focus 8% of the time. Examples included Gore's wooden posture or his convention kiss and Bush's facial gestures.

When the comedians focused on individual traits, the humor had high (16%) or moderate (43%) levels of sophistication, high (15%) or moderate (39%) levels of informative utility, and high (16%) or moderate (35%) levels of truth (hypothetical). When issues were focused on, they were broken into two main categories: issues surrounding voting (5%) and issues surrounding the debates (5%). While the humor was mostly low in sophistication (82%) and truth (80%), coders rated the information value to be more diverse, with high (41%) and moderate (29%) utility in the majority of instances.

DISCUSSION

The purpose of this research was to analyze the nature of humor in late-night television programming. The analysis revealed that humor on late-night television comedy shows during the Election 2000 period helped reshape and amplify some key candidate character traits and issues. Humor itself certainly took on new importance as the previous night's Top Ten list was rebroadcast on the morning news shows. Prestigious media outlets such as the *New York Times* covered the latest jokes from the comedy circuit. A reporter from *60 Minutes* was even caught blowing bubbles during an interview with John Stewart, host of *The Daily Show.* The candidates themselves got involved with appearances on David Letterman's show. Humor took on a variety of shapes and sizes, but was, for the most part, benign.

Nonetheless, humor was relentless in its pursuit of new ways to ridicule Al Gore's woodenness and tendency to exaggerate and George W. Bush's incompetence. The comedians would, in relatively equal percentages across formats of skits, monologues, and conversations, look mostly for daring and outrageous ways to get laughs. This was most evident in *Saturday Night Live* skits and during conversations on *Politically Incorrect.* For example, skits would accentuate candidate traits. Of all the shows, the most off-the-wall was *Saturday Night Live,* which created fictitious scenarios. *Saturday Night Live* offered a "glimpse of our presidential future" with all three candidates. Ralph Nader was impersonated in the Oval Office with pigs flying in the background and devils shivering. Al Gore was impersonated in front of a supercomputer as he lectured from a thick economics textbook, before he was rudely interrupted by a Bill Clinton impersonator (with beer in one hand and chips in the other). George W. Bush was impersonated climbing up from behind the Oval Office desk as the Capitol building burned in the background. Beer cans and garbage littered the office as the Bush imperson-ator drank from binoculars.

This may at first glance appear to support the assertions of those who lament the decline of political campaign discourse. However, when one considers the nature of the 2000 election, the humor may have been amplifying, reinforcing, and stimulating the communication content from other media. Election 2000 was a very close election, conducted during a time of relative prosperity (Wayne, 2001). In such close elections, images can become very important and reassuring to voters in their political decision making (Hollihan, 2001).

The humorous skits and conversations contained important kernels of infor-mation that were salient symbols or frames in voters' minds. Nader had been cas-tigated for letting his ego ruin Gore's chances of getting elected. Gore's seriousness had been lampooned as a handicap in his quest for presidential charisma. Bush's intelligence and frat-boy image were the source of angst for many in the media. Consequently, the humor was not as "useless" as it might appear at first glance because of its outrageous packaging. These humorous images were identifying with salient symbols and presenting them to voters in a new light. The humor had the potential to both reinforce images and stimulate new discussion. The best example of this can be seen in recent criticism of Bill Maher's "antipatriotic" com-ments about the cowardice of U.S. troops. It should be noted that both Al Gore and George W. Bush made appearances on Jay Leno and David Letterman, and both candidates were particularly adept at self-deprecating humor.

The impacts of political humor on voters should be a topic for future research. Voters obtain most of their political information from the media, especially tele-vision. In addition, future voters (those thirty-four and under) are gathering political information from these new sources. In the wake of the September 11, 2001, attacks, late-night talk shows received their highest ratings ever. One needs to ask if the "new" information is a help or a hindrance to voters. This chapter agrees with the view of Hart (1982) that one should not be monolithic in viewing political communication discourse. Political communication is a social act and humor plays a vital social role, especially as images continue to dominate. Elec-tion 2000 was a race in which both major candidates were perceived equally, with similar stances on the issues. In close elections, with peace and prosperity, humor may be a key deciding factor in elections. Myers (2001) notes that as the stakes of politics have shrunk, so has the seriousness with which we treat politics.

When elections or politicians are faced with instability and economic down-turns (as the United States has faced since September 11), humor may be less appropriate as a rhetorical tool. This is evidenced by Jay Leno and David Letter-man not appearing for a week after the September 11 attacks, and when they did reappear, their comedy was muted and more respectful of the president.

Nonetheless, humor will remain a vital and energetic component of political life. Future research should attempt to uncover how this form of political infor-mation differs from other forms. Most importantly, if people are getting their political information from late-night shows, researchers should delve into whether this is a sole or primary source, whether it is an activator and reinforcer of schemas, or whether it is merely a supplementary, lighthearted diversion from mainstream news. In any case, politics is still inherently entertaining. As former President Ronald Reagan showed, politicians can be more effective if they combine politics and entertainment. Political talk shows need to hold people's attention. Myers (2001) quotes the observation by Chris Matthews of the MSNBC/ CNBC talk show *Hardball* that talk shows need to provide both "bread and circus" (p. 6). Fact-based politics gets our attention; fiction-based politics provides a compelling, dramatic background. The danger arises when traditional news shows move too close to entertainment. Viewers then may seek fictional venues to find out about real issues. The key is to differentiate between fact and fiction.

Humor should maintain a place in the body of research on political communication. It can be an effective, motivational tool in at least two key ways. First, humor directed at a favorite candidate can outrage a voter to an extent that he or she may vote. Election 2000 certainly shows that every vote counts. Second, the stereotypical attributes attached to candidates in jokes could help facilitate quicker information processing by voters. Schematic processing such as this is not all bad and may actually help voters manage complexity. The lasting power of humor may best be explained with a quote from David Letterman's Top Ten Dumb Guy Ways to Solve Presidential Election Confusion. His first solution was "Solve it? Are you nuts? This is great!"

REFERENCES

Barney, T. (2001). Celebrity, spectacle, and the conspiracy culture of Election 2000. *American Behavioral Scientist, 44,* 2331–2337.

Bennett, L. (1996). *News: The politics of illusion.* New York: Longman.

Boller, P. (1984*). Presidential campaigns.* New York: Oxford University Press.

Delli Carpini, M., & Keeter, S. (1989). *What Americans know about politics and why it matters.* New Haven: Yale University Press.

Doppelt, J., & Shearer, E. (1999). *Nonvoters: America's no-shows.* Thousand Oaks, CA: Sage.

Edwards, J. (2001). Running in the shadows in Campaign 2000: Candidate metaphors in editorial cartoons. *American Behavioral Scientist, 44,* 2140–2151.

Eliasoph, N. (1998). *Avoiding politics: How Americans produce apathy in everyday life.* London: Cambridge University Press.

Entman, R. (1993). Framing: Toward clarification of a fractured paradigm. *Journal of Communication, 43,* 51–58.

Graber, D. (2000). *Media power in politics.* Washington, DC: Congressional Quarterly Press.

Hart, R. (1982). A commentary on popular assumptions about political communication. *Human Communication Research, 8,* 366–389.

Hart, R. (2000). *Campaign talk: Why elections are good for us.* Princeton, NJ: Princeton University Press.

Hollihan, T. (2001). *Uncivil wars: Political campaigns in a media age.* Boston: Bedford/St. Martin's.

Iyengar, S. (1991). *Is anyone responsible?* Chicago: University of Chicago Press.

Jamieson, K. (2000). *Everything you think you know about politics . . . and why you're wrong.* New York: Basic Books.

Jenkins, R. (1994). *Subversive laughter: The liberating power of comedy.* New York: Free Press.

Kat, J. (1992, Mar. 5). Rock, rap, and movies bring you the news. *Rolling Stone, 33–40.*

Lefcourt, H. (2001). *Humor: The psychology of living buoyantly.* New York: Kluwer.

Markiewicz, D. (1974). Effects of humor on persuasion. *Sociometry, 37,* 407–422.

Moy, P., & Pfau, M. (2000). *With malice toward all? The media and public confidence in democratic institutions.* Westport, CT: Praeger.

Myers, D. (2001, Sept.). Political stars and TV stripes. *USA Weekend,* 6–7.

Ostrom, C., & Simon, D. (1989). The man in the Teflon suit? *Public Opinion Quarterly, 53,* 353–387.

Paletz, D. (1990). Political humor and authority: From support to subversion. *International Political Science Review* 11: 483–493.

Paletz, D. (1999). *The media in American politics.* New York: Longman.

Perry, S., Jenzowsky, S., King, C., Yi, H., Hester, J., & Gartenschlaeger, J. (1997). Using humorous programs as a vehicle for humorous commercials. *Journal of Communication, 47,* 20–39.

Powell, C., & Paton, G. E. C. (1988). *Humour in society: Resistance and control.* New York: St. Martin's Press.

Purdie, S. (1993). *Comedy: The mastery of discourse.* Toronto: University of Toronto Press.

Rosen, J. & Taylor, P. (1992). *Perspectives on the news: The new news v. the old news: The press and politics in the 1990s.* A 20th Century Fund paper.

Schudson, M. (2000). Image: The Kennedy-Nixon debates. *Media Studies Journal, 14,* 122–124.

Sears, D. (1987). Political psychology. *Annual Review of Psychology, 38,* 229–255.

Sella, M. (2000, Sept. 24). The stiff guy versus the dumb guy: The power and prejudice of political comedy. *New York Times Magazine,* 72–82, 102.

Smith, K., & Ferguson, D. (1992). Voter partisan orientations and use of political television. *Journalism Quarterly, 67,* 864–874.

Swanson, D. (2001). Political communication research and the mutations of democracy. In W. Gudykunst (Ed.), *Communication Yearbook 24* (pp. 189–206). Thousand Oaks, CA: Sage.

Trent, J., Short-Thompson, C., Mongeau, P., Nusz, A., & Trent, J. (2001). Image, media bias, and voter characteristics: The ideal candidate from 1988–2000. *American Behavioral Scientist, 44,* 2101–2124.

Udall, M. (1988). *Too funny to be president.* New York: Henry Holt.

Unger, L. (1995). Observations: A cross-cultural study on the affect-based model of humor in advertising. *Journal of Advertising Research, 35,* 66–71.

Wayne, S. (2001). *The road to the White House 2000: The politics of presidential elections* (postelection ed.). Boston: Bedford/St. Martin's.

Zelizer, B. (2001). Popular communication in the contemporary age. In W. Gudykunst (Ed.), *Communication Yearbook 24* (pp. 297–319). Thousand Oaks, CA: Sage.

NEW TECHNOLOGIES

12

Organizing an Online Campaign
The Legacy of McCain2000.com

James E. Tomlinson

When John McCain formally announced his candidacy for president in September of 1999, he was faced with several obstacles. The senator was from a small-population state (Arizona), while his chief opponent for the Republican nomination, George W. Bush, was governor of a much larger and more delegate-rich state (Texas). Bush had already begun to garner official endorsements from Republican leaders across the country, benefited from high name recognition, and had already accumulated a substantial campaign war chest worth over $50 million (Bruni, 1999). However, Senator McCain entered the contest with some considerable assets. He was regarded by many as a genuine American war hero, had served first in the House and then in the Senate, displayed a passion for his message of reform, and had shared an enthusiasm for digital communication technologies with his very Internet-savvy campaign advisers. Of those advisers, his Internet director, Max Fose, would earn a reputation as one of the most skilled and important figures in Campaign 2000. It would prove to be a historic campaign effort.

The research presented here has been undertaken to document the innovative uses of digital technologies by the McCain campaign in 2000 through a series of interviews with those who created and operated the McCain online effort, a review of archived campaign e-mail from McCain2000, and my own experiences as a member of the Pennsylvania State Committee of Citizens for John McCain. The focus will be on how the national campaign integrated the use of the Internet into the very fabric of the campaign's organization and established a model to which other campaigns aspire.

McCAIN INTERACTIVE

The original version of McCain2000.com was online and attracting modest attention through the latter part of 1999, but Max Fose and the McCain team were planning to implement an ambitious strategy that would dramatically alter the way political professionals and candidates would view the Internet. On December 7, 1999, McCain Interactive was launched, coinciding with the senator's major campaign address to honor veterans. This new version of the McCain website established sections for each state to provide an online location for developing a grassroots campaign effort across the country. This effort appeared reminiscent of the efforts of another Internet guru, Phil Madsen, who ran the website for Jesse Ventura's surprising and successful campaign for governor of Minnesota in 1998. Madsen argues that one of the most important aspects of using the Internet in a campaign is to recruit and organize volunteers (P. Madsen, personal communication, May 4, 1999).

John McCain himself, in an e-mail to supporters on December 12, 1999, noted that the website was a vital element in the campaign's efforts to "recruit supporters, spread the message, and help raise funds." The McCain Internet effort was not simply a component of the campaign but was fully integrated into all aspects of the organization. One prominent commentator observed that the McCain Web campaign was characterized by a flat decision-making authority with a direct connection to a candidate who was eager to explore the possibilities of these new technologies (Fineman, 2000).

USE OF THE WEBSITE TO ORGANIZE VOLUNTEERS BY STATE

This use of a national website allowed state organizations to have, without any costs to themselves, a location in cyberspace to list meetings and event locations and coordinate efforts to maximize campaign resources. State groups would send messages requesting that McCain supporters from other locations send volunteers or materials when they were needed. For example, when John McCain was scheduled to visit Boston, the Massachusetts team sent an "alert" message via e-mail dated February 24, 2000, inviting supporters from other states to organize a trip to the event. One team sent out an urgent message March 13, 2000, that it was in need of bumper stickers and yard signs. The team requested that other state organizations send any materials they could spare to help the cause in Illinois.

Some truly innovative use was made of these new technologies by a state organization in Pennsylvania. Tom Pelikan, political director for the state campaign, was pleasantly surprised to find an online chat room for county chairpersons had been organized by a volunteer. On Thursday evenings at 7 P.M. EST, McCain coordinators from across the commonwealth could "chat" about campaign events and organizational issues. The use of this chat room allowed the McCain county chairs to meet without the investment of time and money it would take to arrange a meeting in a physical location.

The Pennsylvania McCain team also established an e-mail list of contacts in every county in the commonwealth that allowed for a level of direct contact with no expenditures of the meager funds the state organization had accumulated. The national McCain organization had been able to direct no funds and very few materials to the Pennsylvania committee, as the campaign was being intensely contested in other states with primary elections well before the election in the commonwealth. Thus, McCain supporters relied on an e-mail campaign through which individuals created their own campaign signs and bumper stickers, which they shared with one another as e-mail attachments (T. Pelikan, personal communication, June 30, 2002).

Just as in other states, the Pennsylvania team established a growing list of supporters by county. While Max Fose at McCain2000.com would forward information on volunteers who had contacted the national organization through the website, local county chairs and state officials were also attracting supporters through a campaign of letters to the editor and news organizations reporting on the formation of local McCain committees. Pennsylvania McCain workers were urged to announce the McCain2000.com Web address and have a local campaign representative's e-mail contact information available at every public pronouncement or media event. As a result, many local campaign chairs found that most contacts for new volunteers were being generated by e-mail and website contacts. Some county chairs orchestrated e-mail campaigns to persuade their local elected Republican officials to endorse Senator McCain. The state campaign was organizing a coordinated series of media events at which these local officials would simultaneously announce their endorsement of the candidate. These plans were for naught, as before the Pennsylvania primary in May 2000, Senator McCain suspended his campaign as a result of Governor Bush's victories in the Super Tuesday primary contests. However, these efforts seemed to attract people who relished the innovative ways the technology could be used to organize and energize supporters.

McCAIN2000.COM: INNOVATIONS IN INTERNET CAMPAIGN ORGANIZATION

In the "old" political model, a candidate would have to invest considerable resources to sponsor a fund-raising event. The campaign would have to determine locations where there was the greatest likelihood of fund-raising success, have an advance team set up publicity, obtain a location, attract press attention, schedule interviews, provide refreshments and entertainment, try to persuade local political figures, party officials, and celebrities to participate and support the event, and ensure that there would actually be people who would attend and contribute. Then the campaign would have to manage the candidate's busy schedule and make travel arrangements and often overnight accommodations for the staff and the candidate. All of these preparation steps involve hours of planning, coordination across often contentious and competing elements of the campaign team, and lots of money.

By February of 2000, John McCain's webmaster was organizing live Internet campaign fund-raising events. Using Web tracking data helped the campaign choose the day and time most likely to attract an audience for the candidate. This format allowed the candidate to meet live (in cyberspace) with contributors from Maine to California, without any overhead costs. Those with high-speed connections were able to access live video as well as audio to chat with the candidate. The format was so popular that additional online chats for campaign supporters were organized including special events featuring the candidate's wife, Cindy McCain (M. Fose, personal communication, June 22, 2001).

In addition, McCain operatives were learning from the mistakes of others. One of those lessons resulted from the Dole96.com debate disaster. Robert Arena, Internet consultant to Dole96, recalls how Bob Dole promoted his website address during the first debate with President Clinton. The increase in traffic to the site was so heavy that it was overwhelmed and froze out uncounted numbers of potential visitors. It became clear that a campaign must anticipate the volume of Web traffic and ensure that there is sufficient server capacity to handle projected visitors (R. Arena, personal communication, Februrary 12, 2002). Max Fose watched the tracking polls of New Hampshire voters with great interest. He realized that if the campaign's poll numbers were accurate, Senator McCain was about to score a surprising victory. He anticipated that the publicity from this victory could generate the same problem for McCain that had caused the Dole site to crash four years earlier. Thus, the night before the New Hampshire primary the McCain campaign more than quadrupled its server capacity and the next day found that to be a wise investment.

When the national media began to announce the dramatic results as John McCain won the New Hampshire primary by a historic margin, traffic to McCain2000.com increased by the hour. The McCain campaign, which had been accepting donations online for several months, found itself receiving contributions at rates as high as $50,000 an hour. In less than twenty-four hours, the campaign had raised $500,000. In just forty-eight hours, that figure exceeded $1 million. Within one week of the New Hampshire victory McCain had received over $2 million in online contributions. Becky Donatelli, one of John McCain's campaign strategists, noted that these contributions averaged under $100 per individual, with 60% of the donations coming from persons aged under forty-five; nearly one-half were from persons who were first-time donors to a political campaign (B. Donatelli, personal communication, March 3, 2000). While the

McCain team had raised $1 million online by January 1, 2000, this represented only 5% of the over $21 million the campaign had raised. However, by the end of February, the funds raised online accounted for 25% of the campaign's income (M. Fose, personal communication, January 20, 2001). The McCain team established for the first time that online contributions were not just feasible but could become a major fund-raising mechanism.

The impact on the campaign went far beyond fund-raising. When I first joined the McCain campaign team in October of 1999, I found myself part of a national e-mail list that totaled 127 persons. By the time of the first presidential primary in February, the campaign e-mail listing of volunteers had grown to 60,000. Just two weeks after the New Hampshire victory, the campaign had attracted over 40,000 new volunteers. By the end of February, an additional 20,000 persons joined the McCain team. McCain's community of online supporters more than doubled in one month, swelling to over 125,000 people (M. Fose, personal communication, January 20, 2001).

The McCain2000.com political website clearly took advantage of new tracking technologies. After accessing the site and registering, visitors would find that with each subsequent visit they would be greeted with a "Welcome (your name here)." This became possible because the software could recognize the visitor's IP (Internet protocol) address and had a name to attach to it.

Tracking software can determine if someone is a first-time visitor to the site or how many times previously that IP has visited. This presents the potential for e-mail and other responses to be tailored to the number of visits as well as to the specific pages a visitor has viewed. The availability of tracking software at affordable prices ensures that political campaigns will use such data to target messages more precisely than ever before.

The McCain campaign chose to post on its website some of its tracking data. During the last week of October 1999, the site data showed the number of "visits" and revealed that the single most frequent visitor to the McCain site was the IP address for the George W. Bush for President Committee. The McCain site posted links especially for their "friends" from the Bush campaign to "aid them in their research."

It is clear that the McCain team viewed with pleasure the amount of time the Bush campaign was spending at its site. However, it was understandable that the Bush staff was doing what any well-run political organization should do, gather all the information possible about an adversary's campaign. Today opponent research can be done, at least in part, by regularly visiting the opposition candidate's website.

The McCain campaign established a regular pattern of e-mail contacts to their growing list of online volunteers. With each major news item or press release about the campaign, e-mail messages either included important announcements or asked the recipients to visit linked sections of McCain2000.com to access the information. The Internet team used every opportunity not only to reinforce the candidate's message but also to respond to press attention and the increasingly negative attacks by opponents. When each of the now famous attack ads against John McCain made its appearance, e-mail to campaign loyalists attempted to explain the candidate's position and provide ammunition for supporters to use in letters to editors or e-mail to local news organizations.

Damage control could also be performed using e-mail. When John McCain first denied any knowledge of the "Catholic Voter Alert" phone calls made in Michigan, the campaign immediately tried to explain to its supporters their candidate's confusion over the origin of these messages, indicting Bob Jones University and its association with Governor Bush.

Press attention that favored the candidate was spread to volunteers via the e-mail network as well. When William Safire wrote a stinging condemnation of the negative campaign ads used against McCain in South Carolina and elsewhere, the *New York Times* editorial of March 6, 2000, was sent by e-mail to all McCain supporters. Similar editorials that either praised Senator McCain or complained of the tactics used by the opposition were sent to supporters on the same day they appeared in the print media.

THE JOHN McCAIN WEB RING

In early December of 1999, a computer graphics specialist at Notre Dame University named Jim Weber created a web ring to support Senator McCain's campaign for the presidency. After arranging for the server space and domain name, he began to encourage other McCain supporters to join his web ring. By the end of December, ten other "McCainiacs" had created pages that were then linked to each other via Weber's site.

Political web rings had not yet been organized by campaigns and thus were not part of the official campaign organization. They are more akin to a person simply posting a sign in a shop window or a yard sign on his or her property. Web rings were online during the primary season for Alan Keyes, Al Gore, Bill Bradley, Elizabeth Dole, and George W. Bush.

Weber created the McCain web ring to provide a location for an online community of the senator's supporters (J. Weber, personal communication, December 12, 1999). The web ring grew to twenty-five members by the time Senator McCain dropped out of the campaign after the Super Tuesday primaries, in which Governor Bush won a substantial number of delegates and assured himself of the GOP nomination. There was also a No–John McCain Web Ring that opposed the senator, just as there were web rings of sites against each of the other candidates. While these web rings may not be of significance in the electoral decisions voters make, they are another example of how the Internet provides a new vehicle for personal expressions of support or opposition outside the mainstream political arena.

THE PERMANENT CAMPAIGN, ONLINE

In 1982, Sidney Blumenthal observed that political campaigns were no longer characterized by discrete periods of intense political activity but rather by an unending process of publicity and fund-raising making them "permanent" features rather than seasonal (Blumenthal, 1982). His observations seem even more pertinent in the emerging age of digital politics.

The McCain2000.com website is still available on the World Wide Web but now is a gateway to Senator McCain's Straight Talk America political action committee, which continues to enlist supporters for his message of campaign finance reform. The now permanent use of this domain name appears to be an important lesson. The McCain2000.com name became one of the most widely distributed and recognizable addresses on the Internet during the presidential election. Continued use of the site allows for surfers to that address to be directed to where they can learn about the senator's current Web activities. This lesson has not been lost on others interested in digital politics. The official campaign address for the George W. Bush campaign in the last election, www.georgew bush.com, remains active but as a link to the Republican National Committee. Obviously, continued use of the domain name prevents any mischievous cybers-quatter from stealing the address before the next election and helps the antici-pated reelection effort of the president maintain a consistent Web presence that may help voters remember how to find campaign information during the 2004 campaign.

JOHN McCAIN'S DIGITAL LEGACY

Senator McCain's campaign made an indelible impression on the press, the professional political consulting community, the public, and on both of the major parties. McCain's innovative uses of these technologies, along with publicity about other digital pioneers like Jesse Ventura and Bill Bradley, inspired a dramatic burst of campaign-related activities in cyberspace during 2000.

During the general election, both the Democratic National Committee (DNC) and the Republican National Committee (RNC) began substantial e-mail campaigns as part of their Get Out the Vote (GOTV) efforts. The RNC attempted to target its audience in very specific terms. By analyzing the age, gender, occupation, and veteran status of persons who were registered by e-mail address with state GOP party organizations or the RNC, selected Republican celebrities would send messages to remind voters to support the GOP ticket on Election Day. For example, senior citizens received e-mail from Barbara Bush. Educators received e-mail from Laura Bush. Veterans received a double dose, with messages from John McCain and Colin Powell. While these messages were simply text e-mail, both parties also began using video e-mail messages during the latter stages of the campaign.

Campaign 2000 will be recorded as the year when both major political parties became ISPs (Internet service providers). While they pose no threat to AOL.com or the other commercial entities, it is an interesting venture. Republicans launched their effort on November 15, 1999, by sending an e-mail announcement to GOP activists around the country heralding the website. For $19.95 per month, members could get an e-mail address and Internet access. The RNC-sponsored site is located at www.GOPnet.com. The GOP site offers opportunities for members to chat with prominent Republicans, including the chair of the RNC. The Democratic Party site, www.freedem.com, first appeared on June 9, 2000, and was promoted by the distribution of cards by state and local party organizations. The DNC offered its e-mail and Internet access for free. Members were asked to sign up for the DNC newsletter and answer a number of questions related to policy and political surveys. My repeated attempts to contact the DNC and RNC for information related to the number of hits and membership these sites have attracted has been unproductive. Neither organization has been willing to share its data.

One way to gauge how widespread the use of new technologies in politics has become is to examine the Political Pages Issue published annually by the professional campaign consultant magazine *Campaigns and Elections.* The March 2001 issue compiled a listing of campaign organizations offering their services to candidates and political organizations. The information is categorized by type of service offered, such as:

Direct Mail Consultants	114 listings
Fund-raising Consultants	106
Pollsters	134
Television/Radio Production	114
Speech Preparation	45

In addition to these traditional types of expertise there are a number of categories that did not even appear in the listings until 1998. The numbers for these listings in the 2001 edition were:

Fund-raising Software	27 listings
Internet Campaign Services	43

Many of the companies offering "political voices" (persons who will read and record the script for a radio or TV spot) now offer digital recordings for increased clarity. An additional advantage may be that it is possible to download the recording directly from the Internet rather than waiting for the mail to deliver a video or audiotape.

Another indication that this new technology has become part of the political campaign mainstream is that standards have emerged for the use of websites. Several articles and handbooks have been prepared as how-to manuals for either conducting campaigns or evaluating website use. While there may not yet be universal agreement on what constitutes an effective campaign website, one source that has outlined generally accepted principles is *Winning Campaigns Online,* authored by Emiliene Ireland and Phil Tajitsu Nash (2001). This work has been endorsed and distributed by the American Association of Political Consultants as a useful guide for Internet campaigning. The authors suggest the following as key to a successful campaign website:

- A good domain name that is easy for visitors to find
- Download time of fifteen seconds or less
- Ease of use by visitors
- Secure online fund-raising
- Form to collect e-mail addresses of visitors
- Issues pages
- E-mail form letters to send to friends
- Recruitment of volunteers
- Media kits for the press
- Events calendar
- Top-quality photos and graphics
- Voter registration information (including absentee ballot information)
- Endorsements page
- Well-written and edited home and biography pages
- Privacy policy
- Good site map
- Pages in languages other than English

Most of the recommendations made by the authors are a result of the successful and pioneering efforts of Web innovators like Phil Madsen (for Jesse Ventura in 1998) and Max Fose (for John McCain in 2000). In the 2000 general election, both the Bush and Gore campaigns made a commitment to using the Internet as an integral part of their campaign strategy. Each campaign website also developed websites that employed the standards described by Ireland and Nash.

While not ultimately successful at gaining the nomination for the candidate, the McCain 2000 campaign will be remembered for its innovative strategy and use of the Internet as an integral part of a political campaign. As NBC and *Newsweek* commentator Howard Fineman observed, "Now I know what politics will look like in the Internet Age. It will look like John McCain's campaign" (Fineman, 2000).

REFERENCES

Blumenthal, S. (1982). *The permanent campaign.* New York: Simon & Schuster.

Bruni, F. (1999, Sept. 10). Bush posts campaign donors on Website. *CyberTimes-New York Times on the Web.* [No pagination]. Retrieved December 5, 1999, from www.nytimes. com/library/tech/99/09/cyber/articles/10politics.html.

Campaigns and Elections. (2001, March). *The political pages: Special edition.* Washington, DC: Congressional Quarterly.

Fineman, H. (2000, Feb. 9). McCain: Politician for the digital age. *MSNBC.com.* [No pagination]. Retrieved February 9, 2000, from www.msnbc.com/news/politics/story/ 0,4536,4424,00.html.

Ireland, E., & Nash, N. T. (2001). *Winning campaigns online.* Bethesda, MD: Science Writers Press.

13

Differences and Similarities in Use of Campaign Websites during the 2000 Presidential Election

Robert H. Wicks, Boubacar Souley, and Rebecca M. Verser

This chapter examines the issues, topics, photographs, and images that dominated the 2000 presidential campaign official websites of George W. Bush and Al Gore. Presidential candidates used political websites throughout the 1990s to communicate with voters. However, with users logging on in record numbers, the Millennium Election was the first in which candidates reached so many citizens with so many different types of messages on their websites. As a result, it is important to understand the ways in which candidates for office are trying to take advantage of this new communication technology to advance political communication.

Analysis of content posted on these websites revealed that the official campaign websites of Bush and Gore were quite similar with respect to textual content. Approximately three-quarters of the textual information posted on each website contained negative charges against the opponent, and about one-quarter acclaimed the candidate's own performance. Concerning issues, candidates stuck to relatively safe themes like education, Social Security, and taxes, avoiding controversial issues that could alienate undecided or independent voters.

With respect to imagery, the Bush and Gore campaign websites were quite different. The Gore website presented seven times as many images as did the Bush website. Furthermore, the Gore images tended to portray the candidate as informal and folksy, while George W. Bush images portrayed the candidate as more professional and businesslike. Finally, the images on the Gore entry page of the website changed frequently and often contained motion. A static image on the Bush page remained unchanged throughout the course of the campaign. We believe that these differences may represent a fundamental philosophical difference between the candidates, as Gore billed himself as the "technology" candidate. This chapter analyzes reasons for the similarities and differences between these websites during the 2000 presidential campaign.

ANALYZING CAMPAIGN WEBSITES AND CONTENT

Few citizens would have imaged in 1990 that by the close of the decade, the Internet would compete with newspapers, television, and other media as a primary entertainment and information provider. With respect to political communication, the 2000 presidential election marked a turning point in which candidates used campaign websites in new and innovative ways to provide citizens with news and background information, as well as online photographs, video clips, and other materials portraying the candidates, running mates, and their family members (Harbert, 2000).

The Internet may also be on the verge of becoming more important in campaigns and elections as it enables citizens to obtain information and communicate with other people and the candidates themselves (Selnow, 1998). Exit polls during the 1996 election revealed that approximately a quarter of all voters used online resources, and about 10% reported that the Internet was a primary source of information in their voting decisions (Connell, 1997). By the 2000 election, about half of all Americans had the capability to view campaign websites from their homes (Rumbough & Tomlinson, 2000).

The amount and depth of information available and the relative affordability of the technology may empower people to obtain information that heretofore was available largely through increasingly concentrated and centralized news media. The decentralized nature of the Internet also reduces the agenda-setting power of news media organizations. It enables citizens to learn about politicians and their platforms in a direct fashion. Even individuals who are not especially interested in politics will be more motivated to use the Internet to learn about issues with political implications such as economic downturns or upswings, terrorism, or the environment (Davis, 1999). Furthermore, enabling audience members to access specialized material on websites makes "information transmission more effective" (Graber, 1996, p. 33).

The Bush and Gore websites used similar strategies to spotlight featured information. The center portion of the upper half of the screen on each website presented the most recent news about the candidate. Several lines of text from recent news releases appeared, and visitors to the website accessed the full report by clicking on these headlines. Stories occupying the center location of the entry page changed periodically throughout a twenty-four-hour cycle. Stories were archived in reverse chronological order after being replaced by a new feature story.

Both websites featured photo galleries of the candidates at various stops along the campaign trail. Each candidate offered pictorial screen savers that could be downloaded to a personal computer. Visitors to both websites could access audio and video clips, register for e-mail, get voter registration information, read information in Spanish, and find out how to volunteer. News items typically remained archived in various departments on both websites for approximately one to two weeks. After that, they were either deleted or indexed in various issues categories on the sites.

The Gore website (www.algore2000.com) contained a variety of subsections, such as "get to know us," "take action," "news," "speeches," "town hall," "*en espanol*," "stay connected," "watch and listen," and "more." An "issues" section across the top served as an indexing system in which archived information about thirty topics such as crime, Social Security, health care, and welfare reform was stored. Appearing under the issues section were four additional buttons labeled news, speeches, town hall, and *en espanol*. The Gore website entry page featured regularly changing photographs that often contained motion illustrating the content of the featured press releases.

The George Bush campaign website (www.georgewbush.com) was similar to Gore's with respect to the various departments and the presence of two or three featured stories appearing in the center of the screen. The news button located at the top of the page enabled visitors to access recent information in reverse chronological order. Some of the news releases were also simultaneously sorted into one of four categories: setting the record straight, latest news, fact, and fiction. Throughout the course of the campaign, the Bush entry page featured an unchanging, static photograph of the candidate and running mate Dick Cheney in the upper left-hand corner.

METHOD

To study similarities and differences between the websites, a senior researcher and three graduate students collected news releases and photographs or images on a daily basis during the fifty days prior to Election Day. Beginning September 18 and continuing until November 7, 2000, team members visited the websites each morning and stored each new news release into one electronic text file for Bush and one for Gore. Photographs or images were also collected and stored electronically on a regular basis. However, photographs in the photo gallery did not change with the frequency of the news releases. Instead, most of the images were archived into the galleries for each candidate for viewers to access at any time.

During periods of significant activity such as the days following presidential or vice presidential debates, the websites were evaluated several times throughout the day. Because the archival systems employed by both campaigns typically enabled the news releases to remain on the websites for at least several days (and often for several weeks) and the images remained throughout the entire campaign, the data-collection system employed assured that all releases and photographs or images were collected (McMillan, 2000).

Text Coding

The news releases varied from being one or two paragraphs containing an endorsement to lengthy acclaims, attacks, or rebuttals. The Bush campaign website yielded 259 news releases, and the Gore campaign website yielded 228. The 487 news releases produced two text files in excess of 1,250 pages containing more than 325,000 words. The news releases were analyzed using a coding instrument adapted from the one developed by the Center for Media and Public Affairs (CMPA) in 1996 (Lichter, Noyes, & Kaid, 1999). The news items posted on the websites were coded into the following twelve categories:

1. *General* stories about the presidential nominees, often about the candidates touring the country to talk about their agenda.
2. *Endorsements,* including releases dealing with the decision by an individual, group of persons, interest group, etc., to vote for a candidate or to support him.
3. *Rebuttals* in which a candidate responds to an attack or tries to deny allegations made by his opponents about him.
4. *Editorials* in which the information content clearly takes a position in favor of a candidate or the cause he is defending. These items can also reflect the point of view of the news organization on a particular candidate, an aspect of his campaign, or his issue proposals.
5. *Polls,* including content dealing with surveys on what the voters think of a candidate or the position of the candidates in the race, what voters think of the issues, what issue they consider the most important.
6. *Statements taking the form of a letter* issued by a candidate, his party, or a group of persons dealing with any particular issue of the campaign.
7. *Candidate interviews* in which a candidate, his campaign representative, or any other person involved in the election process speaks to journalists and answers their questions. This category also includes transcripts of videos or audio interviews.
8. *Onsite campaign reports* from journalists following the candidates throughout the country and reporting on their activities, meetings, and speeches.
9. *Statements by the candidate* made directly to his voters or to the citizens in general. These can be print, audio, or visual or transcripts of radio or television statements.
10. *Statements by campaign representatives* speaking on behalf of a candidate

or on behalf of the campaign and dealing with any of the aspects or issues of the presidential race.

11. *Reports on campaign advertisements* by journalists dealing with the new ads launched by candidates, the content of an actual commercial, the target of a commercial, the reaction of people about a new campaign ad, etc.

12. *Other, a category including,* releases that failed to fit the categories above.

The releases were also coded to: (1) evaluate *primary issue* or *topic;* (2) assess whether the news release contained an *attack;* (3) assess whether the news release addressed *personal characteristics/deficiencies* of candidates.

Attacks are defined as stories that focus mainly on personal aspects of a candidate, including his honesty, experience, record, background, sincerity, attitude, and tactics. Attacks also focus on a candidate's family members and friends. Attacks can also refer to rebuttals (e.g., when a candidate responds to an attack or tries to set the record straight by saying that the attacking candidate is a liar). As emphasized in the CMPA codebook, the candidates' discussions of the election issues (education, taxes, social security, etc.) can also have a negative tone. This may include negative references to what effect a candidate's program would have if enacted. Thus, statements that a proposal would cost jobs, create a drag on the economy, cost lives, or otherwise increase the risks or hazards faced by Americans have all been coded as attacks in this study.

The senior researcher supervised and monitored the coding of the textual content. Text coding was performed by one research associate who received twelve hours of training during a one-week period using news releases randomly selected from various political websites. The research associate coded each of the news releases, and the principal researcher coded 10% of the total population of news releases (Kaid & Wadsworth, 1989; Riffe, Lacy, & Fico, 1998). The coding categories included both dichotomous values such as whether the news release did or did not contain an attack and other categories that required coding from longer lists of items. These coding decisions included *type* of news release (i.e., twelve items addressing whether the release was a statement, an onsite campaign report, a rebuttal, etc.), whether *personal characteristics* were addressed (i.e., twenty-eight items addressing issues such as the honesty or integrity of a candidate, etc.), and *main topic* (i.e., sixty-one topics such as governmental spending, Social Security, taxes, etc.). Scott's pi yielded intercoder reliability values of .78 for whether a news release contained an attack, .90 for personal attributes/deficiencies of the candidates, .85 for type of news release, and .91 for main topic of the news release.

Image Coding

Photographs and images were evaluated using systems that had been devised to evaluate visual communications appearing in news magazines (Moriarty & Garramone, 1986; Moriarty & Popovich, 1991). Only photographs containing a candidate and/or running mate were coded. Photographs showing both the presidential candidate and his running mate were coded twice (once for each person) and treated as two separate photographs in this analysis. The unit of analysis was the photograph or visual image, which was coded to identify twenty-eight attributes intended to tap dimensions associated with behavior, context, and perspective (e.g., visual acuity). The variables coded were activity, posture, arms, hands, eye contact, pleasure, domination, approachability, interaction, political, issue versus image focus, leadership, attention, distance, friendliness, speech, props, setting, family, dress, time, camera angle, camera focus, light level, light direction, background, portrayal, and color.

One researcher coded the entire set of photographs, and a research associate coded seventy-five photographs (11%) that were selected randomly to assess intercoder reliability (Riffe, Lacy, & Fico, 1998; Wimmer & Dominick, 2000). Analysis using the Scott's pi formula (Scott, 1955) produced intercoder reliability coefficients between .90 and .91 for three variables, between .80 and .89 for seventeen variables, between .75 and .79 for five variables, and between .69 and .70 for two variables. Because these two variables (approachability and friendliness) did not achieve the acceptable Scott's pi level of .75, they were not included in this study.

ANALYSIS AND RESULTS

The websites yielded a total of 487 news releases and presented a total of 569 photographs featuring the two candidates. Many of the releases appeared first on the initial entry page containing the primary URL address and were later archived in various locations on the website. Other releases were placed initially in the website archival locations. The photographs and images were archived in the photo galleries.

Analysis of the news releases revealed that they were similar in their propensity to include an attack against their opponent. Specifically, 72% of the Bush news releases and 71% of the Gore news releases contained at least one attack. Conversely, 28% of the Bush press releases and 29% of the Gore press releases were acclaims designed to bolster support for the candidates.

Concerning news pertaining to the personal attributes of candidates, content placed on the websites was once again similar. Seventy-two percent of the Bush news releases dealt with the personal attributes of either Gore or vice presidential candidate Joe Lieberman. Of the 186 Bush news releases dealing with these personal attributes, 92 addressed Gore's strategy and tactics, 39 addressed his campaign conduct, and 23 addressed his professional background and qualifications. Seventy-seven percent of the Gore news releases dealt with the personal attributes of Bush or vice presidential candidate Dick Cheney. Of Gore's 175 news releases dealing with personal attributes, 70 addressed Bush's strategy and tactics, 69 addressed his professional background and qualifications, and 19 addressed his campaign conduct.

Rebuttals were the most common type of news release, totaling 129 for both candidates. The most frequent type of news release on the Bush campaign website was the rebuttal with 78 occurrences (30% of the Bush news releases), followed by editorials with 44 occurrences (17%). The most frequently occurring type of news release on the Gore campaign home page was the onsite campaign report with 58 occurrences (25% of the Gore news releases), followed by rebuttals with 51 occurrences (22%).

The Bush campaign posted only 67 photographs, while the Gore campaign posted 502. The candidates' use of images is a contrast to their use of headlines and news releases. None of the images were used to attack the other candidate, and very few images bore any negative symbolism.

DISCUSSION

The similarity in text but differences in imagery may best be explained in the context of both the competition model of political behavior (Ansolabehere & Iyengar, 1995) and differences in philosophy and orientation of the two candidates. Figure 13.1 illustrates the highly competitive nature of the 2000 presidential race throughout the campaign with neither candidate capable of widening and holding a lead. Following Labor Day, Gore held a slight advantage over Bush, which increased to ten points in the CNN/USA Today/Gallup tracking poll by September 21. But one week later, the candidates were in a virtual tie. On October 5, Gore had again opened up a ten-point lead, but it too dissipated by October 12, the date of the second presidential debate. By late October, Bush had opened up a ten-point lead, but by early November, the election was once again too close to call.

As Benoit and Currie (2001) have noted, candidates for public office have three means by which to persuade members of the public to vote for them: acclaims, attacks, and rebuttals. These three techniques serve as an informal form of cost-benefit analysis because acclaims stress a candidate's own benefits, attacks point out the risks of voting for an opponent, and rebuttals, or refutations, enable a candidate to address deficiencies alleged by an opponent.

Acclaims give voters reasons to vote for the candidate. As this chapter suggests, acclaims accounted for approximately 28% of the information posted on the websites. Candidates can also contrast themselves by criticizing or attacking the performance and positions of their opponents. Attacks give reasons to vote against opponents, and approximately 72% of the news releases posted on the websites included at least one attack on an opponent. Finally, candidates may refute attacks and charges made by opponents. As was also demonstrated, 30%

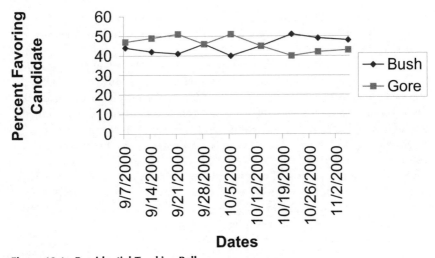

Dates

Figure 13.1: Presidential Tracking Poll

Source: Adapted from a CNN/*USA Today*/Gallup Presidential Tracking Poll; see http://www.cnn.com/ELEC TION/2000/poll/frameset.exclude.html

of the Gore news releases and 22% of the Bush news releases refuted accusations by opponents.

Political theory suggests that candidates in highly competitive races rely heavily on attacks to distinguish themselves from the competition. The political competition model predicts that candidates holding comfortable leads during campaigns tend to present more acclaims in an attempt to promote accomplishments and policy positions, while trailing candidates tend to contrast their positions with those of the front-runners (Ansolabehere & Iyengar, 1995; Haynes & Rhine, 1998; Pfau & Kenski, 1990). In close races without a clear front-runner, each candidate will tend to demonstrate significant attack behavior against opponents because attacks attract media attention and can weaken support for the opposing candidate (Wattenberg & Brians, 1999). Indeed, the closeness of the Millennium Election produced an environment in which negativity would prevail, either on the campaign websites or in other media.

Candidates used imagery quite differently on their websites, perhaps in part because the news media habitually portrayed Al Gore as the stiff and George W. Bush as a somewhat dull and faltering candidate. Through the analysis of the images on both websites, this study indicates that the photographs were intended to serve a public relations function to improve the candidate's image with the media and the public instead of attacking the opposition. Both candidates appear to have tried to counteract the news media through their website images. Bush incorporated many photographs of himself in suit and tie, appearing to be professional, businesslike, and serious. He was shown, along with running mate Dick

Cheney, presenting speeches at large rallies, with various political and issue props in the background. The Bush website presented historical photographs including images of the candidate as a baby with his parents, playing Little League baseball, in college, in the military, in his wedding to Laura, at the birth of his twins, and as governor of Texas. Current pictures of Bush with Laura were also found on the website, but overall, most of his current pictures were of Bush by himself.

Gore's images included the candidate in more casual clothes such as polo shirts and khaki pants. These photos portrayed Gore as more active, with his arms held high, shaking a supporter's hand, holding children, patting someone on the shoulder, or leaning in to hear supporters during casual conversations at restaurants, schools, and nursing homes. By far, Gore's website gallery had more photographs of him interacting with other people than did the Bush gallery. Gore appeared to be focused on his past political career and the current election rather than his personal past or present. He did integrate images of his daughters and wife, including the infamous kiss with Tipper, but nearly all of those photographs were from the current campaign for president, and nearly all were from campaign stops during state-to-state tours.

The difference in the number of photographs posted on the two websites may reflect the degree to which the Gore campaign is focused on Internet technologies. Top computer scientists assert that Gore played a key role in helping the Internet to evolve by lobbying for governmental financing and support. Vint Cerf and Bob Kahn, technologists who wrote the protocols in 1973 that first allowed diverse computers to network, leading to the eventual evolution of the Internet, have acknowledged Gore's contributions as a congressman and senator and as vice president. Cerf and Kahn write, "No other elected official, to our knowledge, has made a greater contribution over a longer period of time" in pushing for government support that would accelerate the growth of the Web (quoted in Thompson, 2000, p. B15). Hence, it is not surprising that the Gore campaign would endeavor to take full advantage of the Internet technologies at their disposal including significant use of photo galleries. Also noteworthy was the use of animation and imagery to support the news releases presented.

CONCLUSION

The Millennium Election may have signaled an important turning point for the Internet as a political communication tool. Recognizing its potential, both candidates attempted to use the Internet to bolster their campaigns through acclaims, but it was also used to a significant extent to both attack opponents and attempt to respond to charges from opposing candidates. With respect to the use of text, both campaigns used the Internet in a similar way. Concerning images, the Gore campaign presented many more and attempted to use pictures both to maintain the attention of audiences through moving images and to illustrate themes presented in text. Future research on campaigns and elections should continue to evaluate the ways in which images are employed to enhance political communication.

REFERENCES

Ansolabehere, S., & Iyengar, S. (1995). *Going negative: How attack ads shrink and polarize the electorate.* New York: Free Press.

Benoit, W. L., & Currie, H. (2001). Inaccuracies in media coverage of the 1996 and 2000 presidential debates. *Argumentation and Advocacy, 38* (1), 28–39.

Connell, M. (1997). New ways to reach voters and influence public opinion on the Internet. *Campaigns and Elections, 18* (8), 64–68.

Davis, R. (1999). *The web of politics: The Internet's impact on the American political system.* New York: Oxford University Press.

Graber, D. A. (1996). The "new" media and politics: What does the future hold? *Political Science and Politics, 29,* 33–36.

Harbert, T. (2000). Election 2000: A high-tech watershed. *Electronic Business, 26,* 70–78.

Haynes, A. A., & Rhine, S. L. (1998). Attack politics in presidential nomination campaigns: An examination of the frequency and determinants of intermediated negative messages against opponents. *Political Research Quarterly, 51,* 691–721.

Kaid, L. L., & Wadsworth, A. J. (1989). Content analysis. In P. Emmert & L. L. Barker (Eds.), *Measurement of communication behavior* (pp. 197–217). New York: Longman.

Lichter, S. R., Noyes, R. E., & Kaid, L. L., (1999). No news or negative news: How the networks nixed the '96 campaign. In L. L. Kaid & D. G. Bystrom (Eds.), *The electronic election: Perspectives on the 1996 campaign communication* (pp. 3–14). Mahwah, NJ: Lawrence Erlbaum Associates.

McMillan, S. J. (2000). The microscope and the moving target: The challenge of applying content analysis to the World Wide Web. *Journalism and Mass Communication Quarterly, 77,* 80–98.

Moriarty, S. E., & Garramone, G. M. (1986). A study of newsmagazine photographs of the 1984 presidential campaign. *Journalism Quarterly, 63,* 728–734.

Moriarty, S. E., & Popovich, M. N. (1991). Newsmagazine visuals and the 1988 presidential election. *Journalism Quarterly, 68,* 371–380.

Pfau, M., & Kenski, H. C. (1990). *Attack politics: Strategy and defense.* New York: Praeger.

Riffe, D., Lacy, S. D., & Fico, F. (1998). *Analyzing media messages: Using quantitative content analysis in research.* Mahwah, NJ: Lawrence Erlbaum Associates.

Rumbough, T., & Tomlinson, J. (2000, November). *Internet 2000: Evolution of Internet content and effects.* Paper presented at the National Communication Association Convention, Seattle.

Scott, W. A. (1955). Reliability of content analysis: The case of nominal scale coding. *Public Opinion Quarterly, 17,* 321–325.

Selnow, G. W. (1998). *Electronic whistle-stops: The impact of the Internet on American politics.* Westport, CT: Praeger.

Thompson, C. (2000, Oct. 15). Net cetera: The Al Gore Internet is not as crazy as it may seem. *Newsday,* p. B15.

Wattenberg, M. P., & Brians, C. L. (1999). Negative campaign advertising: Demobilizer or mobilizer. *American Political Science Review, 93,* 891–899.

Wimmer, R. D., & Dominick, J. R. (2000). *Mass media research: An introduction* (6th ed.). Belmont, CA: Wadsworth.

14

Prelude to a Divide

Who Had Access in 2000?

Thomas P. Boyle

As a prelude to a consideration of knowledge gaps between individuals, access to media has been explored and the emergence of the World Wide Web has piqued interest in media access (e.g., Bucy, 2000). Media scholars have investigated the "gaps" of knowledge and information attributed to media exposure or attention for decades. Tichenor, Donohue, and Olien noted the gaps found by early media researchers and were the first to use the term the " 'knowledge gap' hypothesis" (1970, p. 160). The researchers investigated the hypothesis in two communities during a newspaper strike in 1959 and in two other studies (1970, p. 161). They posited that "communication skills, prior knowledge, social contact, and attitudinal selectivity" all increased the gap in knowledge between groups of different educational levels (1970, p. 163). Across all the three communities, Tichenor, Donohue, and Olien confirmed a relationship between exposure and attention to the print media, education, and increasing gaps about significant issues.

In a later study of nineteen communities, Tichenor, Donohue, and Olien identified three areas where different groups might be limited to knowledge: "access, distribution, and reinforcement" (1980, p. 184). Since then the results of ninety-seven knowledge gap studies found that gaps existed in one-time and across-time studies (Gaziano, 1997). Gaziano noted that *access* to the media was one of a number of "external barriers to knowledge acquisition" (Gaziano, 1997, p. 246). Clearly, access is a major first step to any knowledge gap that might occur.

Since the seminal work by Tichenor, Donohue, and Olien, newer media have held promise as a way to level the socioeconomic playing field and promote greater access. In fact, Tichenor, Donohue, and Olien note the great promise of television to narrow the gap (1970, p. 170). They say that "other mass information delivery systems may be required" to reduce knowledge gaps (1970, p. 170). Gaziano notes that while television may increase the distribution of knowledge to different segments, its ability to narrow knowledge gaps is unproven (1997, pp. 249–250). The results from the studies she considered may be—at least in part—based on television's inability to explain complex issues (1997, p. 250). Media scholars have begun only recently to study the impact of access to the Web. For example, a study of the 1996 presidential election using the American National Election Study data found gaps based on demographic and newspaper-use variables, but Web use was not considered (Eveland & Scheufele, 2000).

Like television before it, the use of the Web has been heralded as a way to provide parity of information access to differing socioeconomic groups. Coming into the 2000 presidential election season, researchers discussed the promise of cyberpolitics. Examining the previous presidential election, studies noted that websites provide a myriad of political information and explored their use through focus group methodology (Jacques & Ratzan, 1997; Kern, 1997; West, 1997; Whillock, 1997). One researcher described how a candidate website "has the potential for leveling the playing field for less well-funded candidates and small parties" and therefore increase the ability to exchange political information (Just, 1997, p. 100). Many scholars discuss the potential of the Web to change the way voters go about obtaining information (Whillock, 1998, pp. 187–188).

Scholars began to study the emerging technology in the late 1990s (Bucy, 2000; Loges & Jung, 2001). In two statewide surveys conducted in 1998, Bucy found that age had a negative relationship and education had a positive relationship with use of the Web (2000, p. 59). In addition, variables measuring income and talk radio exposure were positive and significant predictors of Web use, while local news exposure was a negative predicator in data from Indiana (2000, p. 59). Bucy concluded that "the Internet is not yet a medium of the masses" and "there may be a looming information gap" based on access (2000, p. 59).

Loges and Jung found income and education had a positive relationship with Web access while age and gender (female) had negative relationships with access (2001, p. 552). The researchers found that across seven communities sampled during 1998–1999, age was a major and consistent predictor of access even when numerous other variables were held constant (2001, p. 554). Using an extensive index to measure Web access and use, they found that older respondents had "lower overall Internet connectedness" (Loges & Jung, 2001, p. 556). In fact, Loges and Jung found that younger and older respondents used their time on the Web differently with respect to functions like e-commerce (2001, pp. 556–557). The researchers conclude that as more experienced Web users age, the disparity between age groups might decrease, but they caution that it might be an oversimplification to call it "a generational phenomenon" (Loges & Jung,

2001, p. 559). They note that seniors a generation from now might—like seniors in the study—be less likely to share financial information and seek out information about the world around them via the Web (Loges & Jung, 2001, p. 559).

A study by the Pew Research Center found that 18% of consumers went online to gather information about the presidential candidates late in the campaign 2000 (Pew, 2000, p. 1). The 18% marks a 14% jump over a similar study done in 1996 (Pew, 2000, p. 1). In addition, almost 70% were interested in candidate issue information, and 43% said that information was used in their choice of candidates (Pew, 2002, p. 1). With large numbers of potential voters using the Web as an information source, examining what variables led to the ability to access the Web in 2000 is significant.

This study explores the following three hypotheses:

H₁: Age will be a negative predictor of Web-based political information gathering during the 2000 presidential campaign.

As explored extensively by Loges and Jung (2001), age has a consistently negative relationship with Web use. They note that older individuals differ significantly in the quantity and quality of time online. Bucy (2000) also found that age was a negative predictor of Web use.

H₂: Education and income will be positive predictors of Web-based political information gathering during the 2000 presidential campaign.

As noted, researchers have found that education and income have had a positive relationship with Web use (Loges & Jung, 2001; Bucy, 2000). This study investigates whether those relationships existed during the final weeks of the 2000 presidential election.

H₃: Print attention and campaign interest will be positive predictors of Web-based political information gathering during the 2000 presidential campaign.

Since access is crucial to information gathering and, later, potential knowledge gaps, it is of interest to explore other influences on the gathering of political information. Tichenor, Donohue, and Olien identified attention to newspapers as a significant way to learn about issues (1970). Also, Gaziano noted that issue interest has been shown to be "a knowledge gap leveler" in knowledge gap studies over the past three decades (1997, pp. 247–248). An overall interest in the campaign would be expected to lead to higher levels of Web attention in the presidential election of 2000.

DESIGN AND METHODS

To consider these questions, primary data were collected through telephone surveys of Pennsylvania adults in October and early November, 2000.[1] The calling sessions from a Pennsylvania university resulted in an approximately 50% completion rate and 392 completed surveys. This sample size is similar to other political communication studies (e.g., Drew & Weaver, 1998). A random-digit-dialing system used all available area codes and exchanges in the state.[2] To ensure a random member of the household was surveyed, the callers used the last-birthday method of choosing the adult respondent. Questions were similar to those in other political communication studies, including the media questions asked as part of the National Election Studies survey questions (Miller et al., 1993).

A series of thirteen questions asked about the respondents' media use during the past week. Respondents were asked how many days in the past week they read a daily newspaper, watched the news on television, or saw a talk show or political advertisement on television. Respondents were also asked how much attention they paid to the 2000 presidential race on a five-point media scale. In addition, respondents were asked how much attention they paid to stories on the radio about the presidential race and whether they saw any of the presidential debates or the vice presidential debate. Unlike some previous studies that inquired only about traditional media, in this study three questions asked about Web-based political information.

Web-based political information gathering was measured by three separate questions: exposure, attention, and visiting a candidate's website. Respondents were asked how many days in the past week they used the Internet and how much attention they paid to Web information about the presidential race; a dichotomous question asked if they visited any of the official websites of any presidential candidates.

In addition to the media questions, respondents were asked to rate their overall interest in the campaign on a five-point scale. The next block of questions asked which of the candidates held various positions on several major issues. Based on these six issues, a candidate issue index was constructed with a 1 given to every respondent answer identifying the correct position of the candidate. If respondents did not know which of the two major candidates held this position or if they answered incorrectly, their response was given a 0. This scoring procedure gave the index a range of 0 to 6. The mean of the index was 4.2, giving the researcher some confidence that the candidate issues queried were well known to the public.

Another index was composed of four questions addressing the likelihood that a respondent would vote. These four dichotomous questions asked if they had voted in previous elections and planned to vote in the November 7 presidential election. The range of this index was from 0 for four "no" responses to 4 for four "yes" responses.

Also, respondents were asked a series of demographic questions. This last set of questions dealt with gender, education level, age, race, and income. The ranges of these variables indicated a cross section of the voting public. Respondents in the sample ranged in age from eighteen to eighty-eight with an average age of forty-seven years. Education levels ranged from those with some high school education to those with graduate degrees. On average, respondents had some college education. The average income of those in the survey was in the $40,000 to $49,999 salary range. Women composed 58% of the sample and men 42%. Of the respondents, 90% self-identified as Caucasian, and 6% and 2% identified as African American and Hispanic, respectively.

RESULTS

As one might expect given general media usage patterns for political information, the average respondent reported paying "very little" attention to radio reports of campaign 2000 coverage, with slightly more attention to print and somewhat more attention to television coverage.

Before reporting the statistical responses to the hypotheses, some general survey results for the variables under analysis (age, education/income, and interest) will be described.

Age

Table 14.1 provides a cross tabulation of the percentages of the most general of the three Web variables, exposure. Respondents were asked how many days in the past week they used the Internet. The age group reporting the largest percentage (87%) with no exposure to the Web was those sixty-six years or older. In fact, as table 14.1 shows, the percentage reporting no Web exposure grew consistently among the various age groups defined in this survey from a low of 15% for those age eighteen through twenty-five years old to a high of 87% for those sixty-six years or older. Thus, as much as 85% of the younger respondents reported Web use as a form of campaign exposure.

Table 14.2 shows the cross tabulations for the other two Web variables: attention and visitation. Attention to the campaign on the Web is measured on a five-point scale from none to a great deal, while the Web-visitation variable asked respondents if they visited one of the official websites of any of the presidential candidates. Ninety percent of those aged fifty-six to sixty-five and 89% of those sixty-six and older paid no attention to campaign 2000 on the Web. While table 14.1 shows that younger respondents reported high levels of exposure, the attention variable is not as encouraging. In fact, the percentages that reported high levels of attention on the Web barely broke 10% for each of the three age groups covering eighteen- to forty-five-year-olds. Only among the twenty-six to thirty-five-year-olds did more than 5% of respondents report paying a great deal of attention to campaign information on the Web. As table 14.2 shows, the candidate websites may not be a large percentage of voter information, considering

Table 14.1   Cross Tabulations of Web Exposure and Major Variables (%)

	Web Exposure			
	None	*1–2 Days*	*3–4 Days*	*5–7 Days*
Age				
18–25	15	5	12	68
26–35	27	11	20	43
36–45	32	11	15	43
46–55	40	10	15	35
56–65	64	4	8	25
66+	87	3	3	7
Education				
Some H.S.	77	5	5	14
H.S. Dip.	7	8	13	12
Some Coll.	33	4	17	47
Coll. Dgr.	28	13	15	44
Grad. Dgr.	21	7	10	62
Income				
< $20,000	70	0	2	28
$20–$29,999	65	8	11	17
$30–$39,999	52	16	12	20
$40–$49,999	39	8	10	44
$50–$59,999	32	10	20	39
$60–$69,999	39	0	19	44
$70,000+	19	7	18	57
Gender				
Women	49	10	12	29
Men	37	5	12	46
Race				
Caucasian	45	9	12	35
Minority	34	5	15	46
Interest				
None	50	6	11	33
Very Little	45	8	11	37
Some	45	8	13	34
Quite A Bit	43	11	15	8
Great Deal	43	6	10	6
Print Attn				
None	39	9	5	47
Very Little	42	11	13	33
Some	55	5	12	28
Quite A Bit	39	11	18	32
Great Deal	37	2	15	46
TV Attn				
None	37	10	8	46
Very Little	58	5	5	32
Some	42	7	15	37
Quite A Bit	49	12	13	27
Great Deal	35	8	11	47
Radio Attn				
None	51	7	8	35
Very Little	50	9	9	33
Some	41	8	14	38
Quite A Bit	34	13	19	34
Great Deal	18	9	21	52

that not even 25% of respondents in any age group reported visiting one of the candidates' official websites.

Education/Income

The breakdown by education and income indicates that these are also important variables in political Web use. For example, table 14.1 shows that respondents with only some high school were much more likely to report no Web exposure than those with advanced degrees, 77% to 21%, respectively. Likewise, increases in income generally translated to more Web exposure. The group with the highest education level also had the highest percentage of those with heavy Web exposure. Those reporting high household income also had the highest exposure to the Web (57%).

As table 14.2 shows, those with the lowest amount of education (some high school) were least likely to pay attention to the campaign on the Web. On the other end, more than 10% of respondents with graduate degrees reported that they paid "a great deal" of attention to the campaign on the Web. Those with a higher income also reported paying more attention to the campaign on the Web.

As with Web attention, those reporting the highest level of education had the highest percentage of respondents (13%) reporting at least one visit to a candidate's website. The two groups representing the highest levels of income had the highest percentage who visited a candidate site (19% and 21%).

Race/Gender

Interestingly, there appears to be a slight gender divide in exposure to political information on the Web. Nearly 49% of women reported no exposure compared to only 37% of men. Twenty-nine percent of women and 46% of men reported heavy Web exposure. Some gender differences were apparent with regard to attention to political information on the Web, with women reporting that they paid less attention to the campaign on the Web than did men. As with other measures, women were less likely (11%) than men (17%) to visit a candidate website.

Somewhat surprisingly, given general Web use patterns, Caucasians in this survey were less likely than minority respondents to indicate exposure to the Web. In fact, nearly 45% of Caucasians reported no Web exposure, compared to only 34% of minorities with no exposure. Thirty-four percent of Caucasians and 46% of minority groups reported heavy Web exposure in the previous week. Differences in Web attention based on ethnicity were less apparent than those identified for gender.

Of those identifying with a minority group, 14% visited sites, while 10% of Caucasians reported such visits.

Table 14.2   Cross Tabulations of Web Attention and Major Variables (%)

	Web Attention					Web Visit	
	None	*Very Little*	*Some*	*Quite A Bit*	*Great Deal*	*No*	*Yes*
Age							
18–25	49	17	20	10	3	78	22
26–35	70	6	8	11	6	76	24
36–45	62	14	9	11	4	85	16
46–55	83	5	7	1	4	93	7
56–65	90	4	2	0	4	92	8
66+	89	6	2	2	2	100	0
Education							
Some H.S.	89	0	6	0	6	89	11
H.S. Dip.	87	5	3	4	1	89	11
Some Coll.	73	11	10	3	3	86	14
Coll. Dgr.	66	10	12	10	3	88	13
Grad. Dgr.	59	12	9	9	11	77	23
Income							
< $20,000	76	12	7	5	0	88	12
$20–$29,999	82	2	7	2	7	89	11
$30–$39,999	85	4	6	2	2	85	15
$40–$49,999	76	5	8	8	3	95	5
$50–$59,999	68	12	10	7	2	90	10
$60–$69,999	68	10	10	3	10	81	19
$70,000+	61	15	10	8	6	79	21
Gender							
Women	80	6	5	6	3	89	11
Men	67	12	10	6	5	82	18
Race							
Caucasian	76	8	7	6	4	90	10
Minority	60	13	15	10	3	86	14
Interest							
None	94	6	0	0	0	100	0
Very Little	76	8	14	0	3	86	14
Some	71	10	10	8	1	89	11
Quite A Bit	81	8	3	8	2	91	9
Great Deal	66	9	11	6	9	78	22
Print Attn							
None	78	5	5	10	3	86	14
Very Little	78	14	3	3	1	94	6
Some	80	5	8	5	3	87	13
Quite A Bit	69	10	12	7	2	86	14
Great Deal	51	13	18	4	13	69	31
TV Attn							
None	76	8	8	4	4	82	18
Very Little	80	9	6	4	2	87	13
Some	72	9	9	7	3	86	14
Quite A Bit	78	8	3	8	2	93	7
Great Deal	65	9	12	5	9	81	19
Radio Attn							
None	79	8	4	3	5	91	9
Very Little	81	10	4	4	1	86	14
Some	74	5	9	9	3	78	22
Quite A Bit	65	9	13	11	2	96	4
Great Deal	46	15	21	9	9	69	31

Interest

As expected, those who reported no general interest in the campaign reported little Web exposure to political information. Interestingly, those reporting less interest in the campaign, as defined by indicating none, very little, or some general interest in the campaign, had fairly large percentages of respondents who reported high Web exposure. Conversely, the respondents with a great deal of campaign interest were less likely to report heavy Web exposure to political information. Thus, it appears that the Web is more likely a primary source of political information gathering for those less interested in the campaign.

Although some fairly large percentages of the less interested respondents report using the Web for political information, the numbers do not indicate large amounts of attention paid to the political information. Those in the survey reporting the least interest in the campaign in general also had the highest percentage (nearly 94%) of those who paid no attention to it on the Web. Also of note is the finding that only 9% of those reporting a great deal of campaign interest said they paid a great deal of attention to the campaign information on the Web. Considering other media attention, the only group with a double-digit percentage (13%) who paid a great deal of attention to the candidates on the Web were daily newspaper readers. Concerning television attention to the campaign, the group that reported paying a great deal of attention to the campaign on television also reported paying similarly high attention to it on the Web—at 9% this figure is double that of any other group.

As might be expected, campaign interest itself was a good indicator of candidate website visitation. Of those highly interested in the campaign in general, more than 22% visited a website. More than 31% of those who paid a great deal of attention to the campaign in the daily newspaper and on the radio also visited an official candidate website.

Statistical Analysis

Tables 14.1 and 14.2 show some general patterns of Web exposure, attention, and visitation that would appear to indicate reasonable support for the hypotheses under investigation in this study.

As table 14.3 shows, the demographic, campaign, and media blocks of variables regressed on the most general of the Web variables, Web exposure. Throughout the three models, education was consistently statistically significant and positive at .85. Every level of education the respondents reported would predict almost another day in exposure to the Web. The coefficient representing the age variable was consistently significant and negative, but much smaller. Unlike the age groups in the previous tables, the age variable is measured in one-year increments. Consequently, every twenty years in age would predict one less day of Web exposure. Income was also statistically significant and positive at .21.

Every five steps up the income scale would predict one additional day of Web exposure per week.

The dichotomous variable measuring vote decision was large and positive at .73 in the full model. Already having made a vote decision would translate into additional Web exposure. The only other statistically significant variable in that block is likelihood to vote, which is negative at .31 in the second model and .28 in the third model. An increased likelihood to vote would predict less exposure to the Web.

The last block considered a variety of media variables. The coefficient representing advertising attention is -.30. Three increases in the level of attention to television campaign advertising would predict almost one day less of Web exposure. This full model with the media variables has the highest adjusted R^2 of .39.

Findings from the Web attention variable were also analyzed (not shown here). This variable asked respondents how much attention they paid to the presidential campaign on the Web. As seen in the previous analyses, age and education were statistically significant across the models. Ranging from .19 to .23, the

Table 14.3   Hierarchical Regression Analysis of Predictors of Web Exposure

Predictor Variables	Regression 1	Regression 2	Regression 3
Constant	2.82	2.03	3.13
Gender (male)	.15	.14	.06
Education	.84***	.86***	.84***
Age	−.06***	−.06***	−.05***
Race (Caucasian)	−.73	−.69	−.83
Income	.21**	.23**	.22**
Campaign Interest		.11	.16
Vote Decision (yes)		.61	.73*
Issue Knowledge		.04	−.01
Likelihood to Vote		−.31**	−.28*
Print Exposure			−.08
Print Attention			.13
TV Exposure			−.11
TV Attention			.07
TV Talk Exposure			−.03
TV Talk Attention			.08
Radio Attention			.06
Debates Viewing			−.04
Advertising Exposure			−.04
Advertising Attention			−.30*
R^2	.37	.39	.43
Adjusted R^2	.36	.38	.39

*$p \leq .05$ **$p \leq .01$ ***$p \leq .001$
N = 392. High levels of multicollinearity are *not* present based on the Variance-Inflation Factor.

education variable would indicate a positive relationship between the level of formal education and attention level to the campaign through the Web. Compared to the lowest level of education (some high school) a respondent would increase nearly one level of attention if they were at the highest level (graduate degree). Age was again a negative predictor of a Web variable, yet the age variable was very small at .01 in all three models.

In the campaign block, the campaign interest variable was a significant and positive predictor of Web attention to the presidential campaign in model 2. In the third model, the only media variable that was statistically significant was print attention at .13. The only other media variable of that size was television talk attention, which was significant at the .06 level. These two variables contrast with all other media variables, which were very small at -.01. The adjusted R^2 for the three models ranged from .11 to .16.

Logistic regressions on the dichotomous variable that asked respondents if they visited an official website of one of the presidential candidates was also considered (not shown here). Like the ordinary least squares models in the previous table, the logistic models show that age was negatively associated with visiting a website. Every year of age would indicate a 3 to 4% reduction in the odds of visiting a website.[3]

Considering the campaign and media blocks, the campaign interest variable is large and significant in both models—.62 and .58. Every increase in the scale measuring campaign interest significantly increases the odds of an individual visiting a candidate website. The variable measuring how knowledgeable about candidates' stands on the issues was also positive and significant. The more knowledgeable individuals were about where the candidates stood on the issues, the greater the likelihood that they would visit a site. Of the media variables, only attention to the campaign in a daily newspaper reached statistical significance; it was positive at .42. For this variable, for every additional level of attention to the campaign in a newspaper, the respondent's odds of visiting an official candidate website would increase by more than 50%.[4] All three of the models correctly predicted the outcomes 85% or more of the time.

CONCLUSION

This study sought to investigate access to the Web during the 2000 presidential campaign with three separate Web measures: exposure, attention, and visits to an official candidate website. The first hypothesis was supported with age being a negative predictor—albeit a small one—for using the Web to gather information about the 2000 presidential campaign. The predictor of age was consistently negative across all three Web measures.

Education and income were hypothesized to be positive predictors of using Web sources. Education was found to be a positive predictor of Web exposure and attention but not for visiting official candidate websites. Income was found to be a positive predictor of Web exposure but not of Web attention or website visits.

The analysis here supports the role of attention to campaign 2000 in daily newspapers as a positive predictor of attention to the Web and visits to official candidate websites but not of Web exposure. Also considered in the third hypothesis was the role of general campaign interest to predict Web use. General campaign interest was found to be a positive predictor of Web attention in one of the two models presented here. Much stronger support was found for the positive ability of campaign interest to increase the odds of visiting one of the official candidate websites.

Other variables in the models that emerged as predictors of Web use in 2000 were vote decision, likelihood to vote, attention to televised campaign advertising, and knowledge about where the candidates stood on the issues. Vote decision and likelihood to vote were supported as positive and negative predictors of Web exposure, respectively. The converse predictive ability of the two variables deserves additional attention in future elections. The positive predictive relationship of having already made a decision about the candidates might indicate that committed voters sought out additional information on the Web to reinforce their beliefs. The negative predictive relationship of likelihood to vote might indicate the influence of younger respondents in the models. Younger respondents are much more likely to be heavy Web users but also are much more likely to lack a history of voting behavior over the past few years as measured by the likelihood-to-vote variable.

The only other variable from the campaign block not already discussed is the positive influence of issue knowledge on visiting a candidate website. Caution should be given to an analysis of these two variables since issue knowledge might be predicted by website visits—a potential digital-divide issue that goes beyond the scope of this analysis. Still, we found that the more familiar respondents were with where the candidates stood on the issues, the greater the odds that they visited an official website of one of the presidential candidates. Along with attention to the campaign in a daily newspaper, the only other media variable that emerged as significant was paying attention to the campaign in television advertisements—a negative predictor of Web exposure. The negative predictive ability of this variable on the most general of the Web variables, exposure, might result from the different nature of access to the two media. One might posit that the negative issue information individuals received from television advertisements might drive down information seeking in other media, but the nature of access to Web exposure involves many other variables (e.g., age) that would have greater influence.

The increase in the use of the Web continues to present great potential for gathering information on presidential campaigns. It still has the ability to empower those with lesser resources—candidates, campaigns, and individuals—

but it was far from providing universal access in 2000. The Web might help level the playing field for those seeking political information in future elections. Yet, this study indicates that in 2000 access was still determined largely by demographic variables (e.g., age) and media behaviors associated with them (e.g., attention to a daily newspaper). The potential leveling ability of the Web remains, but in 2000 it was still a very uneven landscape.

NOTES

1. The author would like to thank Susquehanna University for providing funding for this project.
2. Using standard estimating procedures, this sample size would produce a maximum sampling error of approximately $\pm$ 4.6% at the 95% confidence level (Babbie, 1998, p. 38).
3. This percentage comes from the Exp(B) not shown. See Pampel (2000, pp. 35–36) for additional information about this calculation.
4. This percentage comes from the Exp(B) not shown. See Pampel (2000, pp. 35–36) for additional information about the calculation.

REFERENCES

Babbie, E. (1998). *Basics of social research*. Belmont, Calif.: Wadsworth.
Bucy, E. (2000). Social access to the Internet. *Harvard International Journal of Press/Politics, 5* (1), 50–61.
Drew, D., and Weaver, D. (1998). Voter learning in the 1996 presidential election: Did the media matter? *Journalism and Mass Communication Quarterly, 75,* 292–301.
Eveland, W. P., & Scheufele, D. A. (2000). Connecting news media use with gaps in knowledge and participation. *Political Communication, 17,* 215–237.
Gaziano, C. (1997). Forecast 2000: Widening knowledge gaps. *Journalism and Mass Communication Quarterly, 74,* 237–264.
Jacques, W. W., & Ratzan, S. C. (1997). The Internet's World Wide Web and political accountability: New media coverage of the 1996 presidential debates. *American Behavioral Scientist, 40,* 1226–1237.
Just, M. R. (1997). Candidate strategies and the media campaign. In G. M. Pomper (Ed.), *The election of 1996* (pp. 77–106). Chatham, NJ: Chatham House.
Kern, M. (1997). Social capital and citizen interpretation of political ads, news, and web site information in the 1996 presidential election. *American Behavioral Scientist, 40,* 1238–1249.
Loges, W. E., & Jung, J-Y. (2001). Exploring the digital divide, Internet connectedness and age. *Communication Research, 28,* 536–562.
Miller, W. E., Kinder, D. R., Rosenstone, R. J., & the National Election Studies. (1993). *American National Election Study, 1992: Pre- and Post-Election Survey [Enhanced with 1990 and 1991 Data]*. Inter-university Consortium for Political and Social Research, Ann Arbor: University of Michigan.

Pampel, F. C. (2000). *Logistic regression: A primer.* Beverly Hills, CA: Sage.

Pew Research Center for the People and the Press. (2000). *Internet election news audience seeks conveniences, familiar names. Survey reports, December 2000.* Washington, DC: Pew Research.

Tichenor, P. J., Donohue, G. A., & Olien, C. N. (1970). Mass media flow and differential growth in knowledge. *Public Opinion Quarterly, 34,* 159–170.

Tichenor, P. J., Donohue, G. A., & Olien, C. N. (1980). *Community conflict and the press.* Beverly Hills, CA: Sage.

West, D. (1997). *Air wars: Television advertising in election campaigns, 1952–1996.* (2nd ed.). Washington, DC: Congressional Quarterly.

Whillock, R. K. (1997). Cyber-Politics: The online strategies of '96. *American Behavioral Scientist, 40,* 1208–1225.

Whillock, R. K. (1998). Digital democracy: The '96 presidential campaign on-line. In R. E. Denton (Ed.), *The 1996 presidential campaign: A communication perspective* (pp. 179–197). Westport, CT: Praeger.

IV

SOCIALIZING THE YOUNG VOTER
IN CAMPAIGN 2000

15

Political Discussion and Media Use

Contrasts between Early and Late Campaign Phases

Arla Bernstein

The process of engagement in a political campaign can be compared to diffusion of an innovation, in that during each process, information is disseminated from "experts" to a wider population over a period of time. According to diffusion theory, early adopters of an innovation are more reliant on external information, such as from the media, than on interpersonal communication. Since few people have knowledge about the innovation at the early phase of diffusion, they are more likely to rely on the media than on interpersonal communication. On the other hand, in the latter phases of innovation diffusion, individuals are more knowledgeable about the innovation and are more likely to discuss the innovation with others.

Political campaigns disseminate information about a candidate or campaign issue, and comparing political campaigns to innovation diffusion suggests that political engagement and communication behavior during a campaign may vary between early and late phases of a political campaign. A related area of inquiry is whether people are more likely to engage in interpersonal communication or "talk politics" in the later phase of a campaign as compared with their media use (an external source of information) for obtaining news about the campaign. News media exposure is a universal trigger for political conversation, and both news media use and political discussion are considered significant predictors of political engagement (Kim, Wyatt, & Katz, 1999).

Political talk or discussion as a micropolitical process influences important decision-making processes during electoral campaigns (Huckfeldt & Sprague,

1995; Kenny, 1998). Genuine discourse among friends and family members transmits political information and is a form of social interaction that has significant political consequences (Kenny, 1998). It is a form of social interaction that democratic theorists regard as important because discussion is the "soul of democracy" (Kim et al., 1999, p. 362) and allows people to "share ideas, formulate political positions, and come to understand alternative points of view" (Burns, Schlozman, & Verba, 2001, p. 311). However, the occurrence of political talk is a politicizing experience that may have diminished in recent years owing to the dominance of television watching, which has displaced much civic engagement (Putnam, 1995). On the other hand, a longitudinal study from the late 1950s to the early 1990s indicates stability in the frequency of discussion-based political engagement (Bennett, Flickinger, & Rhine, 2000). The current study investigates not only the frequency of political discussion during an electoral campaign overall but also the occurrence of informal political discussion in social relationships as it contrasts with other forms of political engagement during the 2000 electoral campaign.

Political discussion as a form of political participation is embedded in the contrast between active and passive political engagement. For example, whereas following political campaigns through the mass media is generally considered "a passive form of political participation" (Bucy, D'Angelo, & Newhagen, 1999, p. 338), political discussion in its various forms is one type of active political engagement (Bennett et al., 2000). This study examines contrasts between active and passive forms of engagement during early and late campaign phases. It also addresses gender differences in political engagement as they relate to these contextual processes.

In recent decades, the gender gap in political engagement may have narrowed in terms of voting turnout, but gender differences in other areas of political involvement endure. Studies have indicated that women—especially young women—are less interested than men in following politics in the media, engaging in political discussion, and getting involved in campaign activities (Bennett et al., 2000; Capella & Jamieson, 1996; Conway, Steuernagel, & Ahern, 1997).

POLITICAL ENGAGEMENT IN EARLY
AND LATE CAMPAIGN PHASES

To contextualize political discussion as an active form of political engagement and political interest as passive political engagement, a useful starting point is the possible variation of overall political engagement from early to late campaign. Based on the logic that political engagement overall increases as an election becomes more imminent, the following hypothesis is proposed:

H_1: Political engagement occurs at a higher level during the latter phase of a campaign than during the early phase.

Furthermore, given that previous research indicates a gender difference in political engagement, the following question is put forth:

RQ$_1$: Does a gender difference exist for this campaign phase effect?

Active versus Passive Political Engagement

While it is generally agreed that political discussion improves the quality of public opinion and enhances civic-mindedness (Bennett et al., 2000), there may be variation in its role during the early and late phases of an electoral campaign. Although this variation could have significant implications for political campaigns, a dearth of research exists in this area. Passive political engagement in this study is defined as a composite measure of general political interest, interest in presidential campaigns, interest in congressional campaigns, and following political campaigns. Active political engagement is defined as political discussion. Along the lines of diffusion theory, it is expected that:

H$_2$: Political engagement is more active in the late campaign than in the early campaign.

A concern for gender differences suggested the first research question:

RQ$_2$: Does a gender difference exist for this campaign phase effect?

The fact that politically oriented, interpersonal communication may be higher late in the campaign when citizens' knowledge of candidates is higher led to the third hypothesis and a second research question:

H$_3$: Generally, people are more likely to "talk politics" in the latter phase than in the early phase of a campaign.
RQ$_3$: Does a gender difference exist for this campaign phase effect?

Contrasting Political Discussion with Media Use during Early and Late Campaign

Political discussion often occurs in the private sphere, but information is fed into it from the public sphere—including the media. Given that reliance on news media use relative to interpersonal communication may be higher early in the campaign when citizens' knowledge regarding candidates is low, the following hypothesis and research question are proposed:

H$_4$: The ratio of news media exposure to political discussion is higher in the early campaign than in the late campaign.

RQ_4: Does a gender difference exist for this campaign phase effect?

Given that newspaper reading and Internet browsing are generally considered more active than television watching, the fifth hypothesis and a related research question are suggested:

H_5: Newspaper reading for news and Internet browsing for news are more predictive of political discussion than is television watching.
RQ_5: Does a gender difference exist for the relationship between political discussion and different types of news media exposure?

A Contextual Model of Political Discussion

To contextualize campaign phase as a predictor of political discussion in a model of relative strength of the predictor variables, a regression analysis was conducted with the following variables: campaign phase, gender, newspaper reading for news, television watching for news, and Internet browsing for news.

RQ_6: Is campaign phase a stronger predictor of political discussion than is gender or media exposure?
RQ_7: Is there a gender difference in the relative strength of campaign phase and media exposure as predictors of political discussion?

METHOD

The study sampled college students to examine political engagement among young adults who have access to the Internet. Given the interest in Internet browsing for news that is a component of this study, the use of college students ensures a sample that has easier access to media technology than does the general population. A survey-based study of political engagement was conducted among 525 undergraduate students at a large northeastern university during the 2000 presidential and congressional campaign. Students in nine different communication courses were asked to voluntarily participate in a survey regarding social and political views. The two-phase, cross-sectional survey was administered during the spring (N = 289) and fall (N = 236) of the 2000 campaign. The survey questionnaire included items regarding political engagement and media use.

Dependent Variables

The survey questionnaire was designed to provide data pertaining to political interest and activity, including the dependent variables of political discussion (active political engagement), ratio of news media exposure to political discussion, and passive political engagement. Passive political engagement included the following four variables: general political interest, interest in the presidential election, interest in the congressional election, and following political campaigns. For each question pertaining to the political engagement variables, respondents were asked to select responses from a five-point scale ranging from "none" to "a great deal."

For the first hypothesis, which pertains to overall political engagement, active political engagement and passive political engagement variables were combined into one composite variable or index. The factor analysis for this political engagement index indicated a one-factor solution for the five items (table 15.1) with factor loadings of .79 and higher, and an internal consistency analysis was conducted resulting in a Cronbach's alpha of .91, explaining 73% of the variance. For the second hypothesis, which compared active and passive engagement, a passive political engagement index was constructed as previously described. A factor analysis indicated that the four items had factor loadings of .82 and higher, and an internal consistency analysis was conducted resulting in a Cronbach's alpha of .89, explaining 75% of the variance.

The ratio of news media exposure to political discussion was calculated by dividing each of the news media exposure variables by the amount of political discussion. News media exposure was calculated as: average number of hours per week reading newspaper news, average number of hours per week watching television news, and average number of hours per week browsing the Internet for news.

Table 15.1 Means and Standard Deviations for Political Engagement and Media Use Items

	Females (n = 326)		Males (n = 194)	
	M	SD	M	SD
Political engagement, passive				
General political interest	2.8	.85	3.1	.99
Interest in presidential election	3.2	.95	3.4	1.06
Interest in congressional election	2.2	.81	2.3	.94
Follow political campaign	2.6	.92	2.9	1.03
Political engagement, active				
Participate in political discussion	2.6	.92	2.9	.87
Media type				
Browse the Internet for news	0.9	.91	1.3	1.11
Watch television for news	1.5	.94	1.7	.99
Read the newspaper for news	1.5	.84	1.6	1.03

Note: For political engagement items: 1 = none, 2 = very little, 3 = some, 4 = quite a bit, and 5 = a great deal. For media exposure items: 0 = 0 hours, 1 = 1–2 hours, 2 = 3–4 hours, 3 = 5–6 hours, and 4 = 7+ hours.

Independent Variables

Independent variables included gender, campaign phase, and news media exposure as predictors of political engagement. Campaign phase was conceptualized as early and late phases of the 2000 presidential and congressional campaigns. The early phase was operationally defined as spring 2000 and the late phase as fall 2000. Media exposure variables included browsing the Internet for news, watching television news, and reading newspaper news.

Data Analysis

In this study, five hypotheses were posited to explain the relationship between political engagement and campaign phase and between political engagement and media use. The first four hypotheses were tested through the analysis of variance (ANOVA) approach. ANOVA was also used to test gender differences in these relationships. The fifth hypothesis was tested using a regression analysis. Finally, a contextual model for campaign phase effects was explored through regression analysis addressing the last two research questions (6 and 7).

RESULTS

Descriptive Analysis

In addition to overall levels of political engagement and media exposure for the total sample, the responses of males and females were analyzed separately for the components of the political engagement indices and news media exposure (means in table 15.1). Women were found to have less general political interest than men, $F(1,520) = 10.99$, $p < .01$; discuss politics less than men did, $F(1,520) = 7.45$, $p < .01$; and follow political campaigns less than men did, $F(1,520) = 6.42$, $p \leq .02$. Regarding news media exposure, women were found to watch television news and browse the Internet for news less than men, $F(1,519) = 7.42$, $p < .01$ for television watching, and $F(1,519) = 26.52$, $p < .01$ for Internet browsing.

Results for Hypotheses

As expected, overall political engagement was found to be higher in the late (fall) phase of the election campaign, $F(1,522) = 10.89$, $p < .01$ (means in table 15.2). Therefore, H_1 was supported. No interaction was found between campaign phase and gender for overall political engagement. Therefore, no gender difference was found for the effect of campaign phase on level of political engagement. The second hypothesis posited that political engagement would be more active in the late campaign phase. Findings indicated that the ratio of active engagement (political discussion) to passive engagement (political interest) did indeed increase, or become more active, from spring to fall, $F(1,520) = 5.44, p < .05$ (means in table 15.2). Therefore, H_2 was supported. No interaction was found between gender and increase in active engagement; however, males were found to be more active overall in their engagement for both early and late campaign phases, $F(1,520) = 9.18, p < .01$.

The third hypothesis posited that people are more likely to "talk politics" in the latter phase than in the early phase of the campaign. Findings indicated an increase in talking politics over the life of the campaign, $F(1,524) = 8.21, p < .01$. Therefore, H_3 was supported. As for gender difference, findings indicated that men are more likely to discuss politics in both campaign phases, $F(1,522) = 6.81, p < .01$, and no interaction was found between gender and campaign phase. Therefore, both males and females are likely to increase political discussion in the later phase of a campaign.

For the fourth hypothesis, a ratio of news media exposure to political discussion was calculated to determine the proportional relationship between media use and interpersonal communication. Next, the ratios were compared to determine any changes between the early and late campaign. For the Internet news browsing–to–political discussion ratio and the newspaper reading–to–political discussion ratio, no differences were found for campaign phase. However, for the television news watching–to–political discussion ratio, a campaign phase effect was indicated. It was found that for the spring the proportion was .68; the proportion dropped to .57 in the fall, indicating a decrease in television news watching in relation to political discussion (or conversely, an increase in political discussion relative to television news watching). The difference between the spring and fall ratios was found to be statistically significant, $F(1,521) = 7.69, p < .01$. Therefore, H_4 was supported for television news watching. The research question was asked as to whether a gender difference exists for the decrease in the ratio of media use to political discussion. ANOVA findings indicate that no interaction was found between gender and campaign phase effect for the ratio of

Table 15.2 Regression Models: Media Use Variables to Predict Political Discussion

Independent Variables	Model a (all)		Model b (female)		Model c (male)	
	B	Beta	B	Beta	B	Beta
Read newspaper news	.17**	.17	.23**	.21	.21**	.25
Browse Internet news	.14**	.16	.17**	.16	e	e
Watch television news	.01*	.11	e	e	e	e
R-square	.10		.09		.06	
Adjusted R-Square	.10		.08		.06	

*$p<.05$ **$p<.01$
e = excluded

news media exposure to political discussion. Therefore, there was no difference between males and females for this effect.

The fifth hypothesis posited that newspaper reading and Internet browsing are more predictive of political discussion than is television watching. Findings from regression analysis (table 15.2) indicated that H_5 was supported. In a regression model testing the three media exposure variables, the strongest predictor of political discussion is reading newspaper news, with a beta coefficient of .17, p < .01, and the second-strongest predictor is browsing the Internet for news, with a beta coefficient of .14, p < .01. Watching television news had a very small beta coefficient of .01, p < .05. This model accounts for 10% of the variation in political discussion.

To address RQ_5, separate regression models were run for women and men. Results indicate that for females, reading newspaper news is the stronger predictor with a beta of .23, p < .01, and browsing Internet for news was the second-strongest predictor with a beta of .17, p < .01. This model accounts for 9% of the variance in political discussion for females. For males, reading newspaper news is the only predictor of political discussion with a beta of .21, p < .01. Television viewing was not a predictor. This model explained 6% of the variance in political discussion for males.

Finally, to answer RQ_6, a contextual model for campaign phase effects was explored to determine the relative effects of campaign phase, gender, and media exposure on levels of political discussion. A regression analysis (table 15.3) indicated that campaign phase is the strongest predictor of political discussion, with a beta of .22, p < .01; reading newspaper news is the second predictor of political discussion with a beta of .17, p < .01; and Internet browsing for news is the third predictor, with a beta of .14, p < .01. This model accounts for 12% of the variance in political discussion by the total sample of males and females.

To address RQ_7 regarding a gender difference in the relative strength of cam-

Table 15.3   Regression Models: Campaign Phase and Media Use Variables to Predict Political Discussion

Independent Variables	Model a (all)		Model b (female)		Model c (male)	
	B	Beta	B	Beta	B	Beta
Campaign phase	.22**	.12	e	e	.29*	.17
Read newspaper news	.17**	.17	.23**	.21	.16**	.19
Browse Internet news	.14**	.16	.17**	.16	e	e
Watch television news	.01**	.11	e	e	.14*	.16
R-square	.12		.09		.11	
Adjusted R-Square	.11		.08		.09	

*p<.05   **p<.01
e = excluded

paign phase and media exposure as predictors of political discussion, separate models were run for women and men. Results indicated that for females, reading newspaper news is the strongest predictor of political discussion with a beta of .23, $p < .01$, and Internet browsing for news is the second-strongest predictor with a beta of .17, $p < .01$. Campaign phase is not a significant predictor for females and is excluded from the model. This model accounts for 9% of the variance in political discussion for females. For males, campaign phase is the strongest predictor with a beta of .29, $p < .05$; reading newspaper news is the second-strongest predictor with a beta of .16, $p < .01$; and television watching is the third-strongest predictor with a beta of .14, $p < .05$. This model accounts for 11% of the variance in political discussion for males.

DISCUSSION

This study examined contrasts between active and passive forms of engagement during early and late campaign phases and investigated not only the frequency of political discussion during an electoral campaign overall but also the occurrence of informal political discussion in social relationships as it contrasts with media exposure during the early and late phases of the 2000 electoral campaign. In each case, campaign phase effect was tested for interaction with gender in order to determine any gender differences between the campaign phases. Finally, a contextual model for campaign phase effect on political discussion was explored.

As predicted, campaign phase effects were found for overall political engagement, active versus passive political engagement, and level of political discussion, with increases in the fall or late campaign phase. In other words, not only does the level of political engagement increase as the campaign progresses toward the primary and general elections, but also the type of engagement changes, with more active participation in the form of political discussion. Although males were found to have higher levels of both passive and active engagement, no gender differences were found in the campaign phase effect for levels of either.

In terms of the relative involvement in media use to political discussion, the only campaign phase effect found was for the ratio of television news watching to political discussion, with a decrease in the late phase (or conversely, an increase in the ratio of discussion to television viewing ratio). Therefore, political engagement became more active not only in terms of the ratio of political discussion to political interest but also in terms of the ratio of political discussion to the most passive form of media use, television news viewing. Both Internet news browsing and newspaper reading—more active forms of media use—held their ground in relation to levels of political discussion from the early to the late phase of the campaign.

Finally, when campaign phase effect was tested within a contextual model of all the predictor variables for level of political discussion, campaign phase was found to be a significant predictor for males only, whereas Internet news browsing was a significant predictor for females only. It appears that the imminence of elections is a catalyst for males to become more actively engaged in a campaign while females have steadier (albeit less) engagement in a campaign. It is important to note that females who have higher levels of browsing the Internet for news also appear to be more actively engaged in political discussion during the life of a campaign.

Implications for Future Research

Given the association between Internet browsing and political discussion by women, future research regarding the interactivity of campaign websites should be particularly sensitive to gender differences. Furthermore, the effects of campaign website links to information about offline political forums should be investigated in terms of aroused interest and motivation to participate.

Implications for Political Campaigns

Given the propensity for both higher levels and more active forms of engagement in the later phase of a campaign, media messages that relate well to interpersonal communication may resonate well with citizens. For example, video messages on television and the Internet that show conversations between candidates and citizens or among citizens could reinforce the propensity for discussion about a campaign. Furthermore, to encourage more political discussion by females, political parties and women's organizations should continue to sponsor and facilitate forums or workshops of particular interest to women of various age and interest groups. After all, both men and women should be actively engaged in political discussion, thereby improving the quality of public opinion and enhancing civic-mindedness.

REFERENCES

Bennett, S. E., Flickinger, R. S., & Rhine, S. L. (2000). Political talk over here, over there, over time. *British Journal of Political Science, 30,* 99–119.

Bucy, E. P., D'Angelo, P., & Newhagen, J. E. (1999). The engaged electorate: New media use as political participation. In L. L. Kaid & D. G. Bystrom (Eds.), *The electronic election: Perspectives on the 1996 campaign communication* (pp. 335–347). Mahwah, NJ: Lawrence Erlbaum Associates.

Burns, N., Schlozman, K. L., & Verba, S. (2001). *The private roots of public action: Gender, equality, and political participation.* Cambridge: Harvard University Press.

Capella, J. N., & Jamieson, K.H. (1996, July). News frames, political cynicism, and media cynicism. *Annals of the American Academy of Political and Social Science, 546,* 71–84.

Conway, M. M., Steuernagel, G. A., & Ahern, D. W. (1997). *Women and political participation: Cultural change in the political arena.* Washington, DC: Congressional Quarterly Press.

Huckfeldt, R., & Sprague, J. (1995). *Citizens, politics, and social communication: Information and influence in an election campaign.* New York: Cambridge University Press.

Kenny, C. (1998). The behavioral consequences of political discussion: Another look at discussant effects on vote choice. *Journal of Politics, 60,* 231–244.

Kim, J., Wyatt, R. O., & Katz, E. (1999). News, talk, opinion, participation: The part played by conversation in deliberative democracy. *Political Communication, 16,* 361–385.

Putnam, R. D. (1995). Bowling alone: America's declining social capital. *Journal of Democracy, 6* (1), 65–78.

Putnam, R. D. (2000). *Bowling alone: The collapse and revival of American community.* New York: Simon & Schuster.

16

Across the Ages

Views of the 2000 Debates from College Freshmen to Senior Citizens

Diana B. Carlin and Karen Anderson

As voter turnout has declined in the United States, the percentage of younger voters relative to the overall voting population has declined exponentially. The *Washington Post* reported, prior to the 2002 midterm elections, that the number of "older Americans who plan to take part in the November 5 elections outnumber people younger than 30 by more than 2 to 1, creating a distorted national politics in which the issues that dominate campaigns and Capitol Hill reflect an ever-smaller slice of the country" (Goldstein & Morin, 2002, p. 1). Thomas Patterson (2002), in his book *The Vanishing Voter*, notes that, "The voting rate of adults under thirty was 50 percent in 1972. It was barely above 30 percent in 2000" (p. 21).

Whether or not the aging of the electorate affects the national agenda is a debate that continues among political scientists and observers of electoral politics (Patterson, 2002, pp. 12–13). Patterson, however, concludes that, "Who votes does matter. As the electorate has shrunk, it has come to include proportionally more citizens who are older, who have higher incomes, or who hold intense opinions on such issues as gun control, labor rights, and abortion" (p. 13). Politicians speak to those who vote, as is evidenced by a study of the political advertising in the 2000 Bush-Gore race. Advertising targeted those over fifty, and 63.8% of the viewing audience for the advertising was over fifty, although they comprise 36.6% of the population (Neglection 2000, n.d., p. 1).

The content of political messages has been shown to impact participation among younger citizens. The reasons frequently given by nonvoters under thirty for their lack of participation include a lack of knowledge about the issues, failure by the candidates to address issues that matter to them, overall cynicism about politics and political institutions, and the lack of relevance of politics to their lives (Carlin, Vigil, & Buehler, 1998; Green & Gerber, 2001; Institute of Politics at Harvard University, 2000; Mellman Group, 2000). However, politicians argue that they speak to those who vote and that until voting demographics change, their messages won't. Putnam (2000) observes that "Voting is by a substantial margin the most common form of political activity, and it embodies the most fundamental democratic principles of equality. Not to vote is to withdraw from the political community" (p. 35). By withdrawing at the ballot box, young Americans have removed themselves from the political dialogue and the opportunity to influence policies that do and will affect them. Success in finding a way to break this cycle has been elusive.

Each election year since 1992 has seen efforts to get out the youth vote. Among the more visible programs are Rock the Vote, Youth Vote 2000, and A Third Millennium Project. These groups attempted to increase voter registration and raise awareness of the impact of the political process on young adults. In 1992, turnout for eighteen- to twenty-four-year-olds increased; however, in 1996 and 2000 the programs had minimal effect as participation levels declined. Along with voter registration drives and Get Out the Vote (GOTV) programs, the Commission on Presidential Debates promoted DebateWatch '96 and 2000 as another solution to increasing voter participation. A study of the 1992 debates, which formed the basis for DebateWatch, found that student voters used the debates as an information source about candidates and issues to assist them in deciding for whom to vote. They discovered that by watching the debates and discussing their content, they were better informed and felt more confident as voters (Apker & Voss, 1994).

This study builds on the previous research and was designed to assess the impact of DebateWatch as an educational tool across ages. Specifically, it sought to determine if there is a difference in how various age groups view issues and how they talk about them within the context of political debates. Since debates are the single most-viewed political event during a presidential election, they provide an excellent vehicle for voter education and increased involvement. To determine the impact of DebateWatch on voter knowledge and motivation, the following research questions are addressed:

RQ₁: How do debates affect voter knowledge, voter choice, and information seeking?
RQ₂: How does discussion of the debates affect voter knowledge, voter choice, and information seeking?
RQ₃: Is there a difference in the issues considered important across age groups?
RQ₄: Is there a difference in the way that issues are discussed across age groups?
RQ₅: Is there a difference in views about politics across age groups?

RQ$_6$: Is there a difference in the way political debates are observed and talked about across age groups?

METHOD

Data were collected nationally as part of DebateWatch 2000. This section explains DebateWatch 2000, provides an overview of the instruments used, and outlines the data analysis process.

DebateWatch 2000

DebateWatch started in 1996 under the sponsorship of the Commission on Presidential Debates. Its purpose is to encourage citizens to watch the presidential and vice presidential debates in small groups and then discuss them. Groups were encouraged to report their conclusions about the debates to the Debate-Watch Research Center at the University of Kansas for compilation and distribution to the national news media. Specifically, the commission wanted to know what issues were important to the viewers, which ones were irrelevant or not helpful, and what viewers still wanted to hear discussed in future debates or in the campaigns. In addition to this information, researchers sought to learn how the debates and the discussions influenced voter learning, voter choice, and information seeking after the debates.

DebateWatch groups were formed through a variety of methods. On campuses faculty members and campus groups organized watches. Over one hundred national organizations such as AARP, the National League of Cities, the NAACP, YouthVote 2000, Rock the Vote, and the American Association of University Women informed members through newsletters and websites. Grass-roots organizers learned about the project through announcements on the commission's website.[1] While the data set is larger than most for a study of this type, we do know that many individuals who host DebateWatches do not participate in the research phase; thus, the full impact of the project cannot be gauged.

Groups watched the debates and then turned off the television and held a discussion. They were instructed not to listen to postdebate spin. After discussions were completed, groups were invited to send a facilitator's report to the research center via the Internet or toll-free fax and phone numbers. Groups ranged in size from four to over five hundred. In the case of large groups, the debates were viewed on large-screen televisions, and then participants were divided into smaller discussion groups of eight to twelve with each group completing a facilitator's report. Thus, some sites submitted multiple facilitator reports. Many of the groups on campuses included students, faculty, and community members. Kids Voting USA also encouraged elementary and secondary students to participate with their parents; thus, some of the data in this report come from students under eighteen.[2] These data were included in the eighteen-to-twenty-five group during the analysis of the facilitator reports. Groups organized by members of organizations and by individual citizens met in homes, community buildings, churches, and schools.

In addition to the reports submitted to the research center, researchers at each of the debate sites taped discussion groups. Elderhostel groups at the Wake Forest and St. Louis presidential debates taped their discussions and submitted them to the researchers. Groups were also taped at the community DebateWatch held at the University of Kansas. The data submitted to the DebateWatch center and transcripts of groups formed the basis for answering the research questions.

Instruments

The DebateWatch 2000 packet that was mailed to individuals upon request included a one-page facilitator's report form. The packet could also be downloaded from the commission's website. It was available in both English and Spanish, and a few Spanish versions were submitted. The facilitator's report was to be completed as a summary of the group's discussion and sent to the research center by midnight after the debate for inclusion in a news release. Facilitator reports received after the deadline were used for postelection analysis. Additionally, individual participant reports were available on the website. Participants' reports were mailed or faxed to the research center and were not examined in the media analysis.

The facilitator's report (see www.debates.org for a copy of the form) asked for information about the group's location and demographics. The group leader was instructed to answer four questions on the basis of the discussion and to ensure group agreement on the responses. The four questions were: (1) "What topics or issues in the debate did participants find most useful or informative?" (2) "Were any issues or topics considered irrelevant or unimportant to participants?" (3) "Did participants want to hear about any topics or issues that were not included in the debate? Please list." (4) "How many members of your group said participating in DebateWatch would influence the way they read about, watch, or discuss the election?"

The participant's survey included three sections. The first section, completed prior to the debate included demographic information, source preference of campaign information, level of exposure to campaign coverage, and candidate preference. The second section, completed after the debate, included a series of five-point Likert-type questions regarding the value of the debates as a voter education tool and the influence of the debate on candidate preference. Following the group discussion the final section of the survey was administered; it included a series of nine five-point Likert-type questions regarding the value of the discussion and the influence of the discussion on candidate preference.

Discussion Groups

Taped discussion groups were held after each of the debates and were conducted either by the first author or by someone trained by the first author. Transcripts for purposes of this study were made of student groups at the University of Massachusetts after the first debate, Wake Forest University after the second presidential debate, Centre College after the vice presidential debate, and the University of Kansas after the third debate. Elderhostel groups in the debate cities were recorded after the second and third debates. A group of young professionals aged twenty-six to thirty-two were taped after the third debate.

Suggested questions in the packet aided in answering the questions on the facilitator's report and in gathering reactions to the format and to the usefulness of the debates compared to other campaign information and other news sources. Questions included: "What role does politics play in your everyday life?" "What did you learn about the candidates or issues that you did not know prior to the debate?" "Did the debate influence your attitudes about the issues or the candidates?"

Participants

Facilitator reports came from 144 groups after the first debate, 81 after the second, 140 after the third, and 27 after the vice presidential debate. One hundred eighty-six reports were from groups that included only eighteen- to twenty-five-year-olds, 179 were from groups with ages ranging from below eighteen to over fifty-five, and 27 were from groups with no one younger than twenty-six. This represented a total of 4,870 individuals or an average of 12 per group.

Data was collected from thirty-one states, the District of Columbia, and Americans living in Canada and Germany. A total of 798 participant surveys were completed. Two hundred sixty-two participant reports were collected from individuals after the first debate, 89 after the second, 421 after the third, and 12 after the vice presidential debate. Fourteen surveys did not indicate which debate was viewed. Since a concerted effort was made to involve young voters and because the members of a national research team were on college campuses, the majority of participant surveys were from eighteen- to twenty-five-year-olds. Many of the groups that sent in facilitator reports did not collect participant surveys from group members. The student cohort represented 74% (592 out of 798) of the participant reports and 82% (3,994 out of 4,870) of the individuals in the facilitator reports. Discussion-group members ranged in age from eighteen to over seventy.

Data Analysis

Frequencies were obtained for all demographic categories and attitude measures. Open-ended questions on the facilitator reports were content analyzed by three coders using a coding scheme that was developed from the topics included in the debates. Initial coding was done the night of the debate. As a result of time constraints in doing the coding for release to the news media, interrater reliability was not calculated. However, in preparing this essay, an additional coder checked the categories assigned to open-ended comments and reported an interrater reliability of .98.

A series of chi-square analyses was conducted for the major issues surveyed on the facilitator and participant surveys. Facilitator reports were assigned to one of three groups: 18–25 (included participants twenty-five and younger), mixed (included participants from eighteen to over fifty), and 26 and over. Participant surveys were grouped into five age groups: under 18 (3%, $n = 24$), 18–25 (74%, $n = 592$), 26–40 (10%, $n = 77$), 41–55 (6%, $n = 44$), and 56 and older (6%, $n = 47$).

RESULTS

The first two research questions examined the role of the debates and subsequent discussion as they related to individual participants' candidate preference, information seeking, acquisition of voter knowledge, and attitudes related to the debate across age groups. Prior to the debate, participant's indicated their preference for a candidate. Age groups varied significantly in having a predebate preference for a candidate, x^2 (4, N = 781) = 21.5, $p < .001$. Participants 41–55 (93%) and over 55 (96%) were significantly more likely to have a candidate preference prior to the debate than 18–25 (73%) and under 18 (75%). There was no significant change from predebate preference to postdebate preference across age groups, x^2 (12, N = 619) = 16.2, $p > .05$. There was a significant difference in postdiscussion preference across age groups, x^2 (4, N = 700) = 13.4, $p < .01$. Those participants under 18 (19.0%) were significantly more likely to indicate a change in preference than all other age groups.

Age groups varied significantly in the ranking of their top information source for candidate information, x^2 (36, N = 780) = 73.2, $p < .001$. Specifically, participants 41–55 and over 55 were significantly more likely to gain information from Sunday talk shows, such as *This Week* and *Meet the Press,* than adults 26–40 and 18–25. Conversely, 18–25 and 26–40 participants were significantly more likely to gain information from the Internet than participants 41–55 and over 55. Despite these differences, the most common top-ranked information source was network news, which did not differ significantly across age.

Six of the nine items regarding acquisition of knowledge and voter attitudes about the debates were significant across age groups (see table 16.1). Participants over 55 were significantly less likely to learn something new about the candidates or the issues and to use the debates to clarify understanding of the candidate's position than all other age groups. Additionally, participants 41–55 and over 55 were significantly less likely to evaluate the candidates differently after the debates than participants 26–40 and 18–25 (see table 16.2).

All nine of the items regarding postdebate-discussion knowledge and attitudes were significant across age groups (see table 16.3). In general, participants over 55 were significantly less likely to gain knowledge from the discussion (see table 16.4). Additionally, participants 41–55 and over 55 were significantly less likely to evaluate candidates differently or determine for whom to vote on the basis of discussion than were other age groups.

The third and fourth research questions examined which issues were important and how they were discussed across age groups. While the statistical analysis yielded no significant difference in the issues considered important or unimportant across age groups, analysis of the qualitative focus-group data suggested that the issues were discussed differently. For example, discussions of health care were more likely to center on prescription drugs and Medicare for those over fifty-five, while younger participants were more interested in the rising price of insurance and its availability from employers. Students were more interested in higher education, whereas those with children were more interested in elementary and secondary education. When topics such as teacher testing were discussed, parents addressed the issue from the perspective of quality, and students who were education majors wanted to know the impact on their careers.

Once issues other than the top five (taxes, education, health care, international relations, and gun control) were discussed, differences in importance ratings were observed. Given the large number of issues, it was impossible to calculate statistical significance. However, students were more likely to talk about the environment, energy policy, race relations, and abortion. When all groups discussed topics such as Social Security, younger voters did so to query its relevance to them, while older voters wanted to know what was going to be done. The facilita-

Table 16.1   Voter Knowledge and Attitudes from Debates across Age Groups

Variables	X^2	df	N
Taught me something new about candidate	55.9**	16	761
Taught me something new about issues	76.3**	16	761
Clarified understanding of candidate's position	29.3*	16	758
Reinforced my attitudes about candidate	27.6*	16	758
Caused me to evaluate candidate differently	64.0**	16	758
Helped me to decide for whom to vote	34.2*	16	759
Gave me ideas to discuss in the group	15.8	16	758
Made me more likely to vote	20.3	16	750
Increased my interest in following the campaign	20.9	16	753

*$p < .05$ **$p < .001$

Table 16.2 Voter Knowledge and Attitudes from Debate by Age Group

Variable	Under 18	18–25	26–40	41–55	Over 55
Taught me something new about candidate	0 (0%)	24 (4%)	10 (14%)	6 (14%)	10 (23%)
Taught me something new about issues	2 (8%)	23 (4%)	8 (11%)	3 (7%)	12 (28%)
Clarified understanding of candidate's position	1 (4%)	22 (4%)	7 (10%)	2 (5%)	7 (16%)
Reinforced my attitudes about candidate	0 (0%)	13 (2%)	0 (0%)	2 (5%)	1 (2%)
Caused me to evaluate candidate differently	5 (21%)	52 (9%)	9 (12%)	11 (26%)	15 (36%)
Helped me to decide for whom to vote	3 (13%)	47 (8%)	9 (13%)	11 (26%)	8 (19%)
Gave me ideas to discuss in the group	1 (4%)	7 (1%)	2 (3%)	0 (0%)	3 (7%)
Made me more likely to vote	2 (10%)	62 (11%)	10 (15%)	9 (21%)	10 (24%)
Increased my interest in following the campaign	1 (4%)	31 (5%)	7 (10%)	3 (7%)	8 (19%)

Note: Frequencies and percentages of participants within their age group indicating they strongly disagreed with the statements.

Table 16.3 Voter Knowledge and Attitudes from Discussion

Variable	X^2	df	n
Taught me something new about candidate	65.5**	16	722
Taught me something new about issues	64.1**	16	722
Clarified understanding of candidate's position	55.7**	16	721
Reinforced my attitudes about candidate	51.4**	16	721
Caused me to evaluate candidate differently	66.8**	16	719
Helped me to decide for whom to vote	51.1**	16	716
Understand why others view candidates differently	33.1*	16	718
Made me more likely to vote	56.3**	16	715
Increased my interest in following the campaign	59.3**	16	716

*p < .01 **p < .001

Table 16.4 Voter Knowledge and Attitudes from Discussion by Age Group

Variable	Under 18	18–25	26–40	41–55	Over 55
Taught me something new about candidate	0 (0%)	48 (9%)	7 (12%)	9 (23%)	18 (42%)
Taught me something new about issues	0 (0%)	41 (7%)	8 (13%)	10 (25%)	16 (37%)
Clarified understanding of candidate's position	0 (0%)	35 (6%)	7 (12%)	10 (25%)	13 (30%)
Reinforced my attitudes about candidate	0 (0%)	29 (5%)	6 (10%)	7 (18%)	11 (26%)
Caused me to evaluate candidate differently	3 (14%)	56 (10%)	9 (15%)	15 (39%)	16 (38%)
Helped me to decide for whom to vote	1 (5%)	67 (12%)	9 (15%)	13 (33%)	15 (36%)
Understand why others view candidates differently	0 (0%)	22 (4%)	5 (8%)	3 (8%)	9 (22%)
Made me more likely to vote	2 (10%)	47 (9%)	10 (17%)	9 (23%)	17 (43%)
Increased my interest in following the campaign	0 (0%)	30 (5%)	7 (12%)	5 (13%)	13 (33%)

Note: Frequencies and percentages of participants within their age group indicating they strongly disagreed with the statements.

tor report by American students at McGill University underscores the generational perspective:

> [T]he issues of youth participation and voter apathy were of interest to us; however, we were very disappointed that they were not adequately answered. . . . There was a great deal of stress on the elderly and a resulting lack of attention on "younger" issues. It is hard for a group of students to be extremely interested in Social Security, Medicare, prescription drug costs (the main focus of this campaign)—as they are issues that do not affect us a great deal.

The last two research questions explored the difference in views about politics and the debates, in particular, across age groups. The major difference detected in transcripts of discussions held among college students versus Elderhostel participants was in the level of knowledge about the issues. Students were often struggling with understanding the finer details of the candidates' comments, whereas the seniors were analyzing and referencing positions heard outside the debate. Students were also more likely to discuss tactics used by the candidates and express cynicism about the process. For example, participants in one of the

Lawrence, Kansas, groups after the third debate expressed disappointment and cynicism about what they had observed:

> [M6]: And there was . . . it kind of turned into a fight a lot of the times. It was, "Oh My turn to talk, shut up," or something. I was hoping they weren't going to start picking on each other but . . .
> [F2]: Yeah, at first I was pleased that they weren't doing that, but . . .
> [M6]: Yeah, exactly.
> [F2]: But I think it's just kind of the nature of the debate that it turns into that. But that's one thing that watching this debate I was kind of disappointed and stuff—a lot of things were brought up but no concrete solutions or even ideas for solutions. . . .
> [F3]: I think it would be nice if they just stuck to the issues. . . . But if you just directly attack character, it doesn't . . .
> [M7]: The reason you use attacks is because you don't know the issues, so I think a lot of the time they don't know what's going on, so they just use a personal attack to get them out of it.

A group in Boston that watched on the University of Massachusetts campus during the first debate discussed the candidates' failure to speak to them:

> [F7]: You know something that really struck me was that Gore kept talking about how he wanted to help the middle-class people, but I didn't hear anyone talk about helping the working-class people, which I find ironic on a working-class campus, which is . . . that a lot of our students are immigrants who otherwise wouldn't get a shot, and there's like story after story of people who pull themselves up, the quote– unquote, "American Dream," and these aren't the people they are talking about. They're talking about their children's children—like two or three generations beyond. They weren't talking about the people on this campus.
> [F8]: I was listening to NPR during the day today, and they were talking about the fact that they are talking to the American public *everywhere*, the biggest issue was confusion on the issues. They didn't do one thing to help that, because the sparring back and forth on the numbers and, as you said, how could you walk away from any question involving numbers believing either person?

Research Question 6 was answered directly by the facilitator's report that asked if watching the debate and doing DebateWatch would change the way participants followed the campaign, sought more information, and talked about politics. Comparisons of answers among the three groups found no significant differences for the first debate. However, there were differences for the other three debates. Far more younger voters indicated that they would follow the news more closely or were more likely to make a decision on a candidate or actually vote as a result of the experience. Older voters typically had made their decisions prior to the debate and learned little new after the first debate given their higher levels of attentiveness to the media and the campaigns. Mixed-age groups included comments about votes not changing but learning occurring.

A group with all members over twenty-six from Hurricane, West Virginia, observed after the first debate: "Participating in DW will not affect the ways in which we read, watch, discuss the election. There is no such thing as an 'honest politician.' That phrase is an oxymoron." Their cynicism was in sharp contrast to the remarks of three student groups in College Park, Maryland, after the third presidential debate:

1. Nine members [out of 12] said it would influence the way they view the election. A few said that it was their primary source of information for making their voting decision.
2. They said they were much more informed on the election issues than they were before they came and that being involved would motivate them to (1) read more about the election, (2) watch reruns of the earlier debates (which many of them had not seen) on C–SPAN, (3) register to vote, and (4) actually vote in the election.
3. All 12 of them said that DebateWatch got them interested in politics and the issues surrounding their futures.

Student groups in Bonn, Germany; Lawrence, Kansas; and Fullerton, California, among others, made nearly identical reports.

Comments from mixed groups tended to blend the two perspectives—there was nothing new and they were not influenced—with more positive outcomes. For example, a group in Glendale, Arizona, noted that, "All said they have more interest in the election, but none had their opinions swayed by either or both debates to date." Another group, in Pekin, Illinois, indicated that, "All participants welcomed the chance to view the debates (two did not have television in their homes). Although the debates did not change their minds, they all volunteered that their opinions were now more informed."

DISCUSSION

Not surprisingly the eighteen to twenty-five cohort found the debates and discussion were more helpful in informing them about the candidates and issues—even though they often expressed disappointment about the candidates' debate tactics or failure to address issues of importance to them. The fact that many of them had not followed the campaign closely is the best explanation for simultaneous disappointment and acknowledgment of learning.

Experienced voters, who had followed the campaign more closely, learned little new—especially after the first debate—and did not report that their information-gathering habits would change as a result. For those who were already engaged, there was little more they could do. First-time voters were more likely to have their vote choice influenced by the debates and discussion. In the mixed-age groups, younger voters gained an understanding of why issues were important to them. Thus, the research demonstrates that if campaign issues are explained as more directly affecting younger voters, they are more likely to participate in the process. The research also suggests that in future election cycles, students should not participate in groups solely with other students. There is a level of learning that takes place when the various ages confront one another's issues. In the case of younger voters, they can begin to understand that issues such as taxes and Social Security do impact them. Most importantly, the research showed that younger voters can be motivated to vote and to become informed voters if they are given an opportunity to participate in the process actively. DebateWatch and similar programs can do that. Registering and being told how important it is to vote might not be enough to get younger voters to the polls without sufficient voter education to make the issues more understandable and real to them. Viewing debates that summarize the major issues in the campaign followed by a sharing of views about the debates appears to be a combination that contributes to voter education and political interest, especially among young voters.

NOTES

The authors wish to acknowledge the members of the political debates class and honors tutorial at the University of Kansas who worked in the DebateWatch Research Center and assisted with content analysis. Special thanks go to Shawna Smith, Eric Morris, and Jay Self. We would also like to thank our colleagues around the country who organized groups on their campuses and all of the individuals who submitted data.

1. For a complete explanation of DebateWatch and a list of partners, see the Commission on Presidential Debates website at www.debates.org.

2. Kids Voting USA and its state affiliates work to develop lifelong voters through an age-appropriate curriculum about democracy, voting, and citizens' roles and by having students actually vote at an official polling place along with adult voters. The theory behind Kids Voting is that if children and young adults become comfortable with voting, they are more likely to vote when they turn eighteen. Research since the program's founding in 1991 bears this out. Thus, data from this group is included in our analysis because middle- and high-school students are the next wave of new voters. For complete information about Kids Voting USA, see its website at www.kidsvotingusa.org.

REFERENCES

Apker, J., & Voss, C. (1994). The student voter. In D. B. Carlin and M. S. McKinney (Eds.), *The 1992 presidential debates in focus* (pp. 197–202). Westport, CT: Praeger.

Carlin, D. B., Vigil, T. R., & Buehler, S. E. (1998, September). The disaffected electorate: What separates voters from nonvoters? Paper presented at the Annual Meeting of the American Political Science Association, Boston.

Goldstein, A., & Morin, R. (2002, Oct. 19). Young voters' disengagement skews politics.

Washington Post. Retrieved October 19, 2002, from www.washingtonpost.com/wp-dyn/articles/A53238-2002Oct19.html.

Green, D. P., & Gerber, A. S. (2001). Getting out the youth vote: Results from randomized field experiments. Retrieved December 29, 2001, from www.yale.edu/isps/publication/voter.html.

Institute of Politics, Harvard University. (2000, Apr. 11–12). Attitudes toward politics and public service: A national survey of college undergraduates. Retrieved November 3, 2002, from www.iop.harvard.edu/projects-survey.html.

Mellman Group. (2000). Memorandum to Leon and Sylvia Panetta, Panetta Institute. Retrieved January 11, 2000, from www.panettainstitute.org/poll-memo.html.

Neglection 2000. (n.d.). Analysis of candidate advertising. Retrieved November 3, 2002, from www.neglection2000.org/reports/101500ads.html.

Patterson, T. E. (2002). *The vanishing voter: Public involvement in an age of uncertainty*. New York: Knopf.

Putnam, R. D. (2000). *Bowling alone: The collapse and revival of American community*. New York: Simon & Schuster.

17

The Voice of Young Citizens

A Study of Political Malaise in Campaign 2000

Julia A. Spiker, Yang Lin, and Scott D. Wells

Half of U.S. citizens (100 million people) do not participate in presidential elections. Nationwide, voter turnout was 51.2% in the 2000 election, up 2.2% from 1996, but still ranking the United States at 140th among the world's 163 democratically elected governments. The statistics for young voters are even more disheartening. Only 38% of the eligible youth participated in the electoral process in 2000, and less than 20% voted in congressional elections in 1998 (Aspen Institute, 2000; Hochman, 2001). With few exceptions, the percentage of eighteen- to twenty-four-year-olds who vote has declined in each succeeding election since 1972, when eighteen-year-olds were first eligible to participate (McGregor, 2000; People for the American Way, 1988). Among young citizens, the least likely to vote are high-school dropouts and Hispanics (Faler, 2002). Moreover, as younger individuals grow older, they are not likely to acquire the habit of voting (Lessner, 2000).

The media have often attributed such low voter turnout to the attitude of political malaise, sometimes referred to as "videomalaise." A citizen experiencing political malaise lacks trust in the political system, expresses cynicism toward politics, and experiences low political efficacy and high disapprobation toward candidates (Kaid, Johnston, & Hale, 1989; McKinney, Spiker, & Kaid, 1998; Spiker & McKinney, 1999) and, recently, toward special interest groups. Such skepticism hampers the political process, as is made evident by strained communication between a citizen and government.

BACKGROUND ON POLITICAL MALAISE

Scholars have approached political malaise in various ways, identifying different influences and using different terminology to define the phenomenon. The term "political malaise" is used in the current study as an umbrella phrase to cover and unite differing perspectives. This research defines political malaise as a general sense of citizen uneasiness or ill-being directed toward the political process. Although there is a general agreement that political malaise exists, there is great disagreement over what it is and what its causes are. Possible reasons offered for political malaise are an individual's age, gender, lack of political interest, level of political involvement, and reliance on the media.

Pinkelton and Austin (1998) argue that political malaise among adults, and especially youth, can lead to an inconsolable situation called "spiral of disaffection." Under this scenario, people isolate themselves from political information that heightens cynical perceptions of government, resulting in hardened personal views in opposition to political participation. Over time, citizen anger can snowball, affecting other individuals and groups of people and resulting in a genuine spiral of disaffection. Lessner (2000) claims that today's young people demonstrate negative signs unique to their generation, indicating a permanent voting deficiency. This conclusion is congruent with Putnam's research (2000), which shows a significant disconnect among citizens and a disintegration of civic health across social structures. Furthermore, Bloom (1987) maintains that younger people lack the social and civic skills necessary to fully function in a democracy. Others surmise that Generation X, and certainly Generation Y, will continue to thwart political participation as they fail to see its importance in rectifying current ills (Bucy, 2001; Carlin, 2001; Owen, 1997).

The root causes of political abstention are many. One of the most often cited reasons why young people fail to vote is because candidates pay little attention to them, thus making them feel uninformed and unempowered. Thus, it is no surprise that Allison Byrne Fields, director of the 2000 Rock the Vote campaign, explains that young voters cannot see any connections between what is going on in politics and their everyday lives (Hochman, 2001). Modern political campaigns only compound this problem. The current reliance upon slick television advertisements, packaged candidate communication, professional telemarketing efforts, and mass-produced direct mail (see Clymer, 2000) has undermined the traditional style of campaigning, along with the social benefits of face-to-face political engagement.

Other common explanations for political abstention include apathy or the feeling that young people do not care much about politics. Some nonvoters indicate that they do not understand the political process. Other citizens have a difficult time figuring out how to register or do not understand the importance of voting. Additional reasons offered for abstention are reliance on the media, negative political advertisements, past political experiences, the decline of political parties, the absence of a working-class party, the complicated voting system, the increased mobility of citizens, fraying social bonds, and the current state of economic affairs (Friel, 2001; People for the American Way, 1988; Putnam, 2000; Schier, 2000; Spiker, 1998).

Studies reveal that nonvoters tend to be younger and more mobile, have less education and income, and are less involved in partisan politics (Checkoway & Van Tsi, 1978; Kagay, 2000; Luntz & Maslansky, 1992; Toner, 1990; Wellstone, 2001; Wolfinger & Rosenstone, 1980). Several other factors also contribute to a lack of political participation. Specifically, parental, school, and party affiliation, as well as political knowledge, political efficacy, and civic duty are all common *psychological influences* related to voting behavior. *Institutional attributes* affecting voter behavior include *governmental influences* (registration requirements, electoral process, campaign finance system, bureaucratic nature of government), *mass media influences*, and *campaign influences* (campaign style and competitiveness of election). *Cultural influences* are also often credited with affecting voting intentions (see Hunt, 1994; Piven & Cloward, 2000; Seidelman, 1999; Teixeira, 1992).

Many communication scholars have approached the phenomenon of political malaise from the direction of media influence (Holtz-Bacha, 1990; Kaid et al., 1989; Robinson, 1976). As more people have come to rely upon media for political information, political malaise has apparently increased. Television is a key communication medium in the democratic political information process, and its influence on the political system is an important area of study. In fact, for many citizens, television is the sole source of political information. Television is also the choice for most political campaign messages. This mutual reliance and its effects sustain the use of the now popular phrase "mediated politics." The initial political malaise study suggested that reliance on television for political information increased malaise levels (Robinson, 1976). Wald and Lupfer (1978) examined televised political debates. Their results indicated a temporary increase of political efficacy after viewing a debate, yet this level dropped a week later.

Some political malaise studies do not support Robinson's original work. O'Keefe (1980) studied the relationship between television reliance and malaise and found that positive political attitudes, such as feelings "that politicians were altruistic and that voting was efficacious . . . [and] positive candidate images" (p. 125), were associated with greater television reliance. Another major study contradicted Robinson's findings of videomalaise. Leshner and McKean (1997) found that relying on television news did not affect cynicism toward politicians. Their study highlighted increased levels of political knowledge for respondents who relied on television news. This study also included newspaper use with similar results. A possible explanation for the contradicting results is the varying levels of television dependence. Another reason might be the varying assumptions underlying the studies (e.g., television is an influence or it is not).

Political malaise is an important social issue, especially in the United States, a representative democracy that relies on its people for governance. This study considers many of the aforementioned variables to examine political malaise among young citizens. For the future of a democratic society, it is critical to understand how the youth intersect with politics.

RESEARCH QUESTIONS

Debates have been examined as a means of educating citizens about government and promoting feelings of civic responsibility (Wald & Lupfer, 1978). The presidential debates are high-profile media events and as such can be considered a valid stimulus for research to examine political attitudes. Second, reliance on traditional media for political information has fluctuated over the years (Williams & Delli Carpini, 2002). Because of the media's powerful influence on political attitudes, it is important to understand the relationship between young citizens, political information, and the media.

The following research questions guide analysis of political malaise in this study:

RQ$_1$: How are young citizens affected by political malaise?
RQ$_2$: Are political malaise levels different based on political party affiliation?
RQ$_3$: Are political malaise levels different based on gender?
RQ$_4$: Are political malaise levels different based on race?
RQ$_5$: Are political malaise levels different based on habits of media use?

This research examines political malaise among young citizens through use of survey data, focus group discussions, and in-depth interviews. It is vital to explore these questions through different venues to gain more reliability and validity in the findings.

METHODOLOGY

National Survey Data

Coinciding with the three presidential and one vice presidential debate of the 2000 election cycle, participants completed a predebate and a postdebate survey. A total of 1,022 participants between the ages of 18 and 26 were selected for this study. The average age was 19.6. Of the 1,022 subjects, 430 (42%) were male and 588 (58%) were female (four participants chose not to indicate either). Forty percent of the participants identified as Democrats, 38% as Republicans, 16% as independents, and 4% as "other." The data were collected from a cross section of thirteen states across the United States: Alabama, California, Colorado, Florida, Idaho, Indiana, Missouri, Ohio, Oklahoma, Pennsylvania, South Carolina,

Texas, and Virginia. Ordinary least squares regression analyses were conducted on these data.

Focus Group Discussions

This research also employs three focus groups to illustrate the typical responses made by young citizens regarding their attitudes toward politics. The focus group discussions were held during the fall of 2000. One focus group in Missouri was conducted on the night of the first presidential debate (October 3). There were fifteen subjects in the Missouri focus group discussion (nine females, six males); eight were Democrats and seven were Republicans. The average age was 21.6, with a range of 20 to 26. The second focus group was held in Ohio on the night of the second presidential debate (October 11). There were six subjects in the Ohio group (two females, four males). The average age in this group was 20.7, with a range of 18 to 27. The party affiliation was three Democrats, one Republican, and two independents. The third focus group was held in Texas on the night of the third presidential debate (October 17). There were seven subjects in this group (five females and two males). The average age was 18.6, with a range of 17 to 21. Four were Democrats, one was a Republican, and two were independents.

In each group, soon after viewing the debates, participants took a short break and then returned to participate in a focus group discussion lasting approximately forty-five minutes. The focus group moderator followed a prepared set of questions related to the debate (voter learning, comparison of sources for political information, role of the media in the political process, and political malaise and community). The focus group discussions were audiotaped in order to document the discussion. A thematic coding scheme was used for analysis.

In-depth Interviews

Finally, in-depth semistructured interviews were conducted to acquire detailed accounts, extended exploration, and specific thoughts about political participation. Discussions of possible remedies for political abstention were also included. For these discussions, a convenience sample of fifty-four interviewees participated during the months of January and February 2001. The sample consisted of undergraduate students enrolled in introductory communication classes at a large midwestern university. Fifty-four percent of the focus group members were female, and of the total sample, 83% were between the ages of eighteen and twenty-four. Volunteers were solicited, but some students were awarded minimal research or extra-credit points for their participation. During the interviews, which lasted no longer than forty-five minutes, open-ended questions were asked. To gain a clearer reasoning about attitudes toward nonvoting, follow-up questions were also used.

RESULTS

National Survey Results

The first set of regression estimates is based upon the preelection survey (see table 17.1). The dependent variable in this analysis is a composite measure of political malaise. The alpha for preelection malaise is .60; for postelection, it is .63. Coefficients show that females have lower levels of malaise than males and whites have lower levels than nonwhites. For partisanship, these estimates indicate the highest levels of malaise among the independents, followed by Republicans, and then by Democrats. With respect to the impact of use of news media, the coefficients for the preelection results show that more reading of newspapers diminished levels of malaise, as did greater viewing of national network news. However, watching more local news contributed to political malaise. Table 17.1 shows that the estimates for the first five coefficients are statistically significant at the .05 level, whereas the final coefficient is significant at the .10 level. The constant and the R^2 are as expected.

The second set of regression coefficients shows results for the postelection survey data (see table 17.1). Controlling for the same variables as in the preelection model, the estimates are quite similar. The results for the postelection model are thus consistent with the preelection data. Females show lower levels of malaise than males; whites show lower levels of malaise than nonwhites. As for partisanship, Democrats indicate the lowest levels, with malaise being higher among Republicans and the highest for independents. The results concerning the habits of using the media are also similar to the preelection numbers. Once again, the coefficients are similarly significant, and the constant and the R^2 are as expected.

Table 17.1   OLS Regression Estimates of Political Malaise: Pre and Post Surveys, 2000 Presidential Elections

	Pre		Post	
	b	*S. E. of b*	*b*	*S. E. of b*
Gender	−.80	.30**	−1.15	.30**
Race	.40	.13**	.30	.13**
Party	.55	.16**	.63	.17**
Reading Newspapers	−.30	.07**	−.24	.07**
Watching National News	−.45	.07**	−.40	.08**
Watching Local News	.13	.07*	.13	.08*
Constant	23.95	.70	23.95	.73
R^2		.09		.08

** = significant at the .05 level; * = significant at the .10 level.

Focus Group Discussion Results

The thematic analysis of the focus group discussion reveals three themes: (1) debates allow for critical evaluation of candidates; (2) participants feel they have low personal political power but express a strong sense of civic duty; and (3) a generation gap exists since politics is perceived as not relating to young citizens.

Debates as means for critical evaluation of candidates. Participants liked having an opportunity to "hear their [candidates'] voices set to the information," as one female stated. The debates also allowed the subjects to learn more about the candidates, as the same female stated:

> [F1]: I thought it was interesting just to see their interaction with each other. It showed a lot about their personalities and how they could in the future handle things. Gore seemed a lot more patient while Bush was really jumpy and overly aggressive.

Some participants indicated that their attitudes toward the candidates were either reinforced or not changed at all. Many views were critical of candidate qualities, as the following two comments indicate. The first comment addresses candidate abilities:

> [F1]: It really made me think just how sad this is that we have a country with millions and millions of people and these are the two people that we narrowed it down to. It's amazing to me, I mean neither of them are very articulate, neither of them really seem concerned about people, about the people that this country is made up of, you know, and that is really disturbing. That is really disturbing to me.

The second comment addresses how the political system influences candidates' performances:

> [M2]: I think the usage of modern polling techniques—I mean these guys base their campaign platforms on whatever CNN/Time Warner poll of the day says. You know there is an old saying that I'm screwing up but it's something like, 'true leaders take an agenda and convince people to come with them whereas false leaders see where the people want to go and then pretend to lead them there.' And I think that both candidates are merely figureheads of their party. Neither of them is truly operating on their own. I don't know if it's possible for a candidate in this day and age to actually have his own personal agenda and say I want to be president and this is what I'm going to do. If you look at all the third party candidates out there right now, I mean you can hardly get on the ballot let alone get elected unless you have a million dollar advertising campaign plus a bus load of lawyers.

The debate of October 11 used a new format. The two candidates sat at a table across from a moderator. A male in the focus group presented a positive perspective on the format:

[M1]: The format does lead to a more friendly tone. Instead of standing there almost lecturing, you can almost imagine yourself sitting down at a table across from them. It does allow for more one on one.

This new format provided an opportunity for participants to critically evaluate the debate, as well as the candidates, as noted by this statement:

[F1]: Well, supposedly it was a conversational format but you noticed that neither of them maintained or attempted eye contact with the other. That was fairly interesting just to see how they were addressing the audience the whole time. And Bush near the end says, "Oh, thank you, Vice-President Gore," as a sort of formality, although he neglected the eye contact and the entire understanding of the entire debate. I didn't think the moderator was very strong either. The questions weren't very strong—they allowed for extremely broad, you know, just kind of sweeping motions as far as the discussion. It was very broad and didn't get into any specifics. And the moderator could have attempted to zero in on some issues. That would have been important.

Trust was an important issue among the young citizens. One male in the group did not trust the candidates or government.

[M2]: They didn't address questions. They didn't address people. I don't think that what they gave as answers is what they truly believe. They gave the answers that they are supposed to give because that's what they represent, but that's not really their ideals and so I don't trust them. . . . Young people feel cynical about the government because they don't feel as if they are being told the truth. They are not being honest.

Participants felt that a neutral third party was needed to tell the public which candidate is lying because candidates cannot be trusted. One male stated:

[M2]: As voters we have no way to verify what they are saying.

This led to a discussion between two participants:

[M2]: I don't trust them—100%—what they say on national television. I don't trust them—100%—what they say in their ads. I would trust more of an unbiased news source maybe like a national network.
[F1]: Yeah, but where are they getting their information?
[M2]: That's true too.

This lively exchange occurred among five of the participants:

[M1]: What's the media good for other than stirring up trouble?
[M3]: I'd prefer just unbiased reporting.
[F1]: But that's not what people are drawn to. People are always fascinated by what other people think. You're always going to get that.

[M2]: I think people should make their own decisions. I mean there are so many ways to influence people through images and colors and symbolism.
[F2]: I don't know. I just want to know the truth. Don't lie to me.

The source of participants' political knowledge included the media (television, newspapers, the Internet), government classes, and talking with people. Young citizens like the timeless nature of the Internet for gathering information.

Low personal political power but strong sense of civic duty. Typical responses as to why young people do not vote included:

[F1]: I think that . . . people don't care . . . people don't think that their vote matters.
[M2]: Even if all of us voted [young people], it wouldn't even make a dent in our parents' vote.
[F1]: 'Cause look who is running the government—it's our parents. [Also] laziness I'm sure. Feeling like you're not involved. If you feel like you're not involved you don't feel like participating in it.
[M1]: I mean people feel there are more important things to do in their lives because they feel my one vote won't count.

Even though they felt their personal political power was not strong, participants did feel a strong sense of civic duty. One male stated:

[M1]: I vote because it's my duty to vote and I want to take advantage of that right.

Participants felt the voting process needed improvement, so some participants offered ways to increase voting. These three participants offered a solution to the process of voting:

[F1]: Make the process easier.
[M2]: I think people should be able to call up and punch in their Social Security number and vote.
[M3]: I support dial up and vote.

A generation gap arising from perception that politics does not relate to young citizens. Participants believed the candidates addressed education and the environment, issues important to young citizens, but also those unrelated to young people (the economy, gun control, and the military). One student wished that the candidates had covered the issues of copyright and freedom of speech, referring to the case with Napster. Others suggested that politics did not relate to them.

One female gave a reason why young people do not relate to politics:

[F1]: I think a lot of people our age have a problem thinking about the future.

Another participant continued with this perspective:

[M1]: I think a lot of people don't feel like they have a stake in it. I mean I don't own a house, I don't pay property taxes. Younger people don't care because they feel it doesn't affect their lives. . . . If you even look at all the ages and break it down by percentages, young people aren't voting, but the old people have nothing better to do.

[M2]: X'ers feel they can't do anything to change what the [baby] boomers want because they [baby boomers] dominate the culture. The process doesn't encourage X'ers to do it [vote], there is no incentive to do it. Participating won't change anything because you really aren't wanted.

[M1]: Why, as an 18 year old, would I vote for a 45-year-old guy? He is going to vote for things like better snow removal in the street. What do I care about better snow removal? I'll just drive right through it.

These two participants offered ways to improve civic community:

[F1]: Start small with the families, with the individuals. If you feel good about your relationships with other people, then it spreads.

[M4]: There should be more dialogue. People need to talk to each other for one. I mean half the time we don't know each other. We need to learn to work together and live together.

[F1]: I think that people are starting to get involved in other ways, especially with like the Internet and everything. . . . you know, people can join groups. . . . [a] lot of young people do that because . . . [they] see the results and [can] be a part of it.

In-depth Interview Results

The reasons for political abstention are cataloged according to the following themes: psychological, governmental, and campaign. Similar theories and ideas voiced in the in-depth interviews are listed together for the purposes of clarity.

Causes of nonvoting: Psychological influences. The main reason for nonvoting cited in the in-depth interviews was a lack of knowledge about the candidates, the political process, and the importance of voting. Nonvoters do not seem to understand how politics affects their daily lives. This sentiment was plainly spoken by a male respondent in a personal interview on March 29, 2001: "Basically, for me to vote more, I would have to have to be educated as to why it is important that I do so, that it does make a difference what I believe."

Of the psychological influences, the second reason for nonvoting relates to political efficacy. During the discussions, subjects often questioned if their vote really mattered. They wondered whether politicians truly cared about them and whether they could successfully influence the political system. Finally, other reasons cited relate to partisanship and parental socialization.

Causes of nonvoting: Governmental influences. The category of governmental influences, specifically the electoral process, covers a broad range of issues pertaining to the act of voting and its effects. The top explanation under this category, closely related to political knowledge and efficacy, is the oft repeated complaint that "one's vote does not really count" in the electoral process. A male respondent stated in a personal interview on April 2:

> I think a lot of people feel that their one little vote isn't going to change anything. I think that is why most people, you know . . . Just a feeling that they [nonvoters] are not going to change anything so it doesn't matter. So I think all that combined rolls into one snowball effect.

Other governmental influences mentioned by the interviewees included the "single party states," the electoral college, the inconvenience of the voting process, and the exclusion of minor parties.

Causes of nonvoting: Campaign influences. Psychological and governmental influences certainly have a significant effect on voting rates. Campaign influences are also a decisive factor in this equation. Within this category, the most common refrain focused on the stakes in the election. Because of perceived similarities between the candidates, several participants openly questioned their need to vote. In addition, discussions recurrently raised talk of the quality of candidates and the divisive discourse common to politicking today.

Causes of nonvoting: Other influences. Besides psychological, governmental, and campaign influences, other causes for nonvoting were cataloged. According to the in-depth interviews, mass media, economic, and cultural influences affect voting behavior as well, but they play a smaller role. The influence of mass media is a primary theme that emerged from the discussions. Included in this cause is criticism of the quality of media coverage, negativity in news reporting, and the heavy reliance on political polls. Within the primary theme of economic influences, several participants reasoned that the relative good times, economic and otherwise, were a reason for the lack of involvement in political affairs. Finally, cultural influences were also cited as contributing to nonvoting. In general, individualistic goals have taken precedence over collectivist concerns. Consequently, the lackadaisical approach to civic matters by the electorate has contributed to declining rates of political participation.

DISCUSSION AND CONCLUSION

The national survey data reveal that the media influence political malaise. The data indicated that young citizens relied across the board on newspapers as one of the main sources for political information. It is a heartening sign that as more young citizens read the newspapers, their malaise levels diminished. The finding that watching national network news lowers political malaise and local news raises malaise is surprising. Future research needs to explore this discrepancy among young citizens.

Focus group discussions reveal that even though young citizens may experience a low sense of political power, they do feel that participation is important. Young citizens also reveal a healthy distrust of candidate rhetoric, so they look to the media for objective reporting. A sense of civic community is vital to young citizens, even if they do not believe politics directly relates to them. Perhaps most striking in the focus group discussions was the emergence of a generation gap. Young citizens display a lack of understanding of a more senior generation by making comments like "older people have nothing better to do" than vote. Future studies of young citizens' attitudes toward politics need to address the differing perspectives among generations. Also, future questions should be phrased positively to avoid putting participants on the defensive. As one female stated: "Whenever you ask people the question, 'Why don't you go vote?' it puts them on the defensive. . . . you don't want to say oh . . . just 'cause I don't have time. Like many people our age, that would be the reason, but they're not going to say [that, they give] some other reason."

Finally, the in-depth interviews provide some practical advice on how to reengage young citizens in the political process. Overwhelmingly, discussants repeatedly voiced a need for more communication about political campaigns and candidate stances. As one subject described the situation on March 28, "You have to make people understand politics more. . . . Make it less peripheral and more attached to their life. Politics is not making it in [to the nonvoters' thoughts] every day." In addition to greater communication needs, respondents consistently called for more contact with politicians. They want to get to know the political candidates and interact with them. Besides remedies regarding political information and contact, many subjects emphasized the simple solution of eliminating obstacles to voting. They believe that making the process less costly and less prohibitive would entice more voters. Recommendations for technological innovations (e.g., Internet voting) were also common.

In the end, the three different forms of data employed in this study reveal that while young citizens do indeed experience malaise about politics, they consistently indicate that politics and politicians do not connect with them. The youth, when pressed, do appear to recognize the importance of politics but believe that the "process" or the "system," defined broadly, is ill suited to their generation. In focus groups and in-depth interviews, young citizens recommend certain steps that might make the democratic process more relevant to their daily lives.

REFERENCES

Aspen Institute. (2000). *Voters: A candidate's toolkit for reaching young Americans.* Washington, DC: Council for Excellence in Government.

Bloom, A. (1987). *The closing of the American mind.* New York: Touchstone.

Bucy, E. P. (2001, May 26). Participation by digital means? The (dis)engagement of Generation Y. Paper presented at the International Communication Association Convention, Washington, DC.

Carlin, D. (2001, May 26). Youth disaffection in the 2000 election. Paper presented at the International Communication Association Convention, Washington, DC.

Checkoway, B., & Van Tsi, J. (1978). What do we know about citizen participation? A selective review of research. In S. Langton (Ed.), *Citizen participation in America*. Lexington, MA: Lexington Books.

Clymer, A. (2000, Jan. 2). The body politic: Nonvoting Americans and calls for reform are drawn into stark focus in 2000 races. *New York Times*, pp. 1, 24.

Faler, B. (2002, June 24). The young and restless don't get out the vote. *Washington Post*, p. A5.

Friel, B. (2001, Aug. 11). Why Americans still don't vote: Book review. *National Journal* 33 (32): 2560–2562. Review of Piven, F. F., & Cloward, R. A. (2000). *Why Americans still don't vote: And why politicians want it that way*. Boston: Beacon Press.

Hochman, S. (2001, Feb. 19). Rock the Vote sees new relevance for youth activism in the wake of the 2000 election. *Los Angeles Times*. [online version], p. F1. Retrieved from Lexis-Nexis.

Holtz-Bacha, C. (1990). Videomalaise revisited: Media exposure and political alienation in West Germany. *European Journal of Communication, 5*, 73–85.

Hunt, R. A. (1994). *The lonely American voter: Geography and turnout in American presidential elections, 1940–1992*. Unpublished doctoral dissertation, Pennsylvania State University.

Kagay, M. R. (2000, Aug. 27). The nation: Tune in, turn out, turn off; the mystery of nonvoters and whether they matter. *New York Times*, D1–2.

Kaid, L. L., Johnston, A., & Hale, L. (1989). Mass media and political disapprobation. *Political Communication Review, 14* (2), 51–72.

Leshner, G., & McKean, M. L. (1997). Using TV news for political information during an off-year election: Effects on political knowledge and cynicism. *Journalism and Mass Communication Quarterly, 74*, 69–83.

Lessner, L. (2000, Jan. 23). Young adults prefer to make a difference through volunteering, not voting. *Milwaukee Journal Sentinel* [online edition], p. 21A. Retrieved from Lexis/ Nexis.

Luntz, F. I., & Maslansky, M. (1992). Who really votes? Predicting turnout. *Polling Report, 8* (20), 1, 8.

McGregor, P. (2000, Oct. 15). Mobilizing young voters no easy task. *Cleveland Plain Dealer*, p. 1E.

McKinney, M. S., Spiker, J. A., & Kaid, L. L. (1998). DebateWatch '96 and citizen engagement: Building democracy through citizen communication. In T. J. Johnson, C. E. Hays, & S. P. Hays (Eds.), *Political engagement, alienation, and reform: Media and politics in the 1996 elections* (pp. 185–193). Lanham, MD: Rowman & Littlefield.

O'Keefe, G. J. (1980). Political malaise and reliance on media. *Journalism Quarterly, 57*, 122–128.

Owen, D. (1997). Mixed signals. In S. C. Craig & S. E. Bennet (Eds.), *After the boom: The politics of Generation X* (chap. 4). Lanham, MD: Rowman & Littlefield.

People for the American Way. (1988). *The vanishing voter and the crisis in American democracy: New strategies for reversing the decline in voter participation*. Washington, DC: People for the American Way.

Pinkelton, B. E., & Austin, E. W. (1998). Media and participation: Breaking the spiral of disaffection. In T. J. Johnson, C. E. Johnson, & S. P. Hays (Eds.), *Engaging the public: How government and the media can reinvigorate American democracy* (pp. 75–86). New York: Rowman & Littlefield.

Piven, F. F., & Cloward, R. A. (2000). *Why Americans still don't vote: And why politicians want it that way.* Boston: Beacon Press.

Putnam, R. D. (2000). *Bowling alone: The collapse and revival of American community.* New York: Simon & Schuster.

Robinson, M. J. (1976). Public affairs television and the growth of political malaise: The case of "The Selling of the Pentagon." *American Political Science Review, 70,* 409–432.

Schier, S. E. (2000). *By invitation only: The rise of exclusive politics in the United States.* Pittsburgh: University of Pittsburgh Press.

Seidelman, R. (1999). Bringing non-voters in would transform American politics. In B. Miroff, R. Seidelman, & T. Swanstrom (Eds.), *Debating democracy: A reader in American politics* (2d ed.) (pp. 187–198). New York: Houghton Mifflin.

Spiker, J. A. (1998). *Effects of debate viewing and citizen discussion on political malaise.* Unpublished doctoral dissertation, University of Oklahoma.

Spiker, J. A., & McKinney, M. S. (1999). Measuring political malaise in the 1996 election. In L. L. Kaid & D. G. Bystrom (Eds.), *The electronic election: Perspectives on the 1996 campaign communication* (pp. 319–334). Mahwah, NJ: Lawrence Erlbaum Associates.

Teixeira, R. A. (1992). *The disappearing American voter.* Washington, DC: Brookings Institute.

Toner, R. (1990, Nov. 7). The 1990 election: Nonvoters, turned off by campaigns, or just too busy to vote. *New York Times,* p. B1.

Wald, K. D., & Lupfer, M. B. (1978). The presidential debate as a civics lesson. *Public Opinion Quarterly, 42,* 342–353.

Wellstone, P. D. (2001). *The conscience of a liberal.* New York: Random House.

Williams, B. A., & Delli Carpini, M. X. (2002, April 19). Heeeeere's democracy! *Chronicle of Higher Education,* pp. B14–15.

Wolfinger, R. E., and Rosenstone, S. J. (1980). *Who votes?* New Haven: Yale University Press.

Index

257

About the Contributors

Karen Anderson is a Ph.D. candidate in the Department of Communication Studies at the University of Kansas. She was a research assistant for DebateWatch 2000 and an organizer of the five-hundred-person DebateWatch held at the University.

Mary Christine Banwart is assistant professor of communication studies at the University of Kansas where she teaches courses in political campaigns, politics and the media, and leadership. She has published articles and chapters on political campaigns, women and politics, and politics and the media.

Lauren Cohen Bell is assistant professor of political science at Randolph-Macon College. Her research interests include the U.S. Congress, presidential-congressional relations, and state and federal judicial selection systems. Her work has been published in *Judicature, Political Research Quarterly*, and *Government, Law, and Policy*, and she is the author of *Warring Factions: Interest Groups, Money, and the New Politics of Senate Confirmation* (2002).

Arla Bernstein is assistant professor of communication at Georgia State University. She was growth management director of the city of Miramar, Florida, in the 1980s and community development director of Marion County, Florida, and president of the Women's Leadership Network of Marion County in the 1990s. She teaches mass communication and public relations and does research in political communication, public engagement, gender and ethnic identity. She is certified as a facilitator by the International Association for Public Participation and a planner in the American Institute of Certified Planners. She has published in *Communicating Politics: Engaging the Public in Democratic Life* (ed. McKinney et al.) and in *Communication Quarterly*.

Thomas P. Boyle is assistant professor of communication at Millersville University, where he teaches public relations writing, research, and campaigns. His research interests include political campaign communication, especially its influences on media and public agendas. His work has appeared in *Journalism and Mass Communication Quarterly*.

Dianne G. Bystrom has served as the director of the Carrie Chapman Catt Center for Women and Politics at Iowa State University since 1996. The coeditor and contributing author of two books—*The Electronic Election: Perspectives on the 1996 Campaign Communication* (1999) and *The Lynching of Language: Gender, Politics, and Power in the Hill-Thomas Hearings* (1996)—she has chapters in five forthcoming books on women in the U.S. Congress, the 2000 election, electing the first woman president, civic engagement, and political communication. Bystrom also serves as editor of the newsletter of the Women and Politics Research Section of the American Political Science Association and as vice-chair of the Political Communication Division of the National Communication Association. She is a frequent commentator about political and women's issues for state and national media.

Diana B. Carlin is dean of the graduate school and international programs and a professor of communication studies at the University of Kansas. She coordinated the 1992 study for the Commission on Presidential Debates that led to DebateWatch '96 and 2000 and served as the national coordinator. She is coeditor of *The 1992 Presidential Debates in Focus*. Her research on political debates has appeared in *Argumentation & Advocacy, Political Communication, Rhetoric and Public Affairs,* and *American Behavioral Scientist*.

Alyson Cypher works for Sandia Laboratories in Albuquerque, New Mexico. She was working on a graduate degree at the University of Idaho when this research was done.

Paul D'Angelo is a visiting assistant professor in the Department of Communication at the State University of New York, Albany. His research interests include framing theory, news production processes, and framing and priming effects of self-coverage in political campaign news. His recent research has appeared in *Communication Yearbook 22, Journal of Communication,* and *American Behavioral Scientist*.

Elizabeth A. Dudash is a doctoral student in communication at the University of Missouri, Columbia. Her primary research interests are political campaigns and presidential rhetoric.

Janis L. Edwards is associate professor of communication studies at the University of Alabama, Tuscaloosa. Her research specialties include rhetorical and media construction of candidate images, gender and politics, and visual aspects of political discourse. She has published related articles in such journals as *Communication Quarterly* and *Women's Studies in Communication* and is the author of *Political Cartoons in the 1988 Presidential Campaign: Image, Metaphor, and Narrative.*

Frank Esser is assistant professor in the Institut für Publizistik of Johannes Gutenberg University of Mainz (Germany). He is a graduate of City University, London (England) and was visiting professor in the Department of Communication at the University of Oklahoma in 2000/01. His research interests center around cross-national studies of political journalism and campaign communication. He received two top-paper awards at the annual conventions of the International Communication Association (1996, 2001) and has published three books and numerous articles in international journals including the *European Journal of Communication, Harvard International Journal of Press/Politics,* and the *American Behavioral Scientist.*

Kimberly C. Gaddie completed her doctoral degree at the University of Oklahoma. She teaches public communication at Oklahoma State University in Oklahoma City. She also heads a nonprofit foundation that focuses on civic participation.

Georgine Hodgkinson is professor of communication studies at Cosumnes River College in Sacramento. Her research focuses on the impact of debates in political campaigns and issues related to communication education. Her research on the 1996 election was published in the *The Electronic Election.*

Lynda Lee Kaid is professor of telecommunication and senior associate dean of the College of Journalism and Communications at the University of Florida. She previously served as the director of the Political Communication Center and supervised the Political Commercial Archive at the University of Oklahoma. Her research specialties include political advertising and news coverage of political events. A Fulbright scholar, she has also done work on political television in several Western European countries. She is the author or editor of fourteen books, including *Videostyle in Presidential Campaigns, The Electronic Election, Civic Dialogue in the 1996 Campaign, New Perspectives on Political Advertising, Mediated Politics in Two Cultures, Political Advertising in Western Democracies,* and *Political Campaign Communication: A Bibliography and Guide to the Literature.* She has also written over one hundred journal articles and book chapters and over one hundred convention papers on various aspects of political communication.

Stephanie Greco Larson is associate professor in the Department of Political Science at Dickinson College in Carlyle, Pennsylvania. Her research focuses on the content and consequences of news coverage of political actors and institutions. Her recent focus has been on the way television news covers public opinion. She is author of two books (*Creating Consent of the Governed: A Member of Congress and the Local Media* and *Public Opinion: Using MicroCase ExplorIt*) and numerous journal articles and book chapters. Her publications include studies of how women are represented in television news, campaign brochures, detective fiction, and soap operas.

Yang Lin received his Ph.D. from the University of Oklahoma in 1997. He is currently an assistant professor in the School of Communication at the University of Akron, Akron, Ohio. He teaches political communication, intercultural communication, and communication theory.

Mitchell S. McKinney is assistant professor of communication at the University of Missouri, Columbia. His research focuses on political debates, political campaigns, and presidential rhetoric. He is coeditor of *The 1992 Presidential Debates in Focus*, coauthor of *Civic Dialogue in the 1996 Presidential Campaign*, and author/coauthor of several journal articles and book chapters.

Lori Melton McKinnon is associate professor of advertising and public relations in the College of Communication and Information Sciences at the University of Alabama. She is nationally accredited in public relations (APR). Her research focuses primarily on national and international political advertising, public relations, and political debate coverage. In addition to articles in numerous academic journals, she has published book chapters on various topics in political communication and is the coauthor of a book on the 1996 Romanian presidential election.

Jerry Miller is associate professor in the School of Interpersonal Communication at Ohio University, where he is also the director of forensics. His research interests include media coverage of politics and gender issues in political communication.

James E. Mueller is assistant professor of journalism at the University of North Texas. He is also faculty adviser to *The North Texas Daily*, the university's student newspaper. He has taught previously at Pittsburg State University in Pittsburg, Kansas, and at Eduardo Mondlane University in Maputo, Mozambique, as part of a unique graduate program offered by the North Texas Journalism Department. He has worked as a reporter, editor, and photographer for about ten years for newspapers in the St. Louis, Missouri, area. He has written scholarly articles for a variety of publications including *Mass Comm Review*, the *Journal of Media Economics,* and *Grassroots Editor*. He has contributed an article to *The Media in America*, a popular journalism history textbook, and has written a chapter for

Media Management Review and the forthcoming book *Custer and His Times,* vol. 4. His research interests include journalism history, media management, and political journalism.

Michael Nitz is associate professor in the School of Communication at the University of North Dakota. His research examines media coverage and public communication processes in the areas of political, science/environmental, and international communication. His work has appeared in a variety of national and international outlets, including *Communication Monographs, American Journal of Political Science,* and *World Resource Review.* He was a Fulbright guest professor at the University of Hamburg in 1997–1998.

Tom Reichert is assistant professor in the Department of Advertising and Public Relations at the University of Alabama. His research interests include media and politics, social marketing, and the content and effects of sex in the media. His research has appeared in *Journal of Advertising, Journal of Communication,* and *Journalism Quarterly.* He authored *The Erotic History of Advertising* (2003) and coedited and contributed to *Sex in Advertising: Perspectives on the Erotic Appeal* (2003).

Terry Robertson is assistant professor of communication at the University of South Dakota. His research specialties include gender and politics, media coverage of politics, and political advertising.

Marilyn S. Roberts is associate professor in the department of advertising at the University of Florida. Her research on political advertising and political communication has been published in the journals of *Political Communication, Journalism Quarterly, Communication Research, Mass Communication Review,* and *The Harvard International Journal of Press/Politics.* She also has written book chapters on political advertising and agenda setting. Prior to her academic career, she operated her own advertising and public relations firm and served as a media consultant to a U.S. representative for more than a decade.

Theodore F. Sheckels is professor of English and communication at Randolph-Macon College. The author of *When Congress Debates: A Bakhtinian Paradigm* (2000), he has published on political communication topics in *Communication Quarterly, Southern Communication Journal, Howard Journal of Communications,* and *Rhetoric and Public Affairs.* He is also the author of *The Lion on the Freeway: A Thematic Introduction to Contemporary South African Literature* (1996) and *Celluloid Heroes Down Under: Australian Cinema, 1970–2000* (2002) as well as articles on Canadian authors L. M. Montgomery and Margaret Atwood.

Stacey M. Smith is completing her M.A. in communication at Western Illinois University. Her research interests include presidential rhetoric, campaign biography films, and feminine style. Currently, she is finishing work on her thesis, which involves Hillary Clinton's campaign biography film. Upon graduation, she plans to pursue her Ph.D.

Boubacar Souley is a doctoral student in public policy at the University of Arkansas, Fayetteville.

Julia A. Spiker is assistant professor at the University of Akron in Akron, Ohio. Her political communication research interests and publications include the study of political malaise and political uses of the Internet. She is currently the chair of the Political Communication Interest Group of the Central States Communication Association.

John C. Tedesco is assistant professor of communication studies at Virginia Tech. His research focuses on mass mediated political communication, including advertising, public relations, news, and the Internet in both U.S. and comparative political settings. He has published in numerous journals and has authored a variety of book chapters. He is the coauthor of two books on U.S. politics. Before joining Virginia Tech, he held positions as archive and research specialist and research associate at the University of Oklahoma's Political Communication Center and its Political Commercial Archive. He also has experience as a legislative intern for the Civil Service Employees Association PAC (New York State) and as reporter/editorial assistant for the *Times Herald-Record* (Middletown, New York).

James E. Tomlinson is professor of communication studies at Bloomsburg University in Pennsylvania. Courses he teaches include political communication, organizational communication, and argumentation. He is also project director for Integrating Information Technology into the Communication Studies Curriculum, a $275,000 grant funded by the Pennsylvania Department of Education (2002–2003). He was also research director and author of *Cybercitizens of the Commonwealth: How Rural and Urban Pennsylvanians Access and Use the Internet*, funded by the State Legislature of Pennsylvania (2000).

Rebecca M. Verser is a doctoral student in the Department of Communication at the University of Missouri. Her research interests include political communication and new media technologies.

Barbara J. Walkosz is assistant professor in the Department of Communication at the University of Colorado at Denver. She studies political advertising and the relationship of mass media and politics. She has coauthored studies on the voters' perceptions of political candidates and the role of letters to the editor as an indicator of public opinion.

Scott D. Wells is assistant professor of communication studies at St. Cloud State University. His research interests include political and mass communication with a concentration on civic malaise and campaign strategy. He is the author or coauthor of several journal articles and convention papers and also serves as an adviser for political campaigns.

Robert H. Wicks is associate professor of communication at the University of Arkansas, Fayetteville, where he teaches mass communication courses. His published research focuses on media effects, audience processing of media messages, and political communication. He is author of *Understanding Audiences: Learning to Use the Media Constructively.* He has worked professionally as a television and newspaper reporter and editor.

Andrew Paul Williams is a Ph.D. student at the University of Florida, College of Journalism and Communication. He is currently a Bateman Fellow and serves as a public relations instructor and a research assistant for Lynda Lee Kaid. His primary research areas are political communication, media studies, and public relations.